AMERICAN FOREIGN POLICY OFFICIALS

A Publication of the Mershon Center
for Education in National Security

American Foreign Policy Officials

Who They Are and What They Believe Regarding International Politics

Bernard Mennis

OHIO STATE UNIVERSITY PRESS

JX
1706
.A4
1971

Copyright © 1971 by the Ohio State University Press
All rights reserved

Manufactured in the United States of America
Library of Congress Catalogue Number: 72-163634
International Standard Book Number: 0-8142-0164-4

TO MARILYN
with love and appreciation

CONTENTS

Preface

CHAPTER 1: Distinguishing Military and Nonmilitary Participants within the Foreign Policy Subsystem — 3

CHAPTER 2: The Organizational Location and Functions of Political-Policy Officials — 17

CHAPTER 3: Social Origins — 34

CHAPTER 4: Religion — 88

CHAPTER 5: Political Orientation — 112

CHAPTER 6: Cognitive Style — 128

CHAPTER 7: Foreign Policy Beliefs — 147

CHAPTER 8: Why Political-Military Officers and Political-FSOs Differ with Respect to Foreign Policy Beliefs — 169

CHAPTER 9: A Brief Summary and Implications for Future Research — 180

Appendix — 187

Bibliography — 195

Index — 207

TABLES

TABLE 1: Professional Level Employees Assigned to State Department by Organizational Location, 1962 — 19

TABLE 2: Functional Assignments of FSOs, 1962 — 20

TABLE 3: Organizational Sources of FSO Sample — 26

TABLE 4: Organizational Sources of Military Sample — 29

TABLE 5: Year of Birth — 30

TABLE 6: Grade Distribution of Samples and Departments — 31

TABLE 7: Geographical Background — 42

TABLE 8: Representativeness of FSOs Regarding Geographical Background — 45

TABLE 9: Representativeness of the Military Regarding Geographical Background — 49

TABLE 10: Size of Hometown — 52

TABLE 11: Representativeness of the Military Regarding Size of Hometown — 56

TABLE 12: Representativeness of FSOs Regarding Size of Hometown — 59

TABLE 13: Nativity of Parents — 61

Contents

TABLE 14:	Ethnic Affiliation	63
TABLE 15:	Father's Occupation	65
TABLE 16:	Representatives of the Military and FSOs Regarding Father's Occupation	67
TABLE 17:	Level of Education	71
TABLE 18:	College Attended	72
TABLE 19:	Colleges Attended by FSOs, Career Ministers, and Recruits	75
TABLE 20:	Distribution of Military Officers by Type of Commission	78
TABLE 21:	Religious Affiliation	89
TABLE 22:	Representativeness of the Military and FSOs Regarding Religious Affiliation	94
TABLE 23:	Distribution of Political-Military Officers and Military Career Aspirants by Religious Affiliation, Geographical Background, and Status (High or Low) of Father's Occupation	97
TABLE 24:	Religiosity	102
TABLE 25:	Relationship of Religiosity and Church Attendance, Religious Self-Description, and Variables Pertaining to Social Origins	103
TABLE 26:	Church Attendance	106
TABLE 27:	Religious Self-Description	107
TABLE 28:	Political Orientation	117
TABLE 29:	Relationship of Political Orientation and Variables Pertaining to Social Origins and Religiosity	119
TABLE 30:	Political Ideology Identification	120
TABLE 31:	Political Party Identification	121

TABLE 32: Intercorrelation Matrix of Dogmatism and Rigidity Scales — 135

TABLE 33: Cognitive Style — 137

TABLE 34: Relationship of Cognitive Style and Variables Pertaining to Social Origins, Religiosity, and Political Orientation — 139

TABLE 35: Relationship between Anti-Communism, ACD, Nonalignment, and Foreign Policy Belief System — 162

TABLE 36: Relationship between Beliefs Pertaining to Foreign Policy, Government Involvement in the Economy, and Civil Liberties — 165

TABLE 37: Foreign Policy Beliefs — 168

TABLE 38: Relationship of Foreign Policy Beliefs and Variables Pertaining to Social Origins, Religiosity, Political Orientation, and Cognitive Style — 170

TABLE 39: Relative Power of Religiosity, Political Orientation, and Cognitive Style with Respect to Predicting Foreign Policy Beliefs — 175

ILLUSTRATIONS

FIGURE 1: A Model Indicating the Main Sources of the Compositional Characteristics of Organizations — 36

FIGURE 2: Construction of the Foreign Policy Belief System — 164

PREFACE

This study was undertaken with the intention of gaining an understanding of the background and foreign policy political beliefs of State and Defense Department officials who, because of their positions, are capable of significantly affecting American foreign relations and, therefore, contemporary international politics. The author was motivated by an awareness that despite their importance, little is known about these foreign policy officials. Although evidence regarding the subject is scarce, hypotheses and labels alleged to be descriptive are plentiful. For example, the literature is crowded with terms such as *military mind*. Yet few scholars have attempted to deal with this concept, to translate its intended meaning into a form such that it can be examined in an effective fashion. Consequently, the problem of gathering relevant information actually includes two interrelated objectives: one, to suggest how this concept of the military mind (and similar topics) may be more fruitfully examined; and the other, to provide evidence that is susceptible to objective scrutiny.[1] The findings of such an investigation ought to enable scholars to begin to develop a more ade-

1. "Despite a fairly extensive if scattered literature on expertise, the social background of decision-makers, and such stereotypes as the 'bureaucratic mind' or the 'military mind', no systematic attempt has been made to give these various terms operational definitions or to establish empirical referents for them. Nor has the possible impact of continued professional association been studied" (Richard C. Snyder, H. W. Bruck, and Burton M. Sapin, *Foreign Policy Decision-Making: An Approach to the Study of International Politics*, p. 163).

quate basis for speculating about the impact these two groups of officials have upon foreign policy formulation and execution.

In pursuit of these objectives, ninety-five Foreign Service and military officers were interviewed in 1965. At that time, the task of contacting respondents was considerably facilitated by the assistance given me by Mr. Pio Uliassi of the State Department's External Research Staff; Lt. Col. R. C. Hixon, International Security Affairs; Lt. Col. R. B. Kreutzer, Army, International Policy Division; Capt. D. M. Bagby, Navy, Operations 61; and Col. E. Mikolowski, Air Force, International Affairs Division. Needless to say, I greatly appreciate the cooperation of those officers who consented to be interviewed.

I am indebted also to the many individuals who have helped with the design of the study and the writing of the manuscript. Among them are James A. Robinson, Inis L. Claude, J. David Singer, Harold Karan Jacobson, J. Merrill Shanks, James Rhodes, George L. Kraft, and Michael Kahan. The financial burden assumed in accomplishing the investigation was eased by aid extended by the University of Michigan and Michigan Memorial-Phoenix Project. I especially want to acknowledge the financial support given me by the Mershon Center for Education in National Security at the Ohio State University.

Finally, I thank my wife Marilyn, who encouraged me with ideas and supporting words when they were appropriate, and needling words when they were necessary. It would have been most difficult to continue without each of these inducements.

Bernard Mennis

Philadelphia, Pennsylvania
May, 1971

AMERICAN FOREIGN POLICY OFFICIALS

CHAPTER 1

Distinguishing Military and Nonmilitary Participants within the Foreign Policy Subsystem

In order to participate effectively in international political affairs, nation-states (or any equivalent complex social groups) need to develop, differentiate, and professionalize skill-groups specifically responsible for the conduct of foreign relations. This fact has resulted in the emergence over time of readily identifiable professional-bureaucratic governmental organizations (i.e., structures of roles and relationships) staffed by careerists presumed to have special competence in the area of international politics. Within this context, two major organizational groupings reflecting related yet contrasting functional spheres may be distinguished—the military and the nonmilitary. For the purposes of the present analysis, the formulation suggested by Lewis J. Edinger is followed when he identified the military as "that group in the state which has legitimate, primary, and specific responsibility for the organized and planned employment of the state's physical force against other states. A military man accordingly is any legitimate member of this group—regardless of rank, dress or position. When the military function is institutionalized, we may speak of a military establishment."[1] It should be noted that Edinger focuses attention not so

---

1. Lewis J. Edinger, "Military Leaders and Foreign Policy-Making," *American Political Science Review* 57(1963):396. To this may be added Huntington's more detailed statement that "the responsibilities of the military man to the state are threefold. He has, first, a representative function, to represent the claims of military security within the state machinery. . . . Secondly, the military officer has an advisory function, to analyze and to re-

much upon the actual tasks that military establishments may perform but rather upon the exclusive nature of its formally delegated ultimate responsibility, the externally oriented application of force. With respect to the more mature states, this designation very well describes the bulk of the military establishment's activities. This clearly is not true elsewhere. In many states, a substantial part of the time and attention of "professionals in violence" involves directing force against domestic critics, real and presumed. Thus, the conceptualization of the military establishment employed here effectively distinguishes a specific subsystem but does not claim to entirely summarize its relevant activities. It is almost descriptively accurate when reference is made to the United States; it tends to be descriptively imperfect when reference is made to "unstable" or more "authoritarian" political systems.

The nonmilitary aspect is more difficult to specify. It may be useful initially to think of it as a residual element that, together with the military component, constitutes the operational part of the "collectivity as international actor." As such it represents a nonviolent complement, mainly composed of diplomatic elements that may be employed either as an alternative to, or in conjunction with, physical force as a means of policy execution. Additionally, it offers a variety of competitive alternatives to the military establishment in the area of intelligence and resource procurement and allocation. In contrast to the case in the military sector where the Defense Department alone constitutes the military establishment, no one governmental department in the United States entirely incorporates this type of responsibility. Quite obviously, the Depart-

---

port on the implications of alternative courses of state action from the military point of view. . . . Finally, the military officer has an executive function, to implement state decisions with respect to military security even if it is a decision which runs violently counter to his military judgment" (Samuel P. Huntington, *The Soldier and the State: The Theory and Politics of Civil-Military Relations*, p. 72). Also see Morris Janowitz, *The Professional Soldier: A Social and Political Portrait*, pp. 3–7; Jacques Van Doorn, "The Officer Corps: A Fusion of Profession and Organization," *European Journal of Sociology* 6(1965):262–82; and Philip Abrams, "The Late Profession of Arms: A Study of Ambiguous Goals and Deteriorating Means in Britain," *European Journal of Sociology* 6(1965):28–61.

ment of State has traditionally occupied stage center here; and it would not be wholly incorrect to identify nonmilitary international political activites primarily with it. On the other hand, several other departments and agencies also may be included as part of the nonmilitary establishment (e.g., Commerce, Labor). The involvement of these other departments, however, clearly does not nearly challenge in scope, intensity, and duration that of State.[2]

Governmental organizations such as State and Defense are especially interesting focuses for analysis because they represent the primary and official linkages through which international political participants interact—in this case, with the United States. The activities entered into by them include the following general tasks: first, these organizations are the major means by which the United States gathers, processes, and interprets internationally oriented information, and hence learns about external political events; second, their members often act as official representatives of the government; and, third, they are the central vehicles of policy execution, the expression of national will. Expressing a similar thought, Modelski, after describing policymakers as men entrusted "with the special task of influencing other states," declares:

> Policy-makers are an essential component of the process of making foreign policy. In the absence of representatives, no organized relations between states could be carried on. . . . They constitute an essential instrument whose function is mediation between that community and the outside world. . . . Policy-makers can thus be pictured as occupying that crucial point at which inputs are transformed into outputs, it is this key position that accounts for their importance to foreign policy analysis: Inputs and outputs can be defined only by reference to policy-makers.[3]

2. For example, Robinson and Snyder state that "the major institutions in foreign policy-making are clearly within the executive branch—the Office of the President, the Department of State, and the Department of Defense" (James A. Robinson and Richard C. Snyder, "Decision-Making in Internal Politics," in *International Behavior: A Social-Psychological Analysis*, ed. Herbert C. Kelman, p. 453). It would be desirable, of course, to include the Office of the President and Central Intelligence Agency in the analysis. Due to several practical reasons (e.g., inaccessibility, lack of information regarding organizational structure), it became necessary unfortunately to restrict attention to Defense and State.

3. George Modelski, *A Theory of Foreign Policy*, pp. 3–4. Also see the

The important point to be made is that each international political participant necessarily is engaged in the formulation of foreign policy. The state therefore may be viewed as a decision system. In order to achieve effective processing of decisions, certain governmental organizations must be developed. Members of these organizations are involved in decision-making both as receptors (e.g., information-gathering functions) and effectors (e.g., implementing functions). Thus these officials at the minimum are included in the predecisional and postdecisional stages of decision-making. I say "at the minimum" because many minor to moderately important decisions may be made within the organization without reaching the attention of persons at the super-organization, political leadership level. Lack of formal participation at the decisional stage with respect to major issues ought not lead, however, to a minimization of their importance. It should be kept in mind that the political system's "memory" facilities for the most part are maintained and directly utilized by organization members and, moreover, that it is the latter more often than not who furnish the information required for reasonable selection among the various policy alternatives; who are the first to commit ideas to paper, thereby creating a potential focus for organizing discussion; and who are responsible for executing that decisional alternative which becomes governmental policy. These activities assume special significance when it is recalled that here, is in all human endeavors, factors such as selective attention, perception, transmission, and implementation may be operative. Role occupants within the politically relevant components of these organizations consequently are uniquely situated to be important contributors toward the shaping of the climate of opinion within which discussion of major issues and the suggestion of decisional alternatives takes place and to influence the effects policy may have.

Given their evident importance, one would expect to find that there currently exists a relatively developed and sophisticated lit-

statement concerning foreign policy "linkage groups" by Karl W. Deutsch, "External Influences on the Internal Behavior of States," in *Approaches to Comparative and International Politics*, ed. R. Barry Farrell, pp. 5–26.

erature concerning the background, personality characteristics, and political orientations and belief preferences of State and Defense Department officials. Yet John E. Harr laments that, on the contrary,

> until now, few statistics on the FSO corps have been published. Despite the key position occupied by the FSO corps in United States foreign affairs, the available literature on the corps is minuscule compared to the voluminous literature on the substance of foreign policy itself. Even when scholars deal with such subjects as how diplomacy is conducted, how foreign policy is made, or the administration of foreign affairs, the subject of personnel is only one of a number of topics covered and in some cases a very minor one.[4]

Similarly Snyder and Robinson, after stating that "no lengthy argument is required to establish the central importance of the way in which decision-makers perceive other countries and perceive the behavioral environment in which they must function," go on to suggest that the following questions ought to be carefully looked into:

> What are the theories of international relations which are shared by the total organizations or parts of it? Are there subcultures which consist of different ideologies which function to order and explain the external environment with which the Department must deal?. . . If there are significant variations in the theories associated with different decision-making roles, how do these interact with each other?[5]

A final illustration specifically relating to the "social organization of the military" finds Edinger positing the following research objectives:

> (1) The nature and composition of the military elite. . . . (2) What are the recruitment and mobility patterns of the military elite and the nature of the relationship among its members? . . . (3) What are the attitudes, images and expectations of the members of the military elite relative to their own

---

4. John E. Harr, *The Anatomy of the Foreign Service: A Statistical Profile*, pp. 1–2.
5. Richard C. Snyder and James A. Robinson, *National and International Decision-Making*, pp. 89, 144.

roles? . . . How do they view the internal and external political environment?[6]

Each of these quotes contains a strong allusion to the fact that, thus far, a comprehensive and reliable literature with respect to knowledge about foreign policy careerists is yet to be developed. Perhaps it is this shortcoming that has permitted stereotypes concerning the "typical" State and Defense Department officers to persist. The especially disturbing feature is that these stereotypical images have not been subjected to extensive empirical scrutiny. Very roughly put, the currently fashionable image of the State Department type is that of a fellow who is the son of upper-middle-class, Protestant parents of northwest European (probably British) ancestry. More than likely, so the popular image goes, he was born and raised in an urban(e) setting in New England or the Mid-Atlantic states. This fellow, naturally enough, attended a high-status college, either ivy league or little ivy (e.g. Williams). He attends church occasionally, but one certainly could not call him (in the conventional sense) a highly religious person. Although he probably grew up in a Republican atmosphere, he now claims to be a Democrat, but not an especially strong one. He also tends to think of himself as a liberal, but again not strongly so. On most foreign policy issues, he takes a "soft line"; that is, he definitely is not a "Cold War-rior" and all that that term appears to imply.

In contrast to the above stereotype, the military officer type is presumed to have been born and raised in a rural or small-town environment located in the South. His parents also were Protestant of northwest European ancestry. If he attended college, it was more than likely a military academy. Today, he regularly attends church and perceives himself as possessing a more than average commitment to religious principles. In addition, his political party preference is strongly Republican. He very much identifies himself ideologically with political conservatism. His style of thinking regarding political and social issues may be summarized as rigid and closed-minded. Finally, he takes a hard line on issues involving

6. Edinger, "Military Leaders and Foreign Policy-Making," p. 402.

Distinguishing Participants 9

United States participation in international politics. One would therefore expect his political preferences to be quite different from that of the typical State Department official.[7]

Needless to say, the aforementioned stereotypes often are closely associated with, and strongly colored by, normative elements relating to the issue of civil-military relations and the proper equilibrium of that relationship. However, one should definitely feel uneasy regarding, first, the assumption that the members of these two organizations can be so cleanly separated demographically and attitudinally and, second, the matter-of-factness with which such characteristics are attributed to these particular foreign policy elites.

If there is any theory (or better, generally held bias) operative here, it is that of the "military mind" argument. The latter, when it is employed, tends to focus upon two related aspects of (political) cognition: (1) that the content of military thought about political issues (*what* belief and opinion preferences are expressed) significantly differs from the content of comparable nonmilitary (e.g., State Department) thought; and (2) that the structural quality of military thought (*how* belief and opinion preferences are expressed) significantly differs from the structural quality of comparable nonmilitary thought. Are either or both of these claims descriptively accurate? It is difficult to offer a reply since sufficiently reliable and valid evidence simply is not available either to confirm or reject these propositions.[8]

---

7. For example, Walter Millis states that senior military officers "embody the military mind as it currently concerns us. The great majority come from small-town, small-business, small-professional backgrounds" (Walter Millis, "Puzzle of the 'Military Mind,'" *New York Times Magazine*, November 18, 1962, p. 142). Also see John P. Marquand, "Inquiry into the Military Mind," *New York Times Magazine*, March 30, 1952, p. 53; Hanson Baldwin, "The Military Move In," *Harper's Magazine* 195(December, 1947):481–89; J. Frank Dobie, "Samples of the Military Mind," *Harper's Magazine* 193(December, 1946):529–36; Gene M. Lyons, "The Military Mind," *Bulletin of the Atomic Scientists* 19(November, 1963):19–22; and MacAlister Brown and John W. Masland, "Some Evidence on the 'Military Mind'."

8. Sapin and Snyder say the following about "The Nature of the Military 'Threat'": "The view being set forth here is that the participation per se of the professional military in high-level governmental policy-making is not,

This study consequently attempts to address itself to several of the research questions cited earlier by Harr, Edinger, and Snyder and Robinson, and implied by the "military mind" argument. Before indicating its substantive essence, it should be pointed out that the present investigation consciously does not intend to consider each organization in its entirety. Quite obviously, State and Defense merely are subsystems of the greater national political system. The latter encompasses the former and much more. Similarly, one may partition each organization into "political-policy" and "nonpolitical-policy" parts. The political-policy part consists of that specific subset of roles and relationships within each organization *directly* involving the conduct of foreign political relations. Administration, public affairs, and so on are responsibilities fulfilled within the nonpolitical-policy sector. Actions taken by officials occupying positions within the latter, of course, may at various times indirectly have some political-policy importance. However, these effects not only are unintended but clearly are rather ephemeral when compared with the intensive and continuing efforts of political-policy officers. Including administrative and public affairs officials, for example, consequently would result in the focus of the investigation shifting from foreign relations skill-groups to a more inclusive and functionally ambiguous group of governmental personnel, a tendency we wish to avoid. Hence, what will be of concern here is not so much a question of whether the *Departments* of State and Defense may be demographically and attitudinally contrasted, but of whether the distinctively *political-policy parts* within each differ or are similar in composition.

in essence, what is regarded as dangerous. It is rather those 'military' attitudes, preferences, and patterns of thought and behavior which supposedly characterize the professional officer, and which, it is presumed, he brings with him into policy-making. In other words, it is essentially as the 'carrier' of certain values and attitudes, as the possessor of a 'military mind', that the military man becomes suspect. . . .

"Another obvious and fundamental question is the extent to which American professional military men, in their typical ways of acting and thinking, actually do fit the stereotype of the military man that has been presented" (Burton M. Sapin and Richard C. Snyder, *The Role of the Military in American Foreign Policy*, pp. 55–57).

Distinguishing Participants

The primary substantive focus of this study then is the beliefs of those officials occupying positions within the political-policy parts of the Departments of State and Defense. More specifically, we wish to ascertain whether these two groups of officials possess similar or dissimilar foreign policy belief systems (chapter 7). In order to accomplish this objective, it will be necessary to organize individual political beliefs around three dimensions; that is, beliefs pertaining either to communism, arms control and/or disarmament (hereafter, ACD), or nonalignment. It is proposed that these dimensions will cluster, be significantly intercorrelated, so as to form a coherent belief system. Assuming this is true, the general hypothesis as derived from previous discussion may be stated in the following way: taken as a group, political-military officers significantly more often than political-State Department officers will express beliefs that collectively may be designated as a hard-line belief system. The term *hard-line* is meant to convey a constellation of preferences that, within the time context of the 1950s and 1960s, consists of anticommunism and lack of sympathy for ACD and nonalignment. It is sufficient at this point to remark that such a divergence in viewpoint does in fact develop and that its roots are analyzed in chapter 8. There, a two-step procedure is utilized in an attempt to explain why this attitudinal contrast emerges and persists. First, it will be demonstrated that certain personal attributes and/or experiences are associated with the manifesting of one or the other belief system. Second, the reasons that the political-policy parts of the military and nonmilitary establishments exhibit compositional differences regarding those elements identified as being critical to the formation of political beliefs additionally will be revealed.

Before reaching this stage of the analysis, it will be necessary first to introduce and investigate (in chapters 3–6) those attribute elements that may contribute to our understanding of the formation of foreign policy-oriented political beliefs. The attributes to be considered concern each respondent's social origins (e.g., place of birth, size of hometown, father's occupation); religion (e.g., religious affiliation); political orientation (e.g., party identification, ideological identification); and cognitive style (e.g., the psychological-personality traits of dogmatism and rigidity). Two expectations emerge concerning these attribute variables. One, if the stereotypical images depicted earlier have any validity, analysis should reveal the existence of clearly observable and statistically significant dissimilarities when the demographic profiles are compared. The other, at least several from among the latter attributes can be employed in a fruitful way when attempting to explain the attitudinal divergence that arises.

There is yet another reason for investigating the distribution of these attribute variables. The representativeness of such bureaucratic organizations as the Departments of State and Defense, and the political-policy parts within them is to be considered. This issue has been a salient and controversial one for both professional bureaucracies. Each frequently has been accused of not reflecting the predominant characteristics of the society that it purports to serve. Before one can begin to evaluate these accusations, however, it is necessary to begin to conceptually refine the term *representativeness*. A perusal of the literature[9] indicates that representativeness typically has been conceived of in two ways: in a "compositional" and in an "interest" sense. In the first case, the degree to which any organization (or, for that matter, government) is representative is indicated by the extent to which its attribute profile (i.e., the sociological configuration formed by the distribution of its membership across the alternative categories of one or more social attribute variables such as geographical origins, religious affiliation, race) resembles the attribute profile of society. Democratization often is said to occur when the resemblance is considered substantial (i.e., a "condition" notion) or is noticeably increasing (i.e., a "process" notion); in other words, democratization is present when the "compositional representativeness" of an organization ex-

9. J. Donald Kingsley, *Representative Bureaucracy*; Paul P. Van Riper, *History of the United States Civil Service*, especially pp. 552 ff.; John Porter, *The Vertical Mosaic*, especially pp. 449–51; V. Subramaniam, "Representative Bureaucracy: A Reassessment," *American Political Science Review* 61 (December, 1967):1010–19; and Frederick C. Mosher, *Democracy and the Public Service*, especially pp. 10–14.

ceeds some threshhold or is becoming more evident. The second conception of representativeness is similar except that it focuses attention upon whether the "interests" existing in society are "articulated and aggregated" within the organization in proportion to the support they enjoy within the society. If one or several interests continually receive disproportionate salience within the organization, then that organization is said to be nonrepresentative. Note that the argument is not that each one of the components of an organization need be representative, but rather that every interest in society is given its fair due at the organizational level of decision-making. The nature of the organization's components remains essentially unspecified.

It is quite clear that these two conceptions of representativeness are analytically and operationally distinguishable. Nevertheless, it is also quite clear that many people assume that they are empirically related; that the attitudes and behavior of professional bureaucrats are determined mainly by the social attributes that describe them. The implication of this proposition is that interest representativeness is improbable unless and until compositional representativeness virtually exists. A further step is to connect the notion of the legitimacy of organizational outputs to the degree to which the decisional process is characterized by interest representativeness; deficiencies regarding the latter are perceived and interpreted to seriously undermine the legitimacy of output. Thus, the argument may be made that the legitimacy of an organization's outputs is a function of its interest representativeness, and the latter is unlikely unless compositional representativeness first is achieved. Put crudely: if we do not have our people in there, our view will not be seriously considered; and if our view is not seriously considered, then the decision taken has dubious authority for us.

The analysis that commences in chapter 3 attempts to deal with several, though not all, of the questions raised above. First, an effort is made to give further precision to the notion of representativeness, so that it in fact can be empirically investigated. Second, an attempt is made to determine whether or not the organizations studied are representative in the compositional sense. This is a thread that runs through and connects much of the discussion in chapters 3–5. Finally, a modest effort is made to examine the relationship between compositional and interest representativeness. This will grow out of the investigation of the correlates of foreign policy beliefs, a task mentioned earlier in the chapter where the issue related to explaining the anticipated divergence in beliefs between sample respondents. From the perspective of the representativeness issue, the critical question is whether social attribute variables and beliefs are significantly associated—whether "our people" have significantly different beliefs concerning international politics than "their people."

It should be noted that little will be said regarding the connection between beliefs and behavior. Some discussion of this subject will occur in the final chapter. Several reasons may be cited to justify this rather conspicuous underemphasis. First, behavioral data simply are unavailable given reasons of security and the lack of formal behavioral procedures such as roll-call votes and the like. Second, the paucity of previous work in this area discourages "high-risk" investigations that are not incremental in approach and modest with respect to goals.[10]

It is a major assumption of this study, however, that beliefs, and also political orientations and personality traits indirectly, may exert a profound influence upon the character of behavior. Hence, knowledge about these features ought to enable one to speculate with more confidence about the direction of the foreign political policy contribution of State and Defense Department political officials.[11] Also, it may be worthwhile at this time to make

10. On the credit side, the studies by Huntington, Janowitz, Harr, and Sapin and Snyder, which have already been cited, are impressive contributions. Several other investigations also proved relevant and interesting. They are W. Lloyd Warner et al., *The American Federal Executive*; Morris Janowitz, ed., *The New Military*; John W. Masland and Laurence I. Radway, *Soldiers and Scholars*; Regis Walther, *Orientations and Behavioral Styles of Foreign Service Officers*; Robert Ellsworth Elder, *The Policy Machine: The Department of State and American Foreign Policy*; and Charlton Ogburn, Jr., "The Flow of Policy-making in the Department of State," in *The Formulation and Administration of United States Foreign Policy*, ed. H. Field Haviland, appendix C, pp. 172–77.

11. Matthews, when discussing "Politics and Decision-Making," ex-

Distinguishing Participants 15

the rather obvious point that the stating of one's beliefs and opinions actually constitutes an aspect of behavior. For example, M. Brewster Smith says about his effort with Bruner and White: "Our investigations were long on the description and analysis of *opinions*, but short on the observation of consequential *behavior*, political or otherwise. . . . From a political scientist's standpoint as from a psychologist's, this is certainly a deficiency in our case materials . . . but *expressed* opinions are, after all, a form of behavior, and opinions *held* are but one type of behavioral disposition."[12]

The general aim of the inquiry, then, is to offer an investigation into a number of propositions that it is felt have been generally accepted as valid without the benefit of serious intellectual scrutiny. The paucity of previous work in this area alluded to earlier, however, dramatically underlines the very exploratory nature of the investigation. By "exploratory" I mean simply to forewarn the reader that what follows will not be so much a systematic confirmation (or the contrary) of hypotheses flowing from a formal theory or previous empirical analysis as an offering for consideration of certain conclusions suggested by an analysis of the data. It should be evident, however, that this study goes beyond the predominantly descriptive investigations of elites that have prevailed in the literature[13] by attempting, through explicit hypothesis-testing, to of-

presses a similar thought: "In their efforts to understand political decision-making, political scientists have emphasized the study of institutions rather than the study of men. . . . This approach provides only a partial view of political reality. Important political decisions are made by men interacting within an institutional context. It is the basic premise of this study that the social and psychological characteristics of the individual officials acting within a political institutional framework must be considered before an adequate understanding of politics and government is possible." Later he comments that "the ultimate aim of research on the social backgrounds of political decision-makers is to contribute to a better understanding of their behavior and thus to a clearer view of the entire governmental process" (Donald R. Matthews, *The Social Background of Political Decision-Makers*, pp. 3, 38).

12. M. Brewster Smith, "Opinions, Personality, and Political Behavior," *American Political Science Review* 52(1958):1, 14.

13. For example, Harr, *Anatomy of the Foreign Service*; Warner et al., *The American Federal Executive*; John J. Corson and R. Shale Paul, *Men Near the Top*; David T. Stanley, Dean E. Mann, and Jameson W. Doig, *Men Who Govern*; and Franklin P. Kilpatrick, Milton C. Cummings, Jr., and M. Kent Jennings, *The Image of the Federal Service*.

fer explanations for the descriptive findings that emerge regarding the beliefs of foreign policy officers. At the same time, it points to further subjects for investigation; namely, the precise relationship of beliefs to behavior and the effect of the behavior of such officials upon the general foreign policy process.

CHAPTER 2

The Organizational Location and Functions of Political-Policy Officials

The commentary of the present chapter is devoted to further defining the populations to be analyzed and to indicating the manner in which samples from these populations were selected. Some guidelines relating to this task have already been indicated. The populations are to consist of State and Defense Department careerists who occupy positions with assigned responsibilities directly relating to the conduct of foreign political relations.

With respect to the State Department, specifying "careerists" essentially draws attention to the Foreign Service Officer (hereafter, FSO) corps.[1] This is especially true since Wristonization, which prompted, through the process of lateral transfer, a wholesale absorption of many former Civil Service personnel into the

---

1. "The FSO corps is an institution within the large organization of the Department of State. Although the corps technically represents only one of several personnel categories utilized by the Department, it becomes quickly apparent that the corps occupies a very special position not enjoyed by the other major groups—the Civil Service employees who fill the bulk of the domestic jobs, the Foreign Service Reserve (temporary specialists), and the Foreign Service Staff (clerical and technical employees overseas) and foreign nationals (locally employed at overseas posts). The FSO corps is a professional group . . . it has developed the characteristics of a 'career service' in contradistinction to the general Civil Service" (Harr, *Anatomy of the Foreign Service*, p. 4). For historical treatments concerning the development of the Foreign Service, see William Barnes and John Heath Morgan, *The Foreign Service of the United States: Origins, Development, and Functions;* and Warren F. Ilchman, *Professional Diplomacy in the United States: 1779–1939.*

FSO corps.[2] The result of the Wriston "reform" has been not only a sharp increase in the size of the FSO corps—from about 1,300 officers in 1954 to approximately 3,700 in 1965—but also a situation in which nearly all the major positions below the appointee level in the most politically oriented and prestigious Washington bureaus, the so-called Geographic Bureaus, are now largely staffed by FSOs. Table 1 compares the allocation of FSOs with that of other professional level employees, namely Civil Service personnel of grade GS-9 and above, the Foreign Service Reserve, and members of the Foreign Service Staff of grade FSS-10 and above. Note that the great majority of personnel assigned to the State Department, i.e., 1,755 of 2,546, or nearly 69% of the total group, occupy positions falling under the Functional Bureau designation. Administration alone accounts for approximately 27% of the total. Somewhat different information emerges when employees are distinguished according to whether they are FSOs or not. First, only 32% (or 826 of 2,546) of the professional employees in fact are FSOs. Second, the composition of the Functional Bureaus and Executive Offices on the one hand, and the Geographic (or Area) Bureaus on the other, differs greatly as to the percentage of FSOs and non-FSOs contained within them. In absolute number, more FSOs are found within the non-Geographic than Geographic Bureaus. At the same time, it also is clear that FSOs predominate within the latter (77% versus 23% for the non-FSOs), whereas they constitute only a small minority elsewhere (33% versus 67%, and 21% versus 79%). The great difference in size between Area and non-Area Bureaus should not be allowed to obscure this differential concentration of FSO and non-FSO personnel.

Skill-specialties within these bureaus are formally differentiated by the State Department in terms of eleven broad "functional"

---

2. The report that formed the basis for the State Department reorganization of 1954–58 is commonly referred to as the Wriston Committee Report, after the committee's chairman. The official citation is *Toward a Stronger Foreign Service*, Report of the Secretary of State's Committee on Personnel, Department of State Publication 5458. For a discussion of the effects of Wristonization, see Zara S. Steiner, *The State Department and the Foreign Service: The Wriston Report—Four Years Later*.

TABLE 1
PROFESSIONAL LEVEL EMPLOYEES ASSIGNED TO STATE DEPARTMENT BY ORGANIZATIONAL LOCATION, 1962

	FSO		Non-FSO		TOTAL
	%	N	%	N	N
Executive Offices	33	112	67	227	339
Functional Bureaus					
Intelligence and Research	33	70	67	140	210
Public Affairs	11	10	89	83	93
Educational and Cultural Affairs	27	42	73	115	157
Economic	53	75	47	66	141
Security and Consular	11	43	89	331	374
Administration	12	81	88	595	676
International Organization	43	45	57	59	104
Subtotal	21	366	79	1,389	1,755
Geographic Bureaus					
Inter-American	69	58	31	26	84
European	80	111	20	27	138
Far Eastern	79	67	21	18	85
Near Eastern and South Asian	78	54	22	15	69
African	76	58	24	18	76
Subtotal	77	348	23	104	452
Total	32	826	68	1,720	2,546

NOTE: Adapted from "Table 17, Professional Level Employees by Organizational Location," in Harr, *Anatomy of the Foreign Service*, p. 27. Related statistical information is contained in Harr, *The Professional Diplomat*, pp. 145–67. Percentage rounding may result in totals slightly exceeding or falling short of 100%.

fields. The data in table 2 indicate that only five of the eleven have substantial representation. The functional speciality of direct concern here, the political one, is the most numerous, with 18% representation. Yet, both in terms of absolute number and proportion relative to the total FSO corps, the rather small size of this contingent is surprising, at least to the author. It means that less than one-fifth of all FSOs at any given time are involved with specifically political functions in that part (FSO corps) of that establish-

TABLE 2
FUNCTIONAL ASSIGNMENTS OF FSOs, 1962

ASSIGNMENTS	%	N
Political:		
General	1.0	38
Functional	2.5	90
Area	14.7	541
Subtotal	18.2	669
Program Direction:		
General	7.2	264
Political	1.5	56
Economic	0.4	14
Consular	1.8	68
Subtotal	10.9	402
Economic	13.7	503
Administrative	16.1	592
Consular	15.8	581
Commercial	3.7	131
Labor	1.0	36
International Organization	1.5	54
Intelligence	2.0	74
Public Affairs	0.7	24
Cultural Affairs	1.3	49
Miscellaneous	0.8	28
None	14.3	527
Total	100	3,670

NOTE: Adapted from "Table 9: Functional Assignments of FSOs," in Harr's *Anatomy of the Foreign Service*, p. 17. "Miscellaneous" includes Legal, Science, Geography, and Field Post Operations. "None" includes officers between assignments, in training, or over-complement at posts. Also see Harr, *The Professional Diplomat*, pp. 145–67.

ment (State) centrally responsible for conducting foreign political relations.[3]

The most important feature of the data contained in table 2 relates to the question of where FSOs with political functional spe-

---

3. "The most striking point in this distribution of [State] personnel [in 1948] was the assignment of only 336 [out of 5,905, or 5. 7 percent] to political affairs when there was no question that the one function the Department of State alone was set up to perform was the conduct of political foreign relations" (James L. McCamy, *The Administration of American Foreign Affairs*, p. 57). Hence, the condition does not stem from any recent development.

cialties are to be found. It shows that approximately 81% (or 541 of 669) of those FSOs having political assignments occupy Area Bureau positions. Political FSOs then definitely are not uniformly distributed through the department's bureaus. Harr reinforces this point with respect to domestic duty when he declares that "Washington assignments in the political field are distributed among the five geographic bureaus."[4]

In view of the above pattern and the need for parsimony in sampling strategy, a decision was made to define the relevant population as those political FSOs occupying positions within the Geographic Bureaus. This exclusive attention upon the latter bureaus implies that, first, only those officers who are on Washington assignment may be chosen as sample respondents; and second, political FSOs in the Functional Bureaus and Executive Offices cannot be chosen as sample respondents. The first qualification can only be a serious detriment if it is true that political FSOs on overseas assignments as a group are different in important ways from their counterparts at the State Department. But, because of institutionalized assignment rotation, the contrary situation appears to be more probable. Hence, little if anything is lost by insisting on the more restrictive formulation. The second qualification also does not seem to result in serious consequences. The effect of this restriction is to exclude only about 19% of the total political FSO group. Thus, the overwhelming majority remain as possible sample respondents. For any finding to be adversely affected by

4. Harr, *Anatomy of the Foreign Service*, p. 18. The Bureau of International Organization Affairs sometimes is designated as a "geographic" bureau. Several statements appearing in the academic and governmental literatures, however, led me to think of International Organization as a "functional" bureau, or, at least, as somehow being qualitatively different from the geographic bureaus. Harr, for example, definitely views International Organization as a functional bureau. Elder, on the other hand, first says that "policy-making in the Department of State is centered in five regional bureaus," but then in parentheses adds that "the Bureau of International Organization Affairs is often considered a sixth regional bureau" (*The Policy Machine*, p. 19). Perhaps the strongest argument for excluding International Organization is the fact that the State Department itself, as table 2 indicates, differentiates between political and international organization functional specialties.

this restriction, the 19% (not included) group would have to be sufficiently different from the 81% subset so that the latter is prevented from acting as a satisfactory estimate of the total political group. This possibility seems unlikely given the 81% inclusion ratio and the lack of evidence suggesting such a dramatic contrast in character between the two.

Defining the relevant population in the above way, in addition, implies that some FSOs with "program direction" functional specialties ought to be included. Note that, within the general category, 56 (or about 14%) of the 402 "program direction" FSOs are subclassified as being political. The question emerges as to whether this relatively small group of officers ought to be sampled. Several reasons may be offered to explain why they were not. First, a very practical consideration—most of these higher ranking officials proved to be unavailable for interview. Thus, including only political FSOs (i.e., not including "political-program direction" FSOs) results in working with a known, relevant, and accessible population. Second, the decision appears to be in conformity with a distinction Harr makes based on State's differentiation of functional specialities. He says, when offering a definition of *program direction*, that "for the purpose of this study, executives will be defined as all persons in the home office of the Department in the line of command at the rank of Deputy Office Director or higher; Chiefs of Mission (Ambassadors); Deputy Chiefs of Mission; and Consuls General."[5] The evident implication of the above definition is that there is a functional break in the line of command at the deputy office director level. Positions at this and higher levels now fall under the designation of program direction (as distinguished from political, consular, and so on), with responsibilities that, as the title itself conveys, involve executive or managerial, as well as substantive, skills. Thus, this particular division also has some meaningfulness beyond expediency in that it represents a recognition of different *forms* of activity being performed at different *levels* within the hierarchy of the bureau.

Exclusion of this upper stratum of program-direction officials has

5. Harr, *Anatomy of the Foreign Service*, p. 68.

the effect of narrowing the population for the State Department to one that includes essentially country desk officers and their political assistants (where there are any assigned). The typical responsibilities relevant to this particular level in the line of command within State and its geographical bureaus entail both carrying the brunt of the day-to-day, face-to-face liaison work of intergovernmental relations and participation in the formulation of foreign policy. Needless to say, FSOs occupying such roles have an importance difficult to minimize; especially since it is the very character of the former work (e.g., its central position in the accumulation and dissemination of information) that directly enhances their impact regarding the latter responsibility. For example, Elder remarks:

> A country desk officer in one of the regional bureaus of the Department of State may be low man on the totem pole so far as seniority in policy-making is concerned, yet he wields significant power in the formulation of American Foreign Policy. With a considerable degree of truth, it may be said of him that he is both wheelhorse and sparkplug of the decision-making process. . . . In spite of these changes, the Department's 114 country desk officers remain the eyes and ears, the brain and voice, of America in a troubled world. . . . Almost every scrap of information which government agencies collect on an area and many policy papers from other agencies proposing action in an area cross the country desk. . . . The desk remains the real contact point in the Department for the diplomatic post abroad and the foreign embassy in Washington. As the drafting officer who usually is first to put policy ideas on paper, the desk man is in a sense the initiator of American policy toward his assigned country. . . . The desk man's influence at all levels in the decision-making process stems from his detailed knowledge of an area and his role as a drafting officer.[6]

Former United States Ambassador to Cuba Earl E. T. Smith has a considerably less detached and sanguine opinion regarding the part country desk officers play within the foreign policy process.

> What is really our policy? Who makes it? How is it established? . . .
> I testified to the Senate that I had learned from experience and observa-

---

6. *The Policy Machine*, pp. 19–22. McCamy, writing in 1950, sums up their importance by stating that "political affairs were the product of the career Foreign Service Officers in the key positions on the 'country desk'" (*Administration of American Foreign Affairs*, p. 67).

tion that our policies are determined by influential individuals in the lower echelon of the State Department in their day-by-day actions. By the time the higher officials receive them policies have already been made and they have to live by them. In this book I have quoted from testimony of four other Ambassadors who testified under oath to the same effect. It comes too late to correct the efforts of the desk-men, who often become so devoted to the countries to which they are assigned that they forget that their business is the United States. The Fourth Floor consists of desk-men, as they are called. They are career Foreign Service Officers who frequently look upon political appointees as here today and gone tomorrow. . . .

From my life experience in public service and in business, I have reached the conclusion that the structure of organization in the State Department is faulty by law. No President, no Secretary of State, no matter how sincere and purposeful, can protect the United States from the damage of this day-by-day operation of the lower officials. These men are protected by the Foreign Service Office Law, by the Civil Service Law, by the Veterans Administration Law, and by Congressional pressure. For all practical purposes, they cannot be dismissed. They protect each other as though they belonged to a fraternity.[7]

In his book *Anatomy of the State Department*, Smith Simpson presents a somewhat more balanced assessment of the contributions of country desk officers.

The Department thus consists of a broad, pyramidal structure of geographic and functional bureaus headed by the Assistant Secretaries. The geographic bureaus have in the past borne the brunt of the Department's work of digesting information and making daily decisions, and they still consider themselves the custodians of the Republic's real diplomacy. . . .

At the bottom of the pyramid has traditionally sat the "country desk officer." . . .

The country desk officer gradually receded in importance in our foreign relations generally. Too many other departments and agencies of our government came to have similar officers. . . . In fact, the latter came to be but one element in a vast complex of public and private relationships sustained by our nation with every other part of the world.

But the desk officer remained of crucial importance to the operations of State itself. He could catalyze action if he had the knowledge, imagination, motivation and courage to do so. He could help tie the Department together by systematic, imaginative consultation with his opposite numbers in other bureaus. He could do the same for the entire Federal establishment. On the other hand, he could reduce his Government's performance to superficial, prosaic terms if he lacked these qualities, or dwelt too much

---

7. Earl E. T. Smith, *The Fourth Floor: An Account of the Castro Communist Revolution*, pp. 226–28, 231.

Organizational Location and Functions 25

upon his personal advancement. In fact, the deficiencies of most desk officers were so great as to generate proposals to put more senior officers, even ambassadors, into his job. Secretary Rusk has been one of those thinking along this line.[8]

These three statements are sufficiently detailed to illustrate the importance of the activities of country desk officers within the foreign relations establishment. A list of the names of individuals occupying such positions consequently was developed in order to permit the selection of a representative sample. The main source was the State Department's telephone directory. The list when completed contained 117 individuals nearly all of whom were country desk officers. A small group of FSOs who acted as political assistants to the latter also were included. A random sample of 40 then was drawn from among the 117 names. Of the 40 who were selected, 37 were interviewed, 2 agreed to be but because of time and logistical problems could not be included, and one FSO preferred not to participate, the only such case.

Table 3 describes the organizational sources of this FSO sample. Note that the latter represents approximately 32% of the total political-FSO population as it was defined. The percentage interviewed within each particular Geographic Bureau ranges from a low of 21% for the Far East (or East Asian) Bureau, to a high of 41% for the African one. Because of these differences in interview rates, the actual sample is not exactly similar to what would be, on the basis of the relative size of each bureau, a perfectly proportional sample. The major deviance that emerges is that the African Bureau is somewhat overrepresented whereas the European one is somewhat underrepresented. On balance, however,

---

8. Smith Simpson, *Anatomy of the State Department*, pp. 18–20. Please note that the present discussion uses the year 1965 as its reference point. Comments on organizational structure, names, and so on, therefore, are relevant directly to the period in which sampling occurred, and may not necessarily be entirely accurate today. For example, see Simpson's remarks on the department's attempt to supersede "the desk officer of junior rank with a 'country director' of senior grade" (ibid., p. 21). Also see Harr, *The Professional Diplomat*, pp. 302–11, for a detailed discussion of the "country director" reorganization.

TABLE 3
ORGANIZATIONAL SOURCES OF FSO SAMPLE

GEOGRAPHIC BUREAU	POPULATION		SAMPLE		PERCENTAGE OF BUREAU INTERVIEWED	PROPORTIONAL SAMPLE
	%	N	%	N		
Africa	23	27	30	11	41	9
Europe	30	35	24	9	26	11
Far East	12	14	8	3	21	4
Inter-America	18	21	22	8	38	7
Near East and South Asia	17	20	16	6	30	6
Total	100	117	100	37	32	37

the difference between the actual and proportional sample appears quite small.

The attempt to select a representative sample for the military establishment presented additional problems. The initial intention here was to identify those organizations within the Defense Department primarily and directly involved in foreign political policy formulation.

This meant focusing attention upon five groups of military officers: the Joint Staff of the Joint Chiefs of Staff: International Security Affairs of the Office of the Secretary of Defense (hereafter, ISA); and the political staffs, respectively, of the Army (International Policy Divsion), Navy (Operations 61), and Air Force (International Affairs Division).[9]

---

9. This selection was based on a careful examination of Defense Department organizational charts and some previous work done in this area, especially: Samuel P. Huntington, *The Common Defense: Strategic Programs in National Politics*; Timothy W. Stanley, *American Defense and National Security*; William R. Kintner, *Forging a New Sword: A Study of the Department of Defense*; and H. Field Haviland, *The Formulation and Administration of United States Foreign Policy*. The "political staffs" of the services are not completely comparable because the range and composition of responsibilities are not precisely the same for all three. However, the differences are rather slight, and for the purpose of this analysis may be overlooked. It should also be noted that civilians employed by the Defense Department and assigned to ISA and the three political staffs were not interviewed. Comparison of their backgrounds and beliefs with those of the military

ISA is often referred to as the "Pentagon's State Department" and does in fact bear a striking structural resemblance to State. Aside from a Military Assistance division, it consists of a number of area offices (e.g., Directorate for the European Region, Far East Region, and so on), a Policy Planning Staff, and various (in the State Department sense) functional offices (e.g., Foreign Economic Affairs, International Logistics Negotiations). Each of these units contains a director and deputy director, and a professional staff of military and civilian ("general schedule") careerists. Responsibilities, again with the exception of Military Assistance, parallel the example of State. In 1960, Haviland described them in the following way:

> This office [ISA] has been given clear responsibility for, and control over policy and programming for the military assistance program. At the present time, this program absorbs about one-half of the time and energies of the staff. . . . The second major function is coordinating and supporting the Department of Defense representation on the National Security Council, its Planning Board, and the Operations Coordinating Board. . . . The third major function . . . and in a sense the most basic of its responsibilities, is to develop Department of Defense policy positions on a broad range of politico-military problems in United States relations with other countries.[10]

If ISA is the Pentagon's State Department, then the Army's International Policy Division, Navy's Operations 61, and Air Force's International Affairs Division may be referred to as the Services' ISA. They are organizationally and functionally describable in terms very similar to the plans and area offices component of ISA. Like the latter, they have administrative and other counterparts.[11] In addition, the service staffs have a special relationship with the Joint Staff. They are the prime source of both personnel and ideas for the Joint Staff. According to Huntington, the last feature reflects "the political and legislative character of the strategy-making

officers assigned to these organizations would be an interesting subject for future research.
  10. *Formulation and Administration of U.S. Foreign Policy*, p. 83.
  11. For a discussion of the Service staffs, see Masland and Radway, *Soldiers and Scholars*, pp. 514–15, and Burton M. Sapin, "The Organization and Procedures of the National Security Council Mechanism," in *Formulation and Administration of U.S. Foreign Policy*, ed. Haviland, pp. 167–68.

process. . . . Hence, it is to be expected that original contributions and policy proposals would come from the service staffs rather than the Joint Staff, which functioned as a negotiating agency."[12] To reiterate, these four organizations, plus the Joint Staff, were identified initially as the relevant political-military population. However, paralleling the situation in State, this first formulation had to be modified, in this case because the Joint Staff proved to be unavailable for interview. This unfortunate circumstance not only seriously reduces the size of an already small population but, more importantly, removes from the analysis a prominent part of the political subsystem of the Defense Department. On the other hand, the personnel who are recruited for the Joint Staff very often previously held positions in ISA and/or the service staffs. Thus, it is quite possible that the "political" personnel associated with the Joint Staff, and ISA and Service staff officers, would respond in essentially similar ways. Including rather than excluding the Joint Staff, hence, probably would not produce significantly dissimilar data configurations or statistical findings; in other words, adding the Joint Staff, if it were possible to do so, would more than likely have the effect of promoting redundancy rather than change.[13] With this somewhat comforting argument in mind, a list of the

12. Huntington, *The Common Defense*, pp. 160–70.
13. Two factors would undermine the validity of this argument. First, some dramatic change in attitude occurs between the time an officer serves in ISA and/or the Service staffs and his recruitment into the Joint Staff. This counteridea does not appear to be very persuasive. It takes many years in service to reach the positions that are being considered here; this is especially true regarding ISA and the Joint Staff. Thus, each officer who is recruited for a long time has been exposed to departmental socialization. Nor are Joint Staff role demands so peculiarly different from the others so as to foster a substantial shift in political beliefs. In addition, later data analysis will demonstrate that military newtimers and oldtimers (i.e., defined according to length of service) almost without exception do not differ in their demographic and attitudinal characteristics. Thus, continuity in attribute configuration, not change, is the pattern. Second, the argument would be undermined if the recruitment criteria employed by the Joint Staff resulted in their selecting only a particular class of officers from among those previously with ISA or the Service staffs. The existence of such a selection factor cannot be directly affirmed or rejected since the author does not have pertinent data on the subject.

military officers assigned to "Geographic Area-Political" positions below the deputy director level within ISA and the three Service staffs was obtained in each case from the respective executive officer. Table 4 indicates the composition of the military sample according to organization and branch of service.

TABLE 4

ORGANIZATIONAL SOURCES OF MILITARY SAMPLE

A. By Organization

ORGANIZATION	POPULATION		SAMPLE		PERCENTAGE INTERVIEWED	PROPORTIONAL SAMPLE
	%	N	%	N		
ISA	41	28	41	24	86	24
Army Staff	20	14	22	13	93	12
Navy Staff	17	12	19	11	92	10
Air Force Staff	22	15	17	10	67	12
Total	100	69	100	58	84	58

B. By Branch of Service

ORGANIZATION	ARMY		NAVY		AIR FORCE		TOTAL	
	%	N	%	N	%	N	%	N
ISA	19	11	12	7	10	6	41	24
Army Staff	22	13					22	13
Navy Staff			19	11			19	11
Air Force Staff					17	10	17	10
Total	41	24	31	18	28	16	100	58

From a total population of 69 military officers, 58, or 84%, were interviewed. The particular proportion interviewed in each of the four suborganizational strata varied from 67% to 93%. In order for the interviewed sample to have been perfectly proportional to the organizational composition of the population, one less individual from the army service staff should have been included, one less from the navy, and two more from the air force. The variation of the actual from the proportional sample again appears to be quite small.

More serious is the fact that the sample, strictly speaking, is not a probability one. Yet this objection, though justified, may for the purposes of this analysis be compromised. First, there is no reason to believe that the nonrespondent group basically differs from the sample. The primary reason they were not interviewed was lack of time; that is, their names happened to appear at the end of an alphabetical list. In addition, because all of the military officers who were approached agreed to participate and were interviewed, the nonrespondent group does not include a single self-selected individual. In other words, there is little to suggest that compromise here (i.e., treating for purposes of analysis the actual sample as if it were a probability sample) would especially alter the findings or the interpretation of findings.

Comparing the two samples according to year of birth reveals that the military group is composed of older individuals than the FSO group. Over two-thirds of the military sample, as compared

TABLE 5

YEAR OF BIRTH

YEAR OF BIRTH	MILITARY		FSO	
	%	N	%	N
Prior to 1919	40	23	11	4
1920–24	29	17	35	13
1925–29	22	13	35	13
1930 +	9	5	19	7
Total	100	58	100	37

with 46% of the FSOs, were born prior to 1925.[14] This is not at all surprising, since the conduct of foreign relations is more central to the FSO corps than the military. With the former, political-policy responsibilities involve almost all ranks of the hierarchy. In the

---

14. This contrast in age may play a confounding role in any analysis that attempts to compare the two samples. Age would have such an impact if it were significantly related to the variables being considered. Checking through the data analyses contained in this study, however, reveals that age did not have a disturbing influence on statistical results.

military, on the contrary, it is a position that an officer usually attains after considerable line duty, and only at a relatively late period in his career.

As table 6 illustrates, the military sample is certainly drawn from grade strata representing both a smaller proportion of their organization and the higher levels of the authority structure. For example, only about 5% of the armed forces' officers in 1962 had

TABLE 6

GRADE DISTRIBUTION OF SAMPLES AND DEPARTMENTS

A. The Military

Rank	Sample	Army	Navy	Air Force
General/Admiral		0.5%	0.4%	0.3%
Colonel/Captain	47%	5	6	4
Lt. Col./Commander	22	12	12	9
Major/Lt. Commander	26	17	18	22
Captain/Lieutenant	5	31	26	38
Lieutenant/Lt. JG, Ensign		35	37	27
Total	100%	100%	100%	100%

B. The Foreign Service

Rank	Sample	Foreign Service	
		Political	Total
Career Ambassador			0.02%
Career Minister		0.5%	2
FSO-1		5	9
FSO-2	3%	14	12
FSO-3	46	26	19
FSO-4	24	21	18
FSO-5	14	16	13
FSO-6	14	13	14
FSO-7		4	10
FSO-8			5
Total	100%	100%	100%

NOTE: The data for the Army, Navy, and Air Force grade distributions are cited by Kurt Lang, "Technology and Career Management in the Military Establishment," in *The New Military*, ed. Morris Janowitz, p. 69, table 16, "Grade Distribution of Active Duty Personnel, 1962." Lang states that the relevant data source is the Statistical Services Center, Office of the Secretary of Defense. The "Foreign Service" data are adapted from Harr, *The Professional Diplomat*, pp. 146, 158.

achieved the rank of colonel or navy captain, yet nearly one-half of the entire military sample is composed of officers of such rank. At the other end of the spectrum, 5% of the military sample are army or air force captains, or navy lieutenants, whereas this rank alone accounts for about one-third of all military officers. The lowest officer rank, which accounts for another third of all military officers, is not even represented in the sample. Contrast this with the generally more representative nature of the FSO sample. Note that including "political-program direction" office and deputy office directors probably would have produced a rank distribution with greater FSO-2 and FSO-1 representation. As it now stands, the proportion within the FSO sample who are senior officers (i.e., FSO-4 and above) is nearly equivalent to the Foreign Service-Political figure (73% versus 75%), yet substantially exceeds the total Foreign Service figure (73% versus 54%). Thus, although both samples mainly include officers from the higher ranks (the modal categories clearly being colonel/captain and FSO-3), at the same time, the military is even more selective in this respect than the FSO one.

A highly structured oral interview then was administered to the officers included in the military and FSO samples. It consisted essentially of two sections. A section designed to deal with social origins, political orientation, and cognitive style was composed of a number of rather standard survey questions generally of the fixed alternative or factual variety. The other section related to the respondent's perception and interpretation of international political issues. The questions here were all open-ended ones.

An effort was made to pretest the initial form of the interview schedule. Seven members of the University of Michigan ROTC faculty and several advanced undergraduate students in political science participated. Although some rather obvious changes were therefore made, the procedure was not very successful because of the lack of genuine sample comparability. Also, because of the relatively small size of the FSO and military sample, it was not desirable to utilize the first group of interviews conducted for pretest purposes. As a result, the open-ended belief and opinion

Organizational Location and Functions

questions did not, and under the circumstances could not, benefit from systematic pretest. The interview schedule finally employed is reproduced in the appendix.

CHAPTER 3
Social Origins

The social origins (and religious convictions, political orientations, and cognitive characteristics) of those individuals who collectively constitute the distinctly political policy units within the FSO corps and the Pentagon are of interest on two counts. First, there is the question of whether the two groups manifest significant differences in composition. Second, and of more importance, is the question of the relationship of such features to the formation of particular beliefs concerning international political phenomena. Taking these questions in order, this and the next three chapters will be devoted to the former problem. Hence, the data appearing in these chapters will be utilized for two purposes: first, to provide information concerning the composition of our samples and, second, to serve as possible correlates of attitudinal variables.

Here, then, the primary concern is with whether the FSO and military samples do in fact manifest similar or contrasting profiles with respect to a number of social attributes. The attributes to be considered are grouped into three categories: geographical background, characteristics of the parents (e.g., father's occupation, nativity of parents), and education. The strategy to be employed regarding examination of these variables will be a classical and simple one. In every case, the guiding postulate (i.e., null hypothesis) is that the particular attribute under investigation is distributed similarly through both samples. For example, if only two scores, "plus" and "minus," are possible regarding some attribute variable, then, for analytical purposes, it is postulated that the proportion of FSOs who score plus will be approximately equal to the proportion of military officers who do so. The two samples in terms of their patterns of response consequently are assumed to be the same.

However, since several previous studies and popular stereotypes in general suggest that the officers included in the two samples differ with reference to place of birth, size of hometown, and so on, the actual expectation is that the aforementioned "no difference" hypothesis will be rejected, not affirmed.[1] Rejection would imply that a relationship exists between organizational affiliation (whether the officer is associated with the foreign service or the military) and attribute score.

Secondarily, the analysis will attempt to say something about the "compositional representativeness" of the organizations being investigated. As stated in chapter 1, the degree to which an organization is representative is indicated by the extent to which its attribute profile resembles the attribute profile of society. This can be done by simply juxtaposing the two relevant distributions and measuring the extent of their similarity. What is difficult, and more important perhaps, is the task of explaining revealed "nonrepresentativeness"; that is, why an organization does not exhibit compositional representativeness.

The model depicted in figure 1 attempts to indicate the sources of the compositional characteristics of organizations. Three successive general "filter stages" are identified.[2] The compositional

1. Two statistical tests are primarily employed in this study in order to facilitate making a decision concerning rejection of the "no difference" hypothesis. They are the chi-square coefficient (hereafter, χ^2) and Gamma, a statistic proposed by Leo A. Goodman and William H. Kruskal in "Measures of Association for Cross Classifications," *Journal of the American Statistical Association* 49(1954):732–64. Except where otherwise indicated, they will be applied respectively when the data in question are being treated as either nominal or ordinal.

2. Here, I have borrowed from Lester G. Seligman, "Opportunity, Risk, Selection, and Decision-Making: A Model of Political Recruitments." (Paper presented at the 66th American Political Science Association Meeting, Los Angeles, California, September 8–12, 1970.)

FIGURE 1
THE MAIN SOURCES
OF THE COMPOSITIONAL CHARACTERISTICS OF ORGANIZATIONS

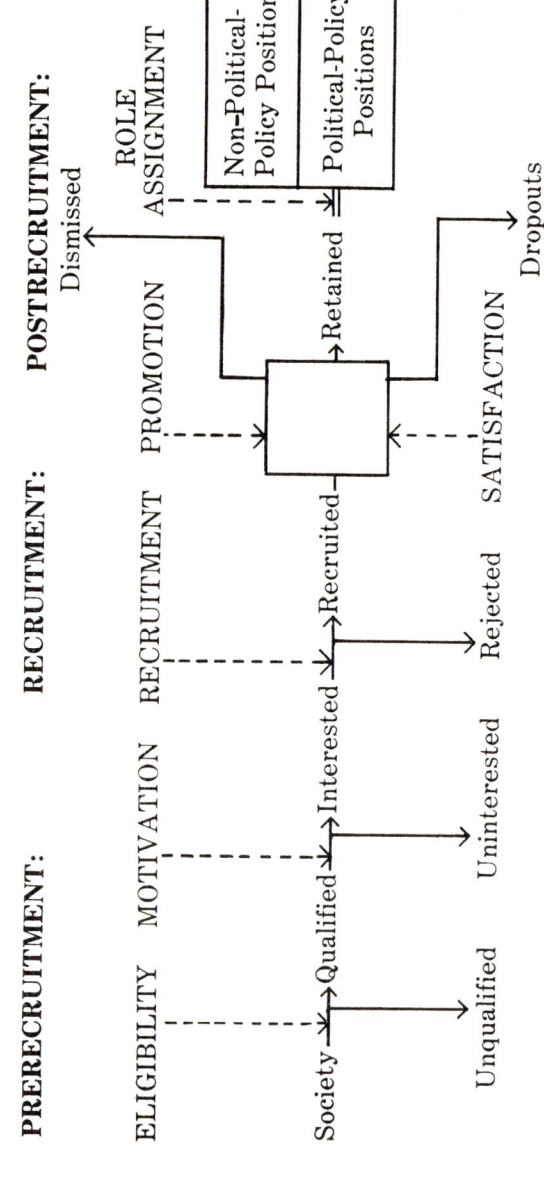

characteristics of an organization is thought to reflect the differentiation of individuals occurring within each of them.

The first identified as prerecruitment, has two aspects: that of eligibility and that of motivation. Each organization, because of the very nature of its responsibilities, requires highly educated officers. Hence, in order for an individual to be eligible as a candidate for recruitment into the organization, he needs to present certain formal education credentials; for example, a college degree. This single "objective" qualification will eliminate a good part of the total population of society from consideration; they are unqualified for candidacy. Those individuals who possess this and other prescribed credentials constitute the qualifying population. A moment's thought would make it clear that the total and qualifying populations may be dramatically dissimilar. Let us assume that once again we are working with an attribute that only has two categories, plus and minus. The above would quite obviously be the case where a far higher proportion of "pluses" graduate from college than "minuses." The second aspect of prerecruitment, motivation, is addressed to an analogous question: What proportion of "plus" and "minus" individuals who qualify as candidates actually wish to become organization officers? Many more (or less) "plus" qualifiers than "minus" ones may aspire to the latter occupation. The aspiring population, the pool from which the organization actually is selecting, consequently, may differ in its proportion of "plus" members from both the qualifying and total populations.

In the second filter stage, identified as recruitment, candidates are differentiated according to whether they are rejected or recruited into the organization. The basis for choice by the organization, whether accomplished by "achievement" or "ascriptive" criteria, is of secondary importance to the analysis. What is critical is the consequence: is the recruited population significantly different from the aspiring one? Or, to use our previous terms, are substantially more plus candidates recruited than minus ones?[3]

---

3. For detailed descriptions of the Foreign Service recruitment process, see Ilchman, *Professional Diplomacy in the U.S.*; Barnes and Morgan, *Foreign*

Postrecruitment, the final filter stage, has two aspects: promotion and satisfaction. Officers may leave the organization voluntarily because they are relatively dissatisfied. These individuals, the dropouts, may either be disenchanted with the organization or perceive that better opportunities exist elsewhere.[4] Other officers may leave because they have to; that is, they are dismissed. Those who do not leave and continue membership in the organiziation form the "retained" population.[5] Quite clearly, the recruited and retained populations may be quite dissimilar if relatively more pluses are retained than minuses. Needless to say, the same reasoning can be extended to the division of the retained population according to whether or not officers occupy positions within the political-policy parts of the Departments of State and Defense.

In sum, the model suggests that the compositional characteristics of an organization is affected by differentiations occurring within three general filter stages. This is not to say, of course, that all three have equal importance. Quite the contrary, the task of explaining the degree of compositional representativeness that is manifested includes attempting to indicate the relative weight of each filter stage. Thus, prerecruitment, recruitment, and postrecruitment, when related to the objective of explaining composi-

---

Service of the U.S.; and Frances Fielder and Godfrey Harris, *The Quest for Foreign Affairs Officers: Their Recruitment and Selection*.

4. See James G. March and Herbert A. Simon, *Organizations* (New York: John Wiley and Sons, 1958), pp. 83–111, for a detailed discussion of "the decision to participate" in an organization.

5. The "retained" population also will include individuals who have undergone "lateral transfer." This form of organizational mobility, where the individual does not join at a low rank but explicitly enters at a level corresponding to that which he already has achieved in another organization, very frequently is distinguished from conventional recruitment. Lateral transfer can be important if those persons who are recruited in this way are significantly different from the conventionally recruited group and are sufficient in number to make a difference with respect to the composition of the total organization. A perusal of our sample respondents reveals that this twofold condition does not prevail here (in spite of the possibility of "Wristonization" having an effect in the Foreign Service sample), and consequently the impact of lateral transfer need not be directly considered in this analysis.

Social Origins

tional characteristics, are visualized as competing hypotheses. Each of these three possible explanations implies a different relationship between the aforementioned populations. The existence of the following relationship supports the contention that prerecruitment is predominant: there is a significant difference between the total and aspiring populations, but no difference between the latter, and the recruitment and retained profiles. The recruitment possibility implies the following relationship: no significant differences exist between the total and aspiring populations and the recruitment and retained profiles; a significant difference emerges between the aspiring and recruitment profiles. The claim of the final contention is enhanced if the only significant difference to be found is between the recruitment and retained profiles. It should be noted that these three theoretical alternatives are not mutually exclusive; more than one may be operative in any given situation. Singly or in combination, such conditions may be detrimental to achieving compositional representativeness of the political-military and Foreign Service, as the term is operationalized here.

Before beginning our analysis, it may be worthwhile at this time to indicate very briefly why the particular set of variables introduced in this and the next three chapters were chosen for examination. Perhaps the most cogent reason for their selection is that, given the experience gained from previous investigations, these variables are expected to provide some clues as to why our respondents express the political beliefs they do. Even a cursory inspection of the literature will reveal that the variables that have been selected very often appear in studies having a substantive focus similar to this one and, more often than not, were shown to be associated in a critical way with the expression of political beliefs. We will refer many times to these other efforts as our investigation proceeds. Presently, by way of example, we may cite the statement of Berelson, Lazarfeld, and McPhee:

> In contemporary America, political events and social differentiation have combined to produce three major types of political cleavage: (1) occupational, income and status cleavages; (2) religious, racial and ethnic cleav-

ages; and (3) regional and urban-rural cleavages. . . . In Elmira, then, it is the socioeconomic classes, on the one hand, and the religious and ethnic groups on the other, that serve as the social carriers of political traditions. In the country at large, to these two kinds of differentiation in the population is added the ecological division of region or size of community (e.g., the metropolitan area as against the small town). In contrast, there are only minor differences in voting between men and women or between young and old or, indeed, on any other characteristic.[6]

Additionally, in one of the most extensive treatments of the subject yet attempted, *The Social Background of Political Decision-Makers*, Donald R. Matthews specifically identifies a father's occupation, race, ethnic origins, religion, education, and occupation as important social background features. The last illustrative example is drawn from a recent contribution by Milton J. Rosenberg concerning attitudes about the cold war. Confronted as we are with the problem of which independent variables to consider, he remarks: "In the following summary, I shall restrict myself to correlates that, with different degrees of reliability, have been able to differentiate between persons who hold to the over-all hard-line or conciliatory approaches respectively."[7] Among the correlates Rosenberg then examines are ethnic affiliation, religious affiliation, class, religiosity, geographical origins, party identification, ideological identification, and "authoritarianism."

It is recognized, of course, that the fruitful employment of these variables in previous research is no guarantee that they will perform the same way with respect to our respondents. But it does seem more reasonable to base our selection of correlates upon the findings of previous research rather than simply ignoring its contributions.

GEOGRAPHICAL BACKGROUND

Regional background and size of hometown are immensely popular variables in social science analysis. Their popularity stems

6. Bernard R. Berelson, Paul F. Lazarsfeld, and William N. McPhee, *Voting: A Study of Opinion Formation in a Presidential Campaign*, pp. 54, 73.
7. Milton J. Rosenberg, "Attitude Change and Foreign Policy in the Cold War Era," in *Domestic Sources of Foreign Policy*, ed., James N. Rosenau, p. 156.

Social Origins

from a number of sources. On the expedient side, information concerning these attributes is unusually easy to accumulate (e.g., only a few moment's of questioning are necessary to gain much background data), process, and employ. A more valid basis for introducing such variables is reflected in the notion that the location and kind of community in which an individual is raised has some bearing on the way he thinks and/or behaves. The underlying idea is that the various regions and communities within the United States represent diverse environmental climates for the formation of political beliefs. The validity of this claim, however, only can be assessed if the geographical backgrounds of the relevant individuals are known.

The location aspect of geographical background is treated in two ways: according to place of birth and where the respondent was raised (i.e., spent most of his precollege years). The two, though conceptually and operationally distinct, of course, are highly related. With respect to this study, 79 (or 90%) of 88 respondents say they were born and raised within the same general (i.e., northeast, south, other) geographical area in the United States.

It may not be intuitively obvious to every reader inspecting table 7 why the specific regions were grouped in the manner they were. The northeast and south are distinguished because they typically are thought to be peculiarly relevant to a consideration of the background of FSOs and military officers respectively. For example, Janowitz, when analyzing the social origins of the military leadership, focuses attention nearly exclusively upon their alleged southern orientation. His findings on the subject are summarized in the statement reproduced immediately below.

> Since the rate of economic and industrial growth in the United States has been unequal, is there any evidence of a regional concentration in the backgrounds of the military elite? To what extent is the South over-represented, not only because of the persistence of a military tradition, but as a consequence of slower industrialization. A regional bias in the background of military leaders should be strongly mitigated by the congressional apportionment system.
> Nevertheless, using the formal definition of the United States Census, there was still, in 1950, an over-representation of southern-born officers in the Army, and, to a lesser extent, in the Navy leadership . . . A fuller

TABLE 7

GEOGRAPHICAL BACKGROUND

REGION	Place of Birth				Where Reared			
	Military		FSO		Military		FSO	
	%	N	%	N	%	N	%	N
Northeast								
New England	12	7	9	3	13	7	9	3
Middle Atlantic	26	15	36	12	24	13	26	9
Subtotal	38	22	46	15	36	20	34	12
South								
Solid South	17	10	9	3	16	9	14	5
Border	5	3	9	3	4	2	14	5
Subtotal	22	13	18	6	20	11	29	10
Other								
East North Central	21	12	21	7	24	13	20	7
West North Central	3	2	3	1	4	2	3	1
Mountain	7	4	6	2	7	4	6	2
Pacific	9	5	6	2	9	5	9	3
Subtotal	40	23	36	12	44	24	37	13
Effective Total	100	58	100	33	100	55	100	35
Statistics	$\chi^2(2)=.532/P=NS$				$\chi^2(2)=.919/P=NS$			
Europe				1				
Middle East				1				
Middle East (Sons of FSOs)				2				
Not Ascertained						3		2
Grand Total		58		37		58		37

NOTE: Again, note that rounding may result in columns totaling slightly more or less than 100%. The Middle Atlantic region consists of the states of Delaware, New Jersey, New York, and Pennsylvania; the East North Central, of Illinois, Indiana, Michigan, Ohio, and Wisconsin; the West North Central, of Iowa, Kansas, Minnesota, Missouri, Nebraska, North Dakota, and South Dakota; the Solid South, of Alabama, Arkansas, Florida, Georgia, Louisiana, Mississippi, North Carolina, South Carolina, Texas, and Virginia; the Border states of Kentucky, Maryland, Oklahoma, Tennessee, West Virginia, and the District of Columbia; the Mountain states of Arizona, Colorado, Idaho, Montana, Nevada, New Mexico, Utah, and Wyoming; and the Pacific states, of California, Oregon, Washington, Alaska, and Hawaii.

The term "P=NS" (i.e., Probability=Not Significant) indicates that the distribution contained in the table has a greater than 10% probability of occurring, as determined by the statistic cited. If a distribution has between a 5% and 10% probability of occurrence, "P=.10" will appear. "P=.05" will indicate that the probability of occurrence is from 1% to 5%. Finally, "P=.01" will indicate a probability of occurrence of less than 1%.

Social Origins 43

measure of the southern component of the military elite can be seen by a comparison with business leaders who come from the South. In Warner's 1952 business leadership sample, only 16 per cent came from the South; in other words, the South was sharply underrepresented in business leadership, as contrasted with its position in the military.[8]

The alleged northeastern geographical bias of the Foreign Service is graphically illustrated by Drew Pearson's statement that the Foreign Service was "a social club whose members are selected from bluestocking Bostonians, wield thin forks with their left hands, and are no more representative of American life than the Redskins whom their ancestors pushed west."[9]

The sample data presented in table 7 nevertheless reveal that, contrary to expectations, no (statistically significant) difference exists between political-FSOs and political-military officers regarding geographical background. Approximately the same proportion within each sample were born and raised in the northeastern (or southern) United States. In general, the marginal distributions in each of the four cases takes the following pattern. The middle Atlantic and East North Central subregions contain the largest number of officers. Together, they account for one-half of the total. Among the three general regions, the South claims about one-fifth representation, with the Northeast and Other dividing about equally the remaining 80%.

Quite surprising is the fact that only 9% of the FSOs, compared with 13% of the military, claim being reared in New England. It is New England that especially is reputed to be the favorite recruitment area of the Foreign Service. On the other hand, the extent (or rather lack of it) of southern representation within the military similarly is unanticipated. The reader familiar with the relevant literature ought to be startled to learn from table 7 that more political-military officers were born in the Middle Atlantic

---

8. Janowitz, *The Professional Soldier*, pp. 87–88. See also Huntington, *The Soldier and the State*, p. 155. All the data reported or cited in this study concerning the military refer only to commissioned officers.

9. Drew Pearson, *Washington Merry-Go-Round*, as quoted in Ilchman, *Professional Diplomacy in the U.S.*, and cited by Daniel H. Willick, *The Recruitment and Promotion of Foreign Service Officers*, p. 1.

section and raised in the East North Central states than were born or raised in the entire southern region. He surely would expect the above ratios to be the reverse of what they are.

Three major findings thus far have emerged: (1) the FSO and military samples manifest similar, not contrasting, geographical background profiles; (2) the FSOs are not unusually more northeastern than their military counterparts; and (3) the military are not unusually more southern than their civilian counterparts.

Knowing this, however, tells us very little if anything concerning whether or not these governmental organizations are representative. More meaning is given to the figures cited in table 7 if additional information about comparable populations is introduced. For example, from the data presented in table 8 we learn that assessing the geographical representativeness of the Foreign Service must involve the distinguishing of several related base populations. When an "Index of Dissimilarity" (ID)[10] is employed and the sample respondents compared with the 1940 United States population distribution, it is found that, among the FSOs, the Northeast is overrepresented whereas the contrary is true for the South (ID:1+7). A similar pattern emerges when the entire Foreign Service (ID:3+7) or recruits (ID:4+7) are considered. In each of these three cases, we are justified in concluding that the Foreign Service is unrepresentative regarding its geographical composition.

This conclusion is refined if our analytical perspective takes into account the matter of educational requirements. It is very obvious that adding the latter qualification has the effect of substantially reducing southern representation, and increasing the proportion

10. An ID is employed in order to compare two columns of data. Following Willick's formulation (*Recruitment and Promotion of Foreign Service Officers*, p. 27), the ID "equals the sum of the absolute differences between two percentage distributions for identical regions divided by two ($\Sigma \mid \Delta\% \mid /2$). For example, in the specific case of "ID:1 + 7" (that is, where the distributions described in columns 1 and 7 are compared for their dissimilarity), the ID "indicates the percentage of Foreign Service Officers who would have to change their region of birth to equal the regional distribution of the U.S. population at their approximate time of birth."

TABLE 8
REPRESENTATIVENESS OF FSOs REGARDING GEOGRAPHICAL BACKGROUND

REGION	Political Officers (1)	FOREIGN SERVICE			ASPIRING (5)	QUALIFYING (6)	U.S. POP. 1940 (7)
		Ministers 1961 (2)	Total 1961 (3)	Recruits 1946–61 (4)			
Northeast	49%	49%	41%	41%	36%	34%	29%
South	14	13	20	14	13	13	29
Other	37	38	39	45	51	48	41
Total	100%	100%	100%	100%	100%	100%	100%
	ID:1+2=1.0		ID:5+6= 5.0			ID:2+7=19.5	
	ID:2+3=8.0		ID:6+7=11.5			ID:3+7=11.5	
	ID:3+4=6.0		ID:1+3= 8.0			ID:4+7=15.5	
	ID:4+5=6.0		ID:1+7=19.5				

NOTE: Several separately derived sets of data are reported in table 8. Unfortunately, the various authors frequently employed different geographical classification schemes. The scheme which most efficiently allowed cross-comparisons to be made was similar to the one previously described, except that the District of Columbia and Maryland now are within the Northeast category. In addition, those reared outside the United States are excluded. An accurate data transformation was possible regarding our sample data. However, estimates needed to be made concerning the "Foreign Service, 1960" and "Foreign Service Recruits, 1946-61" data (the states involved were Arizona, New Mexico, and Virginia). The latter information was taken from Fielder and Harris, *The Quest for Foreign Affairs Officers*, p. 25. The "Foreign Service Ministers" and "Total" data appear in Willick, *The Recruitment and Promotion of Foreign Service Officers*, table 3. Willick's data pertain not to geographical background but to place of birth. Our assumption, based on the pattern of data reported by the respondents in this study, is that these two attributes have sufficient overlap to allow substituting one for the other. Not only here but throughout this analysis, the data for the aspiring and qualifying populations are taken from a study (begun in 1961) of the career decisions of American college undergraduates conducted by James A. Davis and his associates at the National Opinion Research Center of the University of Chicago. The "qualifying" restriction is a college education. This prerequisite *plus* being male and expressing a preference for a career in the Foreign Service (or military) forms the basis for defining an "aspiring" population. Census data for 1940 are reported in the United States Department of Commerce, *Statistical Abstract of the United States* (1966), p. 12. Analogous data pertaining to the region of birth of the FSOs are reported by Har-, *The Professional Diplomat*, p. 175.

of Northeast and Other membership (ID:6+7).[11] This tendency is reinforced when only males who aspire to a career in the Foreign Service are considered. The largest differences concerning geographical representation occurring between contiguous groups are manifest prior to the recruitment step and rest upon the empirical fact that the proportion of southerners who attain a college education and, secondarily, wish to become career FSOs is less than that obtaining for nonsoutherners. The bridge between "who is eligible and wants to enter" and "who actually enters" does not entail notable geographical discrimination (ID:4+5). The pool from which the Foreign Service is selecting initially is biased; consequently, relatively unbiased recruitment from an already unrepresentative residual population leads to an unrepresentative recruited population (ID:4+7).[12]

A major implication of the above is that if the pattern of educational attainment described continues to be manifest (and there is little reason to suspect otherwise), then a more geographically representative Foreign Service (i.e., representative with reference to the United States population distribution) can only be gained if FSO administrators conspire to bias the organization's recruitment process in favor of southerners and against individuals having a northeastern background. Such action naturally raises some obvious normative questions concerning, for example, the principle of equality of recruitment opportunity. It also threatens another

---

11. Incidentally, similar results are achieved throughout even if race is explicitly taken into account. Data from the *Statistical Abstract of the United States*, p. 27, indicate that 31%, 44%, and 25% of the white United States population in 1940 resided respectively in the northeastern, southern, and other regions. Moreover, of the 118 male Foreign Service aspirants, 111 were white; 5 were black; and 2 were oriental.

12. Using similar data, Willick offers a conclusion consistent with the one stated here: "To assert that there is no evidence that Foreign Service recruitment is ascriptive is not the same as saying it is representative. Foreign Service Officer recruits are not representative of the larger society in terms of region of birth or college attended, but there is not evidence that this is due to any organizational policy of the Foreign Service" (*Recruitment and Promotion of Foreign Service Officers*, pp. 8–9). The college attended by military officers and FSOs will be discussed later in this chapter.

Social Origins

principle; the often-expressed aim of professional-bureaucratic organizations to encourage effectiveness of operation by recruiting the "best" individuals available. In sum, biasing recruitment practices in the manner indicated in order to promote representativeness seems neither likely nor desirable from a professional-bureaucratic viewpoint. Future Foreign Service recruits, consequently, probably will continue to be unrepresentative of American society while at the same time they are representative of the Foreign Service aspiring population.

In addition, note that both the sample (ID:1+3) and group of career ministers (ID:2+3) contain a slightly higher percentage of officers of northeastern background than would be expected on the basis of the distribution for the entire Foreign Service. Whether this difference actually is due to ascriptive selection of northeasterners is a difficult question to answer. First, out-recruitment patterns would have to be ascertained. Second, the factor of lateral transfer (i.e., persons moving from non–Foreign Service organizations into the Foreign Service at a rank equivalent to what they held previously) also must be assessed. Third, the proportion of lower grade FSOs from each of the three regional categories who aspire to "political-policy" and "political executive" positions rather than, for example, economic or administrative positions needs to be taken into account. The existence of differential rates regarding any of these features would seriously affect the argument for ascriptive promotion of officers on the basis of their geographical background. One further comment is in order. The manifestation of compositional differences between the presently considered distributions does not by itself prove that the key ascriptive element is geographical background. It may be that the latter is strongly associated with another attribute (e.g., college attended), an attribute that actually is functioning as the ascriptive feature. Willick, in fact, appears to favor such a notion: that more northeasterners than non-northeasterners are Ivy League educated, and it is probably the latter and not former characteristic that is the key selective element.[13] A more detailed examination

13. *Recruitment and Promotion of Foreign Service Officers*, pp. 21–22.

of this argument, however, must wait until the subject of education is introduced later in this chapter.

Turning now to the military, we see in table 9 that among political-military officers the Northeast is overrepresented and the South underrepresented (ID:1+13). In other words, not only is southern membership not exaggerated; but there is, on the contrary, a tendency in the opposite direction. In this respect, civil and military political-policy officers are alike. They differ, however, as to the process within each organization that is responsible for promoting this similarity. This can be shown by juxtaposing relevant subsets of our sample with various comparable populations. A simply way to begin is to work backward from column 13 in table 9.

It immediately is clear that adding the college education qualification once again results in a substantial reduction in southern representation (ID:12+13). However, taking the additional step of specifying that students aspire to a career in the military has the effect of reversing the aforementioned tendency. Contrary to the case with the Foreign Service, the proportion of students raised in the South is higher among military career aspirants than within the general college population (ID:11+12). Using the latter distribution as a guide, we see that whereas more nonsoutherners than expected chose the Foreign Service career alternative, more southerners than expected opted for a career in the military.

The West Point class of 1964 consists of individuals who already have acted with respect to career aspirations. The geographical composition of this committed group of apprentices is shaped mainly by two forces: first, the characteristics of those men who elect to receive their college education at the Military Academy; second, the peculiar nature of the academy's appointment system. Both elements conspire to make a West Point class noticeably more southern in composition than the general college "qualifying" population (ID:10+12), and approximately representative of the United States population distribution (ID:10+13) and "military-aspiring" college group (ID:10+11).[14]

14. "Since congressional representation is principally by population

TABLE 9

REPRESENTATIVENESS OF THE MILITARY REGARDING GEOGRAPHICAL BACKGROUND

REGION	Political-Military Officers					
	College Attended			Service Affiliation		
	Total (1)	West Point (2)	Nonacademy (3)	Army (4)	Navy (5)	Air Force (6)
Northeast	36%	31%	31%	26%	50%	37%
South	44	54	47	57	38	31
Other	20	15	22	17	13	31
Total	100%	100%	100%	100%	100%	100%

TABLE 9 (*continued*)

Region	Military Leaders (1950)			West Point Class (1964) (10)	Aspiring (11)	Qualifying (12)	U.S. Pop. 1940 (13)
	Army (7)	Navy (8)	Air Force (9)				
Northeast	23%	27%	25%	30%	30%	30%	27%
South	43	42	50	36	42	48	41
Other	34	31	25	34	27	22	32
Total	100%	100%	100%	100%	100%	100%	100%
	ID:1+ 7=14.0	ID:3+11= 5.0	ID:7+11= 7.5	ID: 9+13= 9.0			
	ID:1+ 8=11.0	ID:4+ 7=17.0	ID:7+13= 4.0	ID:10+11= 6.5			
	ID:1+ 9=11.0	ID:5+ 8=22.5	ID:8+11= 3.5	ID:10+12=12.0			
	ID:1+13=12.0	ID:6+ 9=18.5	ID:8+13= 1.0	ID:10+13= 5.0			
	ID:2+10=19.0	ID:7+10= 7.0	ID:9+11= 7.5	ID:11+12= 5.5			
				ID:12+13=10.0			

Note: The geographical classification scheme used in this table is exactly the same as the one used in table 7 *except* that Delaware is now considered to be a southern state. Thus, the Middle Atlantic region consists only of New Jersey, New York, and Pennsylvania. The "Military Leaders (1950)" data are from Janowitz, *The Professional Soldier*, p. 88, and refer only to officers who have achieved at least the rank of major general in the army or air force and rear admiral in the navy. The "West Point Class (1964)" data are from Lovell, "Professional Socialization of the West Point Cadet," p. 140.

Social Origins 51

The Armed Forces in their recruitment primarily rely upon these two groups of college students; non-Academy military career aspirants and Academy cadets. The fact that the leadership of the three services and the latter two student collectivities resemble one another suggests that recruitment into, and promotion within, the Armed Forces is relatively unbiased regarding geographical background (ID:7+10, 7+11, 8+11, 9+11).[15] As a result, military leaders will appear to be quite representative when compared with American society (ID:7+13, 8+13, 9+13). At the same time, this group of officers also will appear to contain a disproportionate number of southerners when they are compared with any elite who recruits in a relatively unbiased way from the available undergraduate population (e.g., the Foreign Service and probably business).

The above observations taken together strongly suggest that, in terms of their regional background, military officers with responsibilities directly relating to the formation and implementation of foreign political policy are not typical of the general military establishment. This, in fact, proves to be the case. Political-military officers as a group are more northeastern and less southern than the leadership of the army, navy, and air force (ID:1+7, 1+8, 1+9). With one exception, this finding holds also for each of the parts making up the political-military sample (ID:2+10, 3+11, 4+7, 5+8). Moreover, the lone exception, that sample subset con-

and since 85 percent of appointments to West Point annually are made by United States Senators and Representatives, it follows that the cadet population will closely resemble that of the total U.S. population. Since the distribution of the fifteen to nineteen age group differs little from the distribution of the total population, the former also necessarily resembles the distribution of cadet backgrounds" (John Lovell, "The Professional Socialization of the West Point Cadet," in *The New Military*, ed. Janowitz, pp. 139–40). For data regarding the regional backgrounds of the West Point class of 1972, and also the size of their hometowns and father's occupation, see Capt. Arthur E. Wise, *A Comparison of New Cadets at USMA with Entering Freshmen at Other Colleges*.

15. Note that the "Military Leaders" data refer to the year 1950. They are used because no more contemporary data apparently are available. My guess is that they probably continue to be sufficiently accurate for rough comparisons, but not appropriate where fine distinctions need to be made.

sisting of air force officers, only in part violates the general pattern (ID:6+9). In sum, political-military officers are unrepresentative with respect to both American society and the military establishment. In terms of regional background, they are a decidedly unique group of military officers differing far more significantly from their parent organization than is the case with their counterparts in the Foreign Service.

Until this point, attention has been centered upon the location aspect of geographical background. The focus now shifts to a consideration of another geographical factor, the kind of community in which one is raised. By the term *kind of community* I mean more precisely its population size; whether the respondent's hometown environment was rural, small city, or large city.

An examination of the data presented in table 10 pertaining to

TABLE 10

SIZE OF HOMETOWN

Size	Military		FSO	
	%	N	%	N
Rural:				
Farm	6	3	0	0
Town	13	7	14	5
Subtotal	19	10	14	5
Small City:				
Up to 100,000	38	20	34	12
100,000–250,000	11	6	6	2
Subtotal	49	26	40	14
Large City:				
250,000+	32	17	46	16
Effective Total	100	53	100	35
Statistics	$\chi^2(2)=1.686/P=NS$			
	Gamma$=.225/P=NS$			
Military Installation		5		
Not Ascertained				2
Grand Total		58		37

Social Origins

size of hometown reveals that, despite some percentage variation, the two samples yield essentially similar profiles. Thus, paralleling the case with regional background, the notion that no difference exists between military officers and FSOs cannot be rejected. Once again, the empirically based finding is contrary to expectations. The unexpected element here is the sparse rural representation occurring among the military. The rural figure (19%) "should" have been substantially larger. By way of illustrating the unanticipated quality of this feature, Janowitz after an analysis of similar data concludes:

> From a historical and theoretical point of view, there was every reason to believe that the military would be heavily recruited from nonindustrialized areas—from agricultural communities and small towns. . . . The data on the place of birth of military leaders indicate that they are overwhelmingly of rural and small town origin . . . in 1950 almost 70 percent of the Army leaders came from rural backgrounds, while, as we expected, the naval percentage had declined to approximately 56 percent.[16]

Nevertheless, a bias toward rural representation did not develop with respect to political-military officers, and it is probably this that is responsible for lack of a significant intersample difference.

This, of course, does not invalidate the main point made by Janowitz, that the entire military establishment is disproportionately composed of individuals born and/or raised within a rural environment. In table 11 the data upon which Janowitz has based his inference is compared with the 1950 United States population distribution (ID:7+13, 8+13, 9+13). The emerging dissimilarities confirm the fact of a rural bias within the armed forces.[17]

---

16. *The Professional Soldier*, pp. 85–86. To reiterate, the Janowitz data are not, and should not be considered, strictly comparable to the data presented here. First, Janowitz refers to the size of the community of birthplace, not where raised. Second, there is a fifteen-year difference in time. However, even if we allow for some minor variation regarding the former, and assume a continuation of an urbanization trend implied in the latter, the difference in findings still is quite startling.

17. Certain problems are present when making comparison regarding size of hometown that were not present regarding regional background. On the one hand, there is the long-term quantitative population shift from rural to urban areas, and the corresponding increase in suburban–small city

An equally salient finding is the discrepancy manifested once again between the political-military profile and the military leadership (ID:4+7, 5+8, 6+9). Even after taking into account the influence that the trend toward urbanization would have during the fifteen year interval 1950–65, the extent of the disagreement is of startling proportions. Political-military officers are not only unique as to the location aspect of their regional background but, perhaps to an even greater degree are atypical when size of hometown is considered. The validity of this claim is underlined when the political-military are compared with recent undergraduates throughout the United States and at West Point. Please recall that most sample respondents were raised at a time when nearly one-half of the United States population resided within rural areas. The West Point classes of 1964 and 1965 and the aspiring undergraduate population were raised during a period when the rural proportion of the population fell from 36% in 1950 to 30% in 1960. Yet, the relevant political-military subsets contain approximately the same percentage of rural persons as do the latter two groups (ID:2+10, 3+11).

This congruity with respect to rural representation stands in dramatic contrast to the variation between the aforementioned configurations regarding small-city and large-city representation.

population. The proportion of the population contained within large (central) cities has remained relatively stable over the last forty years. On the other hand, there is the more recent qualitative change in the class, racial, and ethnic composition of large cities. I am referring here to what has often been called the (middle-class) flight to the suburbs. These two trends make it imperative that all comparisons be made with caution. For example, in table 11, the military leaders in 1950 were juxtaposed with 1950 census results. This is not strictly appropriate since the former actually were raised in about the year 1920. In 1920, 49% rather than 36% of the United States population resided in rural areas. By 1930, the rural figure had declined to 44%. In other words, although the extent of rural bias that is observed is moderated by the use of more historical data, the existence of such a tendency continues to be affirmed. One final point needs to be noted. In 1950, the Census Bureau modified its definition of "urban" and "rural" places. The effect of this change was to reduce by about 4% the rural figure that otherwise would have been reported in 1950. If these new definitions were employed in 1920 and 1930, the rural figure cited above probably would be slightly lower.

Here, the timing and extent of the growth of suburbia is clearly established. We already have commented upon the main quantitative change occurring with respect to the United States population distribution; the on-going rural decline and corresponding increase in the number of persons living outside the large central cities but within an urban metropolitan context (for the small-city category, an increase from 36% in 1950 to an estimated 43% in 1960). However, the more important aspect of this population shift appears to be the qualitative one. By this I mean that the large central cities are increasingly populated by groups who, as a general rule, are not proportionately represented among college students. This is even more true when reference is made to the rural areas. The ethnic, racial, and like, groups that are overrepresented to a greater degree than ever before are suburban oriented. As a result, the latter class of communities now contribute 43% of the total college population. This figure is substantially more than the 27% who were raised in large cities and the 23% raised in nonmetropolitan area small cities of less than 100,000 population. What this means is that any organization that requires that prospective candidates acquire a college education in order to be eligible for recruitment will increasingly be admitting individuals who were born and raised within a suburban setting.

The military establishment of necessity is moving in just this direction. As we see in table 11, the 1964 and 1965 West Point classes (column 10) and aspiring population (column 11) in fact already are predominantly composed of persons of small-city, not rural, background. This is the case despite the fact that a mechanism, analogous in form to the one discussed with respect to regional background, partially reverses the tendency toward rural derepresentation. As with persons of southern background, a military career is noticeably more attractive to rural than urban college students (ID:11+12). Such a "vocation" apparently also is relatively unattractive to large-city and suburban persons. It already has been stated that 43% of the qualifying population say they were raised in a suburban environment, compared with 23% who were raised in nonmetropolitan area small cities. Among mili-

TABLE 11
Representativeness of the Military Regarding Size of Hometown

	Political-Military Officers					
		College Attended		Service Affiliation		
Size	Total (1)	West Point (2)	Nonacademy (3)	Army (4)	Navy (5)	Air Force (6)
Rural.........	19%	20%	22%	14%	19%	25%
City up to 100,000.....	38	20	44	38	25	50
City over 100,000.....	43	60	34	48	56	25
Total.....	100%	100%	100%	100%	100%	100%

Social Origins

TABLE 11 (continued)

SIZE	MILITARY LEADERS (1950)			WEST POINT CLASSES (1964–65) (10)	ASPIRING (11)	QUALIFYING (12)	U.S. POP. 1950 (13)
	Army (7)	Navy (8)	Air Force (9)				
Rural	65%	56%	69%	25%	18%	3%	36%
City up to 100,000	} 35	} 44	} 31	48	62	70	36
City over 100,000				26	21	27	28
Total	100%	100%	100%	100%	100%	100%	100%
	ID:1+ 7=46.0	ID:3+11=17.5		ID:7+11=47.5		ID: 9+13=33.0	
	ID:1+ 8=37.0	ID:4+ 7=51.0		ID:7+13=29.0		ID:10+11=13.0	
	ID:1+ 9=50.0	ID:5+ 8=37.0		ID:8+11=38.5		ID:10+12=22.5	
	ID:1+13=17.0	ID:6+ 9=44.0		ID:8+13=20.0		ID:10+13=12.5	
	ID:2+10=33.5	ID:7+10=39.5		ID:9+11=51.5		ID:11+12=14.5	
						ID:12+13=34.0	

NOTE: The "Military Leaders (1950)" data are from Janowitz, *The Professional Soldier*, p. 86; the "West Point class (1964–65)" data are from Lovell, "Professional Socialization of the West Point Cadet," p. 139; the "Total Population (1950)" data are cited by Donald J. Bogue, *The Population of the United States*, p. 38, from the U.S. Bureau of the Census, *United States Census of Population: 1950*.

tary career aspirants, however, the small-city category contains slightly more persons from the latter than from the former class of communities (32% versus 30% suburban). Hence, adding the feature that only those males who aspire to a career in the military establishment be included once again mitigates the full influence that the educational requirement by itself would exert. The aforementioned reversal receives its impetus from the fact that rural and nonmetropolitan area small city residents more often than expected favor pursuing a career in the armed forces. The impact of this pattern of occupational selectivity, however, is not of sufficient extent to offset the potent effect of urbanization, or more precisely, suburbanization, manifested by that group of individuals from which the military establishment necessarily must recruit future officers. Thus, a rural-oriented armed forces is increasingly, if it is not already, a phenomenon of the past.

The advancing influence of suburbia is even more in evidence when the size of the hometown of FSOs is considered. This can be shown in two ways. First, let us compare FSO "newtimers" and "oldtimers."[18] The main disparity between the two subgroups is clear to see: approximately two-thirds of the FSO oldtimers were raised in central cities with a population of over 100,000, whereas a plurality of the newtimers say their hometown was a small city of under 100,000 population (ID:2+3). My guess is that if the background characteristics of current FSO recruits were examined (i.e., if relevant data were available), or that of those officers holding country desk jobs in the Geographic Bureaus ten years from now, the above trend would appear to be much more pronounced. I say this because I know that only a minority of the so-called newtimer subgroup actually were adolescents during the period of accelerating suburban growth and rural and large central city decline. Referring once again to table 5, please note that only seven of the FSOs were born after 1929. Of this group, only

18. "Newtimers" and "oldtimers" are distinguished by the criterion of length of service. The procedure utilized required the accomplishing of two simple steps: (1) ordering all respondents according to their length of service, and (2) dividing them at the median into two subgroups.

Social Origins

TABLE 12
REPRESENTATIVENESS OF FSOs REGARDING SIZE OF HOMETOWN

Size	Total Foreign Service 1966 (1)	Political Officers Total (2)	Political Officers Oldtimers (3)	Political Officers Newtimers (4)	Aspiring (5)	Qualifying (6)	U.S. Pop. 1950 (7)
Rural	13%	14%	12%	17%	10%	3%	36%
City up to 100,000	} 87	34	24	44	77	70	36
City over 100,000		52	65	39	13	27	28
Total	100%	100%	100%	100%	100%	100%	100%

ID:2+5=43.0
ID:2+6=36.0
ID:2+7=24.0
ID:3+4=25.5

ID:3+5=53.5
ID:3+6=46.5
ID:3+7=36.5
ID:4+5=33.0

ID:4+6=26.0
ID:4+7=19.0
ID:5+6=14.0
ID:6+7=34.0

NOTE: The "Total Foreign Service (1966)" data are reported by Harr, *The Professional Diplomat*, p. 175.

two have a post-1935 birthdate; the youngest was born in 1939. The suburban explosion, however, did not really take hold until World War II ended. This means that many included within the newtimer subgroup predate the shifts in residence that commenced in the late 1940s.

Second, note that the dissimilarity between newtimers and the qualifying and aspiring populations, although substantial, still is conspicuously less than between the latter two distributions and the oldtimer profile (ID:3+5, 3+4 versus 2+5, 2+4). The reason for this is the increase in small-city representation as we move from column 2 to 3, *and* from column 5 to 4. The loser each time is the large-city category. Obscured is perhaps the more interesting situation of the change occurring within the small-city category when the "qualifying" and "aspiring" populations are compared. In a previous discussion concerning military aspirants, it was argued that students of suburban background are less attracted to the idea of developing a career in the Armed Services than are students from nonmetropolitan area small cities. This was inferred from the empirical finding that there was a lower proportion of suburbanites among military aspirants than among the entire undergraduate sample. With respect to the Foreign Service, however, the contrary is the case. It will be recalled that 43% of the qualifying students are of suburban background. Yet, 62% of the male students who aspire to a career in the Foreign Service say they were raised in a suburban community. The remaining 38% are distributed nearly evenly among the three additional options. In sum, the already existing bias within the qualifying populations concerning suburban overrepresentation is *reinforced* when the aspiring requirement is introduced and not mitigated as in the case of military aspirants. The inference to be made is clear; while the military establishment is undergoing a transformation involving the loss of its traditional rural orientation, the Foreign Service at a more rapid pace increasingly will be composed (if it is not already) of college graduates raised in suburban rather than large (central) city settings.

Social Origins

NATIVITY OF PARENTS, NATIONALITY, AND OCCUPATION

The data contained in table 7 indicate that individuals who occupy governmental positions relating directly to the conduct of foreign political relations are, in overwhelming number, native-born. The notion of entering a profession involving national service, combined with reasons of security, probably are sufficient grounds to account for such a cirumstance. It apparently is also true that most of these officials are themselves the sons of native-born parents. More precisely, 83% of the political-military group and 89% of the FSOs say that both their parents were born in the United States. By way of comparison, in 1920, 72% of the na-

TABLE 13

NATIVITY OF PARENTS

Parents	Military		FSO		Native-born White U.S. Population	
					1920	1950
	%	N	%	N	%	%
Native-born	83	48	89	33	72	81
Foreign-born or Mixed Parentage	17	10	11	4	28	19
Total	100	58	100	37	100	100

NOTE: The "Native-born White U.S. Population" figures are taken from Bogue, *Population of the United States*, p. 365.

tive-born white population was estimated to have native-born parents. By 1950, the proportion had risen to 81%. Thus, there is little deviation between the officers and a comparable national population regarding this attribute variable.

It appears, however, that the political-policy officers of the Foreign Service and military establishment do deviate substantially from the United States population distribution regarding ethnic affiliation and status of father's occupation. In order to examine the former characteristic, it was necessary to first utilize the data reported above concerning the nativity of parents. If the father was reported to be foreign-born, the country cited as his place of birth was used, provided that the country was not located in either the Western Hemisphere or a (formerly) European colonial area. If the latter was the case, a follow-up question on previous ancestry was asked. A similar follow-up question was employed where the parents were reported to be native born.

Inspecting the relevant data contained in table 14 reveals that an overwhelming proportion of the respondents trace their nationality to northwestern Europe. In fact, approximately one-half of all the officers identified the United Kingdom as the home of their ancestors. The only other noticeably favored ethnic affiliation is the German one, which accounts for another one-fifth of the military and one-seventh of the FSOs. On the other hand, only three of the entire military sample and five of the thirty-five FSOs claim they are of south or east European descent. Although I was not able to acquire an ethnic breakdown of the United States population, it seems safe to say that the aforementioned distribution is not representative of American society. Certainly the south and east European nationalities appear to be underrepresented. Additionally, none of the military officers and only two FSOs are of Afro-American ancestry, compared with an estimated 11% of the United States population.

Yet, the data presented in table 14 also show that more than three-fourths of the qualifying population of college undergraduates is composed of students of Northwest European ethnic affiliation. When the aspiring element is added, the latter figure in each case is increased and now nearly equals the proportions reported earlier regarding the sample respondents (95% versus 90%, and 80% versus 82%). The general similarity between each sample distribution and respective aspiring population lends some support to the claim that the apparent unrepresentativeness of the two governmental groups probably is largely due to differences in educational attainment and career aspiration manifest in our society rather than to recruitment bias on the part of these governmental organizations. This conclusion must be stated in a cautious man-

TABLE 14
Ethnic Affiliation

NATIONALITY	Political Officers				Aspiring		Qualifying
	Military		FSO		Military	FSO	
	%	N	%	N	%	%	%
Northwest Europe							
British, Scottish, Welsh	47	26	51	18	44	39	32
German	20	11	14	5	20	20	25
Irish	7	4	3	1	21	13	12
Other	20	11	11	4	5	10	8
Subtotal	95	52	80	28	90	82	77
South or East Europe	5	3	14	5	6	10	14
African (Negro)	0	0	6	2	2	4	2
Other	0	0	0	0	3	4	6
Effective Total	100	55	100	35	100	100	100
Do Not Know		1		1			
Not Ascertained		2		1			
Grand Total		58		37			

ner since information is not available concerning the ethnic composition of each organization's recruits, membership, or upper-level strata. Quite obviously, pronounced, though divergent, biases may be operative with respect to, on the one hand, recruitment and, on the other, promotion. Or, the effect of a disproportionate out-recruitment pattern may be counter-balanced by differences attributable to the generation gap underlying the comparisons implied in table 14. These types of mutually cancelling tendencies may possibly exist. Nevertheless, my hunch is that each organization's recruitment and promotion patterns are not ethnically selective, and, as a result, the various recruit, membership, and other profiles mentioned earlier very much resemble (i.e., share the same biases as) the aspiring population described in table 14.

The main reason I believe that ethnic bias probably does not play an important role is that the number of students of non–Northwest European ancestry who qualify and aspire to a career in either the military establishment or Foreign Service is relatively so few that it hardly seems necessary for these organizations to do anything other than impartially recruit in order to perpetuate their current ethnic pattern. The (prerecruitment) factors of educational achievement and career choice act to virtually assure that the political parts of the above two governmental organizations will continue to be dominated by officers of Northwest European nationality. The potency of the above two factors is underlined when it is recalled that more than a majority of the political-policy officers were born and raised in the northeastern and east north central United States, and in cities rather than farms and towns, those areas and communities that contained and continue to contain great numbers of new immigrant (i.e., east and south European) citizens. In sum, the political parts of both organizations for the most part are composed of officers who are white, native-born, of northwest European (probably British, possibly German) ethnic affiliation, and the sons of native-born parents. It is more than likely that they will continue to be so characterized in the predictable future.

From this information, it is not too difficult to infer that the

TAPLE 15

Father's Occupation

Occupation	Military %	Military N	FSO %	FSO N
Higher Status:				
Professional and Technical				
Foreign Service Officer	0	0	5	2
Military Officer	10	6	8	3
Other	41	24	32	12
Self-Employed Businessman, Manager, or Official	14	8	30	11
Subtotal	66	38	76	28
Lower Status:				
Clerical and Sales	14	8	5	2
Worker				
Skilled	5	3	5	2
Semi-Skilled	5	3	3	1
Service	2	1	5	2
Unskilled	0	0	0	0
Farmer	9	5	5	2
Subtotal	35	20	24	9
Total	100	58	100	37
Statistics	$\chi^2(1) = 1.099 \,/\, P = NS$ Gamma $= .242 \,/\, P = NS$			

fathers of most of the respondents had high-status and not low-status occupations. The data furnished in table 15 indicate that such an inference is correct. The fathers of two-thirds of the political-military officers and three-fourths of the FSOs fall within the high-status-occupation stratum. The modal occupation in each case clearly is the professional and technical category. Slightly more than one-half of the fathers were engaged in work of the latter nature. Please note that this category includes a small group of respondents who are the sons of military officers and FSOs. The second largest group of fathers were "self-employed businessmen, managers, and officials." The remaining minority are divided not too unevenly among the three lower-status occupations. Aside from some minor percentage variation, the pattern is the same for both groups of officers—in each case, sons of high-status-occupation fathers predominate.

This pattern is shown in table 16 to be very unrepresentative when compared with the occupational distribution of employed males (ID:2+9, 3+9). Approximately four-fifths of the latter population appear to have held lower status positions. The worker category alone accounts for slightly over one-half of all employed males. Moreover, the most heavily represented occupation within our two samples, the professions, is the smallest in size (6%). Much of this difference between the samples and the "employed male" population appears due to the influence of education, the same variable that has proved to be so potent an explanatory factor in previous analyses. The key element again is the existence of differential rates of educational attainment among the subsets of the distributions that are being considered. As would be expected, sons of low-status-occupation fathers are far less likely to attend college than their more privileged peers. This is attested to by the fact that the qualifying population is evenly divided between the two occupational status categories, whereas the more inclusive national distribution is four-fifths composed of males employed in low-status occupations (ID:8+9). The aforementioned dissimilarity obviously is substantial. Yet, at the same time, it is quite evident that its extent is decidedly less than what obtained earlier in this and the previous century when a college education had relevance only for the sons of the relatively privileged few. There also is little doubt that the well-documented trend toward a more representative "qualifying" population will continue. As a greater percentage of the sons of clerks, salesmen, workers, and farmers attend college, the contrast between the student population and national labor force will diminish.

Another interesting point is the differing character of military and Foreign Service aspirants. Pursuing a career within the latter organization is shown to be relatively unappealing to workers' and farmers' sons. The result is that the discriminating influence of education described above is enhanced, and the FSO aspiring population therefore is less representative than college students in

Social Origins

TABLE 16
Representativeness of the Military and FSOs Regarding Father's Occupation

Occupation	Total Foreign Service 1966 (1)	Political Officers			Military Leadership 1950 (5)	Aspiring		Qualifying (8)	U.S. Male Pop. 1950 (9)
		FSO (2)	Military			FSO (6)	Military (7)		
			Total (3)	Nonacademy Grads (4)					
High									
Professional	38%	37%	41%	38%	} 44%	} 27%	} 24%	} 25%	} 6%
Military Officer	3	8	10	3		31	20	24	13
Businessman	31	30	14	16	30				
Subtotal	72	76	66	56	74	58	44	49	19
Low									
Clerk, Salesman	12	5	14	22	11	20	16	12	13
Worker	12	13	12	16	5	21	37	31	53
Farmer	4	5	9	6	10	1	4	7	15
Subtotal	28	24	35	44	26	42	57	50	81
Total	100%	100%	100%	100%	100%	100%	100%	100%	100%

ID:1+2= 4.0 ID:1+9=53.0 ID:2+9=57.0 ID:3+8=16.0 ID:4+7=12.5 ID:5+7=30.5 ID:6+8= 8.5 ID:7+9=24.5
ID:1+6=14.0 ID:2+6=18.0 ID:3+5= 8.5 ID:3+9=46.5 ID:4+8= 6.5 ID:5+8=24.5 ID:6+9=39.0 ID:8+9=30.5
ID:1+8=22.5 ID:2+8=26.5 ID:3+7=22.0 ID:4+5=18.0 ID:4+9=37.0 ID:5+9=55.0 ID:7+8= 6.0

Note: The "U.S. Male Population (1950)" data refer only to the distribution of employed persons, by occupation and sex, and appear in the *Statistical Abstract of the United States*, p. 229. Information concerning the "Military Leadership (1950)" data are reported by Janowitz, *The Professional Soldier*, p. 93. The "Total Foreign Service (1966)" data are reported by Harr, *The Professional Diplomat*, pp. 177, 179.

general (ID:5+8 versus 7+8). The contrary is true with respect to the military (ID:6+8 versus 7+8). A military career appears to be more attractive to students whose fathers were workers than to the sons of high-status-occupation fathers. Interestingly enough, farmers' sons, a group traditionally drawn to the armed forces, currently do not favor a military career, whereas the sons of clerks and salesmen do express such a preference. The latter surprisingly also are attracted to a career in the Foreign Service.

The relationships discussed in the previous paragraphs suggest several things. First, a good part of the apparent unrepresentativeness of the two groups of political officers is eliminated if they are compared with their "relevant" aspiring populations rather than with an occupational distribution of the United States population. By including the term *relevant*, I mean to direct attention to the difference in time periods that underlies the data reported in table 16. It will be recalled that information regarding the career choices of college undergraduates initially was collected in 1961, whereas the political officers making up our samples were interviewed in 1965. However, the reader additionally will recall that the "median" political-military officer and FSO already has served as an officer for about 22 and 13 years respectively. Hence, most of the sample respondents were student aspirants during the 1940s and early 1950s, a period during which probably a somewhat smaller percentage of sons of low-status-occupation fathers attended college than was true in 1961. The earlier FSO and military aspiring populations, therefore, more likely than not contained a larger proportion of sons of high-status-occupation fathers than the 58% and 44% figures reported in table 16. We, of course, do not know exactly how much larger. But it is clear that, given even a modest additional increment, the relevant aspiring populations will begin to resemble our two sample configurations.

It additionally suggests that both organizations, and probably also the political-policy parts within them, are undergoing a similar change in composition. The general trend is toward greater representativeness and heterogeneity in membership through an increase in the proportion of officers who are the sons of low-status-occupation fathers. The specific occupational category that ought to show the largest increase is clerical and sales, a subset of occupations that is often referred to as white-collar, low-middle-class. Furthermore, this trend should proceed at a faster pace within the military than Foreign Service because the particular pattern of career choice pertaining to the latter institution acts to retard the compositional changes described above, whereas in the case of the former institution, career aspiration patterns reinforce it.

The traditional overrepresentation of the high-status occupations and the on-going trend toward greater representativeness and heterogeneity alluded to, in all fairness, are not altogether unexpected phenomena. For example, our findings regarding the military very closely parallel, and are consistent with, those stated by Janowitz in *The Professional Soldier*:

> American military leaders traditionally have come from the more privileged strata. However, recent trends in their social background supply striking confirmation of the decline in the relatively high social origins of the military and of its transformation into a more socially heterogeneous group. . . .
> With regard to specific middle-class occupations, it has been the professional and managerial groups, rather than the business groups, which have contributed to the military, reflecting the clash between business and military values. . . . With urbanization, the percentage of farmers' sons declined. . . . The broadening of social base has brought in the lower middle class, white collar families—sons of salesmen and clerical workers—plus a smattering from the working class.[19]

One final point should be made before this section is concluded. Janowitz contends that businessmen's sons are proportionally less likely than sons of professionals to develop a military career. He attributes this to a traditional "clash between business and military values," a clash that many see as rapidly diminishing in force as the technological imperatives and implications of modern warfare become ever more manifest. Nevertheless, we see from a comparison of military and FSO sample respondents that businessmen's sons are noticeably less prevalent within the former group of officers

19. Pp. 89–92.

(14% versus 30%). Moreover, please note the difference in representation of this occupational category among military and FSO career aspirants. About 24% of the college student population are sons of businessmen; yet only 20% of the military aspirants, as compared to 31% of those who aspire to a career in the Foreign Service, fall within this category. Such differences affirm Janowitz's contention and suggest that his remarks here continue to be valid.

EDUCATION

The present section is concerned with whether our sample respondents differ in the amount of education they receive and the type of college they have attended. A first step to this end is to compare the political officers according to the highest degree level they have attained. The classification scheme utilized involves four categories ranging from high school (graduates) or less to Ph.D., LL.B., or equivalant.

The data contained in table 17 indicate that political-FSOs and political-military officers are not only a highly educated group of individuals relative to the national population but also are unusual in this respect when compared with their fellow non-political-policy officers. About one-seventh of all FSOs in 1962 did not have a bachelor's degree; less than one-third of them had continued their education to the point of securing a M.A. and/or Ph.D. degree or their equivalents. We also see that a rather sizable percentage of military officers on active duty in 1960 within the army (43%), navy (30%) and air force (51%) do not have a B.A. or equivalent degree. By way of contrast, political officers almost without exception have earned four-year college degrees. More than half of them have gone beyond this to do graduate work and eventually attain a M.A. or its equivalent. There even is a small group of four political-military officers and three political-FSOs who have a Ph.D. or law degree. Both groups of political officers, then, offer essentially similar patterns when the variable, years of schooling, is considered—patterns, however, that readily distinguish them from both their nonpolitical fellow officers and the United States population.

TABLE 17
LEVEL OF EDUCATION

EDUCATIONAL LEVEL	POLITICAL OFFICERS				ARMED FORCES (1960)			FOREIGN SERVICE (1962) %	UNITED STATES (1965)	
	Military %	N	FSO %	N	Army %	Navy %	Air Force %		White Male %	Total %
High school or less	5	3	0	0	43	30	51	14	87	91
B.A. or equivalent	35	20	46	17	57	70	49	53	13	9
M.A. or equivalent	53	31	46	17	NA	NA	NA	27	NA	NA
Ph.D., LL.B., or equivalent	7	4	8	3	NA	NA	NA	5	NA	NA
Total	100	58	100	37	100	100	100	100	100	100

NOTE: The data for "Foreign Service (1962)" are adapted from Harr, *Anatomy of the Foreign Service*, p. 39. Information concerning "Armed Forces (1960)" is cited by Lang, "Technology and Career Management in the Military Establishment, p. 55, from the secretary of defense. The "United States (1965)" data are reported in the *Statistical Abstract of the United States* (1966), p. 113. The letters "NA" mean that the original source did not include this category and, therefore, relevant data could not be ascertained.

TABLE 18
College Attended

	Military		FSO	
	%	N	%	N
Ivy League	5	3	35	13
Other Prestige Private	4	2	3	1
Big Ten	5	3	8	3
University of California	9	5	5	2
Washington, D.C., Area	7	4	14	5
Military Academy	42	23	0	0
Other	28	13	35	13
Effective Total	100	55	100	37
No College Degree		3		
Grand Total		58		37

NOTE: The "Other Prestige Private" category includes the so-called Little Ivy League (e.g., Williams, Amherst) and such schools as Chicago and Stanford. Colleges within the Washington, D.C., area such as American and George Washington Universities are separately classed because of their rather unique relationship with respect to the education of both military and civilian governmental officials.

Let us now shift our attention to a consideration of the type of college that political officers attended. The main task here is to describe the composition of the political-policy parts of the Foreign Service and the military establishment. From the data presented in table 18, we see that, in terms of representation, two categories of colleges clearly stand out—the Ivy League schools in the case of the Foreign Service, and the academies in the case of the military. With respect to the former, 35% of the officers received their B.A. or its equivalent from the colleges that together constitute the Ivy League. Of this group, four each are from Harvard or Yale, three from Princeton, and two from Dartmouth. Aside from this category (and perhaps the subset of Washington, D.C., area colleges), no other school or group of schools is conspicuously represented. A similiar pattern is evident within the military with the exception that here academy graduates are the salient group. Twenty-three (or 42%) of the fifty-five political military officers who have college degrees received them from either the United States Military or Naval Academies. Again, no other college or group of colleges is conspicuously represented.

Social Origins

The fact that graduates of Ivy League schools and the military academies are prominent is not at all unexpected. To the contrary, many observers assert that ascriptive practices have been and currently are operative in the recruitment and/or promotion of officers that favor graduates of these institutions. But is the case for ascription proved simply by referring to the large number of FSOs or military officers who attended Harvard, Yale, and the others, or West Point and Annapolis? Of course not. A far more extensive analysis than this based on additional information is necessary in order for it to be demonstrated that "an individual's position in the military [or Foreign Service] depended on his social characteristics, and not on his personal achievements."[20]

In his study of *The Recruitment and Promotion of Foreign Service Officers*, Daniel H. Willick assesses precisely this question: whether the relatively large number of Harvard, Yale, and Princeton (hereafter, HYP) graduates within the Foreign Service is due to selection based upon ascription. The approach he uses is similar in nature to the one employed earlier in this chapter. For the most part, it entails comparing the percentage of FSOs who received a bachelor's degree from HYP within three related populations; the entire FSO corps, FSO recruits, and career ministers. Willick's findings are summarized in the following statement.

> As of 1961 Harvard, Yale, and Princeton men were found both to have entered and to have remained in the Foreign Service in a much greater proportion than is warranted by their share of the American college population. The immediate impulse is to say . . . that ascription still plays a significant role in the entry into the Foreign Service. This conclusion seems unwarranted since, at least in 1961, not only did a larger percentage of the HYP college students aspire to the Foreign Service, but the HYP's who aspired were better academically than the non-HYP aspirants. Therefore, in 1961 a large proportion of HYP college students aspired to the Foreign Service than non-HYP students and the HYP's were more capable of passing the written entrance examination than non-HYP students. This means that the disproportionate contribution of Harvard, Yale, and Princeton to bottom level Foreign Service Officer recruits does not seem to be due to an ascriptive recruitment policy. . . .
>
> The evidence seems to disconfirm the third proposition that advancement within the Foreign Service has become less ascriptive through time.

20. Janowitz, *The Professional Soldier*, p. 60.

> The reverse—a more ascriptive (in terms of college attended) advancement policy—seems to be the case. . . .
> After the drastic changes in personnel policy of 1954, advancement to career minister became more ascriptive.[21]

Willick's conclusion that ascriptive recruitment regarding college attended is not operative, in spite of the fact that this variable is not distributed in a representative fashion through the Foreign Service, is entirely consistent with the findings thus far reported in this chapter. Each time, the total population of FSOs, or some particular part of the latter, appears to be unrepresentative when compared with a more inclusive total (e.g., United States) population. The temptation is to interpret this situation as indicating that the Foreign Service is biased in its selection of recruits. Yet, again and again we see that such an inference is incorrect. The main source of compositional unrepresentativeness is not ascriptive recruitment but rather derives from the combined effect of such prerecruitment factors as education (who receives a college education, which college a student attends, and so on) and career choice.[22]

At the same time, it should be clear that nonascriptive recruitment and ascriptive promotion are not mutually exclusive processes. In fact, relevant data on the subject suggest that these apparently contrary forces not only may be compatible, but actually are descriptive of a trend recently manifested within both the Foreign Service and military establishments. Please note that the data contained in table 19 indicate that the percentage of Ivy League graduates within the upperstrata of the Foreign Service (i.e.,

21. Pp. 6, 21, 24.
22. A parallel conclusion emphasizing career success and the variable of "mode-of-entry" is stated by Martin B. Hickman and Neil Hollander, "Undergraduate Origin as a Factor in Elite Recruitment and Mobility: The Foreign Service. A Case Study," *Western Political Quarterly* 19(June, 1966): 337–53. There most pertinent finding is "that generally within a mode-of-entry group graduation from Harvard-Princeton-Yale was not a factor in success; and that, therefore, the unexpectedly large number of graduates from these schools in the successful population is explained by their concentration in those mode-of-entry groups from which the successful population is normally drawn" (p. 349).

TABLE 19
COLLEGES ATTENDED BY FSOs, CAREER MINISTERS, AND RECRUITS

COLLEGE ATTENDED	POLITICAL OFFICERS	CAREER MINISTERS		TOTAL	RECRUITS
		Pre-1954	Post-1954	1960	1961
Ivy League	35%	41%	48%	22%	30%
Other Prestige Private	3	7	10	8	11
Big Ten	8	4	10	9	8
University of California	5	3	2	3	4
Washington, D.C., Area	14	7	3	9	3
Military Academy	0	3	2	...	2
Other	35	34	27	49	43
Total	100%	100%	100%	100%	100%

NOTE: All the data contained in table 19, with the exception of the "Political Officers" sample, are taken directly from Willick's original code sheets rather than the summary figures reported in *The Recruitment and Promotion of Foreign Service Officers*. This was necessary because in the latter he distinguishes only HYP and non-HYP graduates.

among career ministers) before 1954 was 41%, and more recently was 48%. This increase in Ivy League representation occurred despite the facts that: first, the out-recruitment rate for Ivy League graduates is probably higher than for graduates of other colleges;[23] and, second, the Foreign Service, reacting to both public and governmental criticism, has endeavored to pursue a nonascriptive, nationally oriented recruitment campaign. It is common knowledge, for example, that the rather private recruitment of former years has, under some prodding, given way to a more open system where information about the Foreign Service is distributed, and written examinations and even interviews administered, throughout the United States. Because Ivy League representation among career ministers has increased during the period in which the above features were introduced and implemented, it appears to this author that a more nationally oriented, broadly recruited, and representative membership somehow is perceived within the Foreign Service to be a not very desirable trend and thus is resisted through

23. Ilchman, *Professional Diplomacy in the United States*, p. 232.

ascriptive promotion practices. This rather obvious interpretation of the data is also expressed by Willick.

> This shows that although the formal policies of the organization became less ascriptive certain segments of the organization were acting to perpetuate the traditional type of Foreign Service Officer.
> Bureaucratization at the bottom of the organizational hierarchy was shown to have been caused by external pressures, while debureaucratization at the top seems due to actions taken within the organization in reaction to bureaucratization at the bottom and lateral infusion.[24]

It will be recalled that the relatively prestigious country desk officer positions within the Geographic Bureaus are staffed by middle- to upper-middle-level personnel. As such, they should share the aforementioned ascriptively based bias characteristic of the Foreign Service leadership (i.e., career minister) group, though not to the same extent. If the data contained in column one of table 19 are examined, the reader will find the above to be the case. Of the political-policy officers, 35% are Ivy League graduates as compared with 30% of the FSO recruits, 22% of all FSOs, and 41% and 48% of the pre-1954 and post-1954 career minister groups. Hence, we may conclude that the substantial Ivy League representation manifested within the sample of political officers is due to several things: students who attend HYP and other Ivy League schools more often aspire to a career in the Foreign Service than other college students, they are better qualified academically and thus more likely to pass the difficult impartially administered recruitment examinations and, if they choose to stay within the Foreign Service, are more likely than their non–Ivy League colleagues to be promoted into the relatively prestigious country desk officer political-policy positions.

Turning now to a consideration of political-military officers, it will be recalled that 42% of the sample respondents are academy graduates. No other subset of colleges enjoys more than token representation. In this respect, the two groups of political-policy officers, Foreign Service and military, are similar. However, in the latter case, the overall figure that was cited above obscures an

---

24. *Recruitment and Promotion of Foreign Service Officers*, p. 25.

Social Origins

intrasample difference that corresponds to service affiliation. From the data contained in column one of table 20, we see that academy graduates are not proportionately distributed between the three armed services. Not a single air force–affiliated political-military officer is an academy graduate, whereas 61% of the army and 50% of the navy subgroups received academy commissions. This interservice dissimilarity, of course, is not at all surprising when the age of the sample respondents and the fact that the Air Force Academy has only recently been formed are taken into account. The composition of the air force subgroup, hence, is readily explicable. The matter of academy predominance within the army and navy subsamples is a more difficult question to answer.[25]

The data contained in table 20 suggest that the relatively high percentage of academy-commissioned (army and navy) political-military officers is first of all a reflection of a general phenomenon occurring within the services; that is, the proportion of academy graduates steadily increases as one moves through the ranks of the navy, and probably also the army, from newly commissioned officers to a level corresponding to that achieved by our sample respondents—colonels and lt. colonels or captains and commanders. The reasons for this no doubt are many and complex. For one thing, West Point and Annapolis graduates far more often than ROTC- and OCS-commissioned officers initially intend to (and do) pursue a military career.[26] The great majority of persons within the latter two groups of commissioned officers either adopt a

---

25. Those officers who are reported to have academy commissions are presumed to be graduates of the military academies. Nonacademy officers earn their commissions through either a ROTC or OCS program. According to Zald and Simon, "Career Opportunities and Commitments among Officers," table 5, p. 264, only 29% of OCS-commissioned officers within the entire armed services, as compared with almost all ROTC-commissioned officers, have a bachelor's degree. Furthermore, my guess is that many of the OCS-commissioned officers who have college degrees received them after being commissioned, and probably from the University of Maryland (which operates many centers throughout the world) or other District of Columbia area colleges. It therefore seems reasonable to infer that most, if not nearly all, of the nonacademy political-military officers within the sample have ROTC rather than OCS commissions.

26. Ibid., table 9, p. 273; Lang, "Technology and Career Management in the Military Establishment," table 13, p. 64.

TABLE 20

DISTRIBUTION OF MILITARY OFFICERS BY TYPE OF COMMISSION

	POLITICAL OFFICERS	TOTAL MILITARY	COLLEGE EDUCATED	GENERALS & ADMIRALS		COL. & LT. COL., CAPT., & CMDR.	MAJ. & CAPT., LT. CMDR. & LT.	LT., LT J.G., ENSIGN	COMMISSIONED OFFICERS
	1965	1961	1961	1951	1964	1961	1961	1961	1957–67
Army									
Academy	61%	11%	17%	51%	75%	NA	NA	NA	8%
ROTC	⎱39	48	69	⎱49	⎱25	NA	NA	NA	82
OCS	⎰	41	14	⎰	⎰	NA	NA	NA	10
Total	100%	100%	100%	100%	100%				100%
Navy									
Academy	50%	33%	35%	82%	89%	76%	47%	14%	11%
ROTC	⎱50	28	28	⎱18	⎱11	8	24	35	36
OCS	⎰	39	37	⎰	⎰	17	29	51	53
Total	100%	100%	100%	100%	100%	100%	100%	100%	100%
Air Force									
Academy	0%	4%	9%	51%	38%	6%	4%	5%	5%
ROTC	⎱100	27	58	⎱49	⎱62	15	14	57	64
OCS	⎰	69	33	⎰	⎰	80	83	38	31
Total	100%	100%	100%	100%	100%	100%	100%	100%	100%

NOTE: As in previous cases, comparative data presented for analytical purposes derive from several sources; thus, the figures may not be precisely correct. They represent the "best" estimates this author can make given the nature of the original information. Data concerning the "Generals and Admirals" are taken from David R. Segal, *Selection of General Officers in the United States Armed Forces*, table 1, p. 3. A revised version of this paper appears as "Selective Promotion in Officer Cohorts," *Sociological Quarterly* 8(1967):199–206. With the exception of "Political Officers," all of the other data are adapted from Mayer N. Zald and William Simon, "Career Opportunities and Commitments among Officers," in *The New Military*, ed. Janowitz, tables 1–3, 5, pp. 260–62, 264.

Social Origins 79

"wait and see" attitude or say they will serve only their minimum tour of duty; viewpoints that may be entirely realistic if in fact career opportunities for nonacademy commissioned officers are seriously circumscribed due to the existence of ascriptive promotion practices favoring academy graduates. Segal argues that a bias of this nature is operative. Its main function, he claims, is to enable the army and navy to "maintain their organizational autonomy" during a period of "increasing interpenetration with the civilian sector."[27] Overt manifestations of this "reaction against 'civilianization'" are the more rapid promotion rate of academy graduates and the evident decrease in the percentage of nonacademy commissioned officers among the leadership (generals or admirals) group from 1951 to 1964. I believe the justification for this rests upon the popular presumption that academy officers are more capable than others. This bit of folklore, one that probably contains some element of truth and, additionally, caters to the emotional self-satisfaction and career interests of West Point and Annapolis alumni, serves to perpetuate an environment within which it is assured that academy-commissioned officers are provided with greater opportunities for advancement. For example, academy-commissioned officers are more likely to return to college and attain a master's degree,[28] a feature that is becoming an increasingly important asset with respect to the eventual achievement of

27. *Selection of General Officers*, p. 8. After inspecting the same data, Janowitz arrives at a similar conclusion: "Likewise, the distinction between academy graduates and others generates organizational cleavages. In the expanded military establishment since the end of World War II, the percentage of academy graduates who enter on duty as junior officers each year is only a very small number as compared with those from ROTC and other sources. . . . The basic fact is that all of the armed forces are obliged to make use of cadres of junior and middle level officers who are likely to have limited opportunities for advancement to the highest rank. Academy graduates, marked for longer careers than other types of officers, pass rapidly through the command of smaller tactical units, and are more often provided with some form of technical training" (Morris Janowitz, in collaboration with Lt. Col. Roger Little, *Sociology and the Military Establishment*, pp. 69–70).

28. Zald and Simon, "Career Opportunities and Commitments among Officers," table 6, p. 265.

high rank. The fact that academy graduates more frequently are permitted while in the service to attend school beyond the bachelor's degree is particularly relevant to the filling of political-policy positions. Because of the character of curriculum schedules at West Point and Annapolis, academy students are not able to have extensive exposure to the subject matter of political science, or related social science fields such as economics, sociology, and so on. The opportunity to receive graduate-level education provides the chance for academy-commissioned officers to become proficient in political science; a credential that, although not mandatory, certainly is taken into account when personnel for political-policy positions are being considered. Among political-military officers, seven of the nine West Point graduates and all six of the Annapolis graduates who gained a master's degree received it in political science. In sum, because there are tendencies within the armed forces that favor the advancement of academy-commissioned officers (tendencies which, if anything, are becoming more pronounced), it appears unlikely that the substantial academy representation that existed within the political-policy parts of the military establishment in 1965 has or will in the near future be diminished.

SUMMARY AND CONCLUSIONS

The primary objective of this chapter has been to provide a reasonably accurate social profile of that group of military officers and FSOs within the Defense and State Departments who occupy positions directly relating to international political activities. In order to do this, information concerning three general types of attributes was sought. The first concerned geographical background, and included variables relating to location and size of birthplace and hometown. The second group of attributes pertained to nativity of parents, father's occupation, and ethnic affiliation. The third group concerned amount of education and type of four-year college the respondents attended.

In general, the results reported in this chapter tend to suggest

Social Origins

that, in terms of their social background, political-policy officers in the Foreign Service and military establishment have much in common. Approximately one-half of the officers in both groups were born and raised in the northeastern and east north central United States. The remaining half were rather evenly distributed across the other six geographical regions. The majority of the officers in each case were raised in an urban environment. With respect to nationality, few are other than northwest European; a very small proportion trace their ancestry to southern or eastern Europe. Their native-born parents, for the most part, apparently were financially comfortable. This deducation seems quite reasonable given both the pattern of father's occupation reported and the extent and form (i.e., type of college attended) of education of both groups. In other words, the general tone in each case tends to be northeastern, urban, and upper-middle class. Nevertheless, there certainly are sufficient exceptions to the above pattern so as to make it somewhat hazardous to speak in terms of a "typical" political-military or Foreign Service officer. It is more accurate to speak of "modal" characteristics rather than "typical" officers. "Modality" here refers to those social status characteristics that most frequently occur within the groups that are being investigated.

The fact that the two groups of political-policy officers manifest similar profiles regarding the social characteristics discussed in this chapter (i.e., the modal category was the same for both samples in each attribute case, and, thus, no statistically significant differences arose) has an important implication for later analysis. To reiterate a point made earlier, a major aim of this study concerns ascertaining whether political-military officers and political-FSOs differ with respect to their international political beliefs. Assuming an attitudinal dissimilarity is manifest, a complementary objective then involves explaining the latter in terms of certain social, political, and psychological independent predictor variables. However, as a result of the findings contained in this chapter, it now is apparent that the existence of a significant intersample attitudinal difference cannot be accounted for by referring to the attribute variables thus far introduced. Because they fail to distinguish political officers according to their respective organizational affiliations, they cannot be used effectively when the attempt is made to explain significant contrasts in attitude occurring between representative members of the two organizations.

A large part of this chapter has been devoted to the question of why the profiles took the compositional form they did. The approach employed involved a two-step analysis. We first sought to discern whether the distribution of a particular attribute within a sample was "representative." Representative has been used here to indicate a condition whereby the major divisions in some comparable base population are found to exist in similar proportions within the sample. The base against which each sample initially was juxtaposed usually was the United States population. The relevant distributions then were compared and differences noted. In almost every case, political-policy FSOs appeared *not* to be representative. When compared with the United States population distribution, they are: (1) more northeastern (and correspondingly less southern) in their regional origins; (2) more urban (and correspondingly less rural) regarding the size of their hometown; (3) more old immigrant–northwest European (and correspondingly less new immigrant–south and east European) regarding ancestry; (4) more often the sons of fathers who held high-status occupations; (5) more educated; and (6) to an unusual extent Ivy League educated. The group of political-military officers also appeared *not* to be representative. Their dissimilarity from the comparable base population followed the pattern for FSOs described above, although the extent of their deviations generally was not as great as that of their Foreign Service counterparts, and they tend to be academy rather than Ivy League educated.

The second step entailed an examination of the sources of the observed discrepancies. The aim here involved ascertaining why the political-military officers and political-FSOs were not representative. In order to answer this question, it was necessary to group the possibly contributing factors according to whether their effects primarily are manifest prior to recruitment, during the recruitment process, or after recruitment. Factors falling within the first stage of the sequence mainly concerned differential rates of educational attainment and career choice patterns. The second and third elements of the sequence were organized around the issue of ascription; whether selection into, and/or promotion within, each establishment is based for the most part upon a person's social characteristics or his personal achievements. It was found that, with one partial exception (i.e., college attended), the dissimilarities in composition between political-FSO respondents and the United States population distribution were due largely to prerecruitment factors. Introducing the qualifying elements of educational attainment and/or career aspiration usually had the effect of noticeably diminishing the nonrepresentative quality of the political-FSO sample. By way of contrast, there is little, if any, evidence to suggest that the selection process that occurs during and after recruitment substantially alters the attribute profile already evident among FSO aspirants. Recruitment and promotion practices, by not having an important impact on social composition, consequently serve to perpetuate the biases already wrought by the prerecruitment factors mentioned earlier. In other words, unbiased achievement oriented recruitment and promotion procedures perpetuate the compositional nonrepresentativeness of elite organizations when educational opportunity (and related eligibility criteria that constitute the recruitment rules of the organization) are disproportionately distributed within the society. In point of fact, educational opportunity is selectively distributed. Thus, both political-FSOs and the entire Foreign Service appear not to be representative when the variables discussed in the first two sections of this chapter are being considered. A partial exception to this pattern is the attribute variable pertaining to college attended. I say "partial exception" because once again unbiased recruitment is the case; about the same proportion of Ivy League graduates are recruited into the Foreign Service as can be theoretically expected on the basis of career aspiration patterns and academic ability. On the other hand, a good argument can be made that upward movement within the Foreign Service to higher authority positions depends to some extent upon whether an officer is an Ivy League graduate. Country desks within the Geographic Bureaus usually are occupied by officers with the rank of FSO-3 (or sometimes, FSO-4), and thus may be considered middle- to upper-middle-level positions. As such, they are affected by an ascriptive bias favoring Ivy League graduates and, consequently, contain a very substantial Ivy League representation. This Ivy League bias also accounts for the very slight increase in northeastern representation among political-FSOs and career ministers, as compared with recruits and the entire Foreign Service alluded to earlier in this chapter. The aforementioned difference can be attributed to the fact that Ivy League graduates, not surprisingly, tend more often than other college graduates to have been born and raised in the northeastern United States.[29] Hence, the small increase in northeastern representation is associated in a spurious way with the ascriptive promotion of Ivy League graduates.

The situation with respect to political-military officers is more complex. For one thing, although the prerecruitment period also is important here, the consistency and extent of its contribution is less than what obtained with the Foreign Service. The reasons for this can be traced directly to the manner in which West Point and Annapolis choose their students, and the nature of military career aspirants in nonacademy colleges. Both features conspire to partially reverse the biasing influence that educational attainment promotes and thus make the candidate pool from which the armed forces are selecting officers somewhat more like the United States population distribution (i.e., somewhat more representative) than otherwise would be the case. Similarly to the Foreign Service, the only noticeably ascriptive element occurring within the military establishment during and after recruitment had to do with the college attended variable. In even more dramatic fashion than was true with respect to Ivy League FSOs, graduates of the Military and Naval Academies were revealed to have a much greater chance for advancement to leadership positions than ROTC- and

29. Willick, *Recruitment and Promotion of Foreign Service Officers*, table 12.

Social Origins

OCS-commissioned officers. The proportion of academy graduates substantially increased with each succeeding grade level in the hierarchy. The parallel between the two organizations concerning the college attended variable may be taken one step further. In both cases, the proportion of Ivy League and academy graduates among Foreign Service and military leaders was shown to be greater now (i.e., after 1954 and 1964 respectively) than previously (i.e., before 1954 and 1951 respectively), even though graduates of these institutions were becoming less numerous within each organization. Because political-military officers also occupy middle- to upper-middle-level positions, they are affected by the aforementioned ascriptive bias in much the same way as their counterparts in the Foreign Service. Hence, it is to be expected that the political-military officer group will have a substantial academy representation among its members.

What thus far has not been adequately dealt with are the other discrepancies manifested by political-military officers. It was stated earlier that reference to prerecruitment factors only partially answers the question of why political-military officers are not a representative group. Moreover, we learned in addition that, aside from college attended, no noticeable change in composition occurs during and after recruitment. Attention, therefore, is directed toward the selection of political-military officers, and whether (and how) they differ from their peers with respect to social background. The subsequent analysis revealed that, in general, whereas political-FSOs seemed quite typical of the corps as a whole, political-military officers appear atypical when compared with the armed forces membership. If the theoretical work and data provided by Huntington, Janowitz, Lovell, Lang, Zald and Simon, and the rest can serve as a valid guide regarding the construction of a social profile of the military establishment, then we are led to the conclusion that the military officers who occupy political-policy positions within the Pentagon are significantly more northeastern, urban, upper class, and educated than their non-political-military colleagues. The basis for their uniqueness consequently is a substantive one relating to the particular staff position for which they are selected—a position with role functions directly concerning the formation and conduct of political-military policy. In other words, it is the "political-policy" aspect of the position that apparently is the key element. One result of this pattern of atypicalness is that political-military officers begin to resemble their counterparts in the Foreign Service to the extent that no significant differences are apparent between the two groups. We stated earlier in this study that ISA (and, by implication, the political staffs of the armed services) often is referred to as the Pentagon's State Department. In view of our findings, this association appears to possess an appropriateness that goes well beyond the feature of their sharing similar official responsibilities.

The data presented in this chapter additionally suggested that both organizations are becoming more heterogeneous in their composition.[30] The compositional change from rather exclusive homogeneous collectivities to more broadly based bureaucratic-oriented organizations has come about for various reasons, among them: (1) more persons learned about the Foreign Service and military establishment as foreign policy issues became ascendant during and after World War II, (2) the rapid growth of the Foreign Service and military establishment meant that persons from other than the social groups that traditionally predominated must be recruited, (3) the achievement of a college education now is possible for most high school graduates, and (4) a relatively diverse group of college students compared with what obtained previously

---

30. "The military elite has been undergoing a basic social transformation since the turn of the century. These elites have been shifting their recruitment from a narrow relatively high social status base to a broader base, more representative of the population as a whole" (Janowitz and Little, *Sociology and the Military Establishment*, p. 23). Ilchman comments: "The administration after the Rogers Act succeeded in democratizing as well as further professionalizing the service. 'Democratization,' of course, is not meant in the sense that the service accurately represented every group in American society. It is meant in the sense that the career had a wide recruitment base, that the barriers had been removed from almost every aspect of the service, and that its social character changed markedly from that of its Diplomatic Service progenitor" (*Professional Diplomacy in the United States*, p. 225).

aspire to developing a career within these organizations. It also was found that this increasing heterogeneity has encouraged the army, navy and Foreign Service to intensify the ascriptive selection of academy and Ivy League graduates for leadership positions. For example, the proportion of Ivy League and academy graduates within the latter strata was revealed to be greater now (i.e., after 1954 and 1964, respectively) than previously (before 1954 and 1951, respectively). A similar process can be expected to occur within the air force as the number of its academy graduates increases in the future. But the above bias will not reverse the tendency toward heterogeneity because it additionally is true that the composition of each of the Ivy League schools and academies is itself becoming more varied. These colleges certainly have a more socially heterogeneous student body today than they did in the past. Consequently, social-status characteristics apparently are becoming increasingly irrelevant with respect to the recruitment and promotion of political-military officers and FSOs, even when ascription regarding college attended is admitted.[31]

Yet the question may be raised as to why, coming from similar backgrounds, our respondents made different choices as to the profession they would pursue and, probably as a consequence, selected different colleges to attend (i.e., Harvard, Yale, and Princeton versus West Point and Annapolis)? Furthermore, what prompts some college graduates at Big Ten schools, the University of California, and so on, to enter the Foreign Service, and others to join the armed services? These certainly are interesting research questions. Part of the answer may lie with the particular religious and/or political viewpoints and identifications held by an individual—subject areas to which we now turn our attention.

31. "In terms of ideals and values, the officer-corps seems to remain distinctly separated from the rest of society. Its social origins might have had some significance in the past, but the contrast today between the uniformity within the group and the officers' social background, strongly suggests that the group now derives its main characteristics from a particular culture, developing from occupational activities and quite irrespective of social composition" (Francesco Kjellberg, "Some Cultural Aspects of the Military Profession," *European Journal of Sociology* 6[1965]:285).

CHAPTER 4
Religion

Another group of variables that receives much attention in the literature pertains to religion. Most religion variables can be divided into two classes: one concerned with religious affiliation (What are you?), the other with extent of religious involvement (How religious are you?). Both of these aspects will be examined in this chapter. Following the pattern established in chapter 3, the focus here initially will be upon investigating how each organization's political policy officers are distributed with respect to these characteristics and, second, upon the determinants of the distribution patterns manifested.

Without any delay, let us turn to a consideration of the religious affiliation of political-military officers and FSOs. The data contained in table 21 reveal first of all that the former group is about one-fourth Catholic and nearly two-thirds Protestant. Of the six remaining military officers, four identified themselves as members of nontraditional Christian churches (e.g., Unitarian, Mormon). Approximately two-thirds of the FSOs also claim to be Protestant. Only another three (of 37, or 8%), however, are Catholic. Note that in the military three times that percentage are Catholic. Finally, nearly one-fifth of the FSOs, compared with only 4% of the military, are either Jewish or claim no religion. In sum, Protestants predominate within both groups to about an equal extent. The disagreement that emerges between the two distributions is a secondary one in nature and involves the dissimilar division of the

TABLE 21
RELIGIOUS AFFILIATION

RELIGION	POLITICAL OFFICERS				ESTIMATED DISTRIBUTION U.S. POPULATION	
	Military		FSO		Household head with 4 years of college (1955–56)	Total (1957)
	%	N	%	N	%	%
Protestant						
Episcopal	21	12	30	11	6	2
Presbyterian	10	6	11	4	9	6
Congregational	3	2	8	3	2	1
Methodist	12	7	19	7	15	14
Lutheran	7	4	0	0	6	7
Reformed	2	1	0	0	0.3	0.3
Baptist	3	2	0	0	10	20
Other	0	0	0	0	} 13	} 13
No denomination	5	3	3	1		
Total Protestant	64	37	70	26	61	63
Roman Catholic	26	15	8	3	21	26
Nontraditional Christian	7	4	3	1	3	3
Jewish	2	1	11	4	9	3
Other	0	0	0	0	2	1
No religion	2	1	8	3	4	3
Grand Total	100	58	100	37	100	100

NOTE: The "U.S. Population" figures are estimates derived from data cited by Bogue, *The Population of the United States*, table 23-1, 23-2, 23-10, pp. 689, 691–92, 701. The "Nontraditional Christian" category includes the following religious bodies: Christian Scientists, Spiritualists, Latter Day Saints (Mormons), Unitarians, Jehovah's Witnesses, and Quakers.

one-third minority who are not included within the aforementioned modal category. In the case of the military, most of the non-Protestants are Catholic; in the case of the Foreign Service, there are more Jews or "no religion" respondents than Catholics.

The main feature of Protestant predominance is not unexpected. A contrary result would be greeted with some suspicion since it already has been established that about 50% of the political-policy officers claim British ethnic affiliation, and most of the remaining half trace their ancestry to other parts of northwest Europe. The previous chapter's findings, moreover, enable us also to anticipate the denominational structure of the two Protestant subsets. First of all, we know that Protestant denominations significantly differ as to the income and education of their members. For example, the major denominations, and Catholics and Jews additionally, may be ranked according to whether their memberships are relatively high income-educated (e.g., Episcopal, Presbyterian, and Jewish), or median (e.g., Catholic, Lutheran, and Methodist), or low (e.g., Baptist).[1] We also know that most officers are highly educated and, in terms of their background, from the more privileged social strata (e.g., the great majority are the sons of high-status-occupation fathers). Therefore, one may easily infer that many of the officers either initially were raised within a high-income-educated denominational setting, or, if they were not, are encouraged to join such religious bodies because affilation with the latter churches is prevalent among colleagues and superiors and/or is symbolic of upward social mobility.[2] In any case, the result ought to be that our two samples contain substantial Episcopal and Presbyterian contingents, and few if any officers who identify themselves as Baptists. This is revealed to be the case. Table 21 shows that of 95 respondents, only two political-military officers are Baptists. On the other hand, 31% of the military and 41% of the FSOs describe themselves as members of the former two denominations. If Congregationalists are added, as they probably ought to be, the appropriate figures for the high-income-educated group of denominations reach 34% and 49% respectively. The remaining 21% of the military and 19% of the FSOs who are Protestant may be considered members of "median" denominations.

The above pattern is not of particular interest until juxtaposed with the denominational composition of the United States population. Striking percentage variations then are revealed, the most prominent of which relate to a severe overrepresentation of Epis-

1. See Bogue, *Population of the United States*, pp. 701–8, for a description of the membership of religious bodies regarding the highly associated factors of income and education.
2. Lovell ("Professional Socialization of the West Point Cadet," pp. 137–38) argues that there exists within the military establishment a pressure toward Episcopal affiliation.

copalians and corresponding underrepresentation of Baptists. More precisely, although the Episcopal church claims only about 2% of the total United States and 8% of the Protestant populations, it alone accounts for 21% of the political-military officers and 30% of all FSOs. Contrariwise, the Baptists, who are 20% and 37% of the American and Protestant populations, contribute just two political-policy officers. The extent of these disproportionalities, furthermore, is but slightly diminished when only household heads with four or more years of college serve as the comparable base population. Hence, on the one hand, we see that the aforementioned prominence of Protestants clearly is in keeping with their number within the United States population. On the other hand, we also see that speaking merely of Protestant predominance without reference to denominational composition obscures acute internal disproportionalities. The various Protestant subsets are shown for the most part to contain an unrepresentative abundance of high-income-educated denomination members. This refinement concerning the privileged denomination bias underlying the makeup of the general Protestant group has the advantage of providing the latter with an appearance that is quite consistent with the implied social status set emerging from the previous chapter's analysis.

One minor but interesting point pertains to Jewish representation within the military sample. Only one political-military officer of fifty-eight is Jewish, whereas 9% of those who are household heads with four years of college are of this religion. This apparent underrepresentation is quickly explained if the pertinent data appearing in table 22 are inspected. It shows that Jews are far more likely than non-Jews to attend college. Yet, we also see that scarcely any Jewish college students at all wish to develop a military career. Thus, even a proportion of one Jew among fifty-eight military officers is, if anything, more than should be expected. On the other hand, the 11% Jewish representation among political-FSOs and 8% within the total Foreign Service cannot be so easily accounted for. Note that since few Jewish college students aspire to be a FSO, the factor of career choice does not play a role here.

There are, of course, various alternative explanations. Unfortunately, sufficient data are not available to either affirm or reject with some confidence any of them. One possibility is that fifteen to twenty years ago a higher proportion of FSO aspirants was Jewish than in 1961. A trend of this nature, however, seems unlikely since the last several decades have witnessed a series of organizational reforms that should have made a Foreign Service career more, not less, congenial to Jewish college students. A second reason may be the existence of ascriptive recruitment and/or promotion practices that favor Jews as against non-Jews. Such a pattern also is unlikely for it runs directly counter both to what we know about the Foreign Service (i.e., the Ivy League, Episcopal character of the organization) and popular stereotypical notions regarding this institution. Similarly, arguments based on differential rates of lateral transfer and out-recruitment do not appear either to be appropriate. Perhaps the explanation that sounds most persuasive is the one that directs attention toward the academic rigorousness of Foreign Service examinations pertaining to the selection of officers and the differing academic ability of Jewish and non-Jewish college students. The argument here would be based upon the contention that Jewish FSO aspirants are better students than non-Jewish FSO aspirants and, therefore, more frequently pass the impartially administered and evaluated entrance (especially written) tests. This proposition cannot be readily assessed, however, because only two of the 118 FSO aspirants claim to be Jewish, and we do not have information regarding the religious background of FSO recruits. Nevertheless, information relating to the academic ability of a cross section of college students divided according to religious affiliation is available. In his book, *Undergraduate Career Decisions*, James A. Davis presents data concerning what here has been called the qualifying population that reveal that, as a group, Jewish students score higher on an Academic Performance Index than do Protestant and Catholic students.[3] Thus, empirical support is indirectly provided for the above

---

3. James A. Davis, *Undergraduate Career Decisions*. For example,

Religion

assertion. In addition, such a line of reasoning intuitively appears more reasonable that the alternative explanations previously introduced. Needless to say, even partially satisfactory verification of this contention demands investigation of some obvious intervening links that are as yet unexplored.

A final point has to do with the number of "no religion" respondents among political-FSOs (8%) and FSOs in general (6%) as compared with their corresponding proportion within the United States population (3%). Why this disparity is manifest becomes clear if we inspect the data contained in table 22. We see that 26% of all FSO aspirants refuse to express a religious affiliation. The bulk of this subset no doubt were reared by Protestant parents. Moreover, we probably can assume without much question that, as individuals leave college and later become established, there tends to occur a regression toward religious affiliation. The religious bodies that most likely would gain representation as a result of this regression would be the ones that have been described as high-income-educated Protestant denominations. First, most "no religion" respondents evidently were raised as Protestants (and probably within an Episcopal, Presbyterian, or Congregationalist setting), and the majority can be expected to revert to their background affiliation. Second, those officers of a median or low-income-educated denominational background will be attracted to the high-status denominations partly because most of their peers are of such affiliation and partly because the status of their occupational positions warrants a denominational identification of relatively high status. Thus, it is to be expected that older political-FSOs should exhibit a profile that contains more Protestant affiliators than the FSO "present religious affiliation-aspiring" population, and that the extent of "no religion" representation among the group of political-policy officers should fall somewhere between the present and reared figures cited for FSO aspirants.

The existence of these minor anomalies, though interesting, should not serve to distract the reader from the main findings that

---

see table 1.11, p. 220, where Jews are revealed to perform better academically than non-Jews even when sex and size of hometown are taken into account.

TABLE 22
REPRESENTATIVENESS OF THE MILITARY AND FSOs REGARDING RELIGIOUS AFFILIATION

Religion	Total Foreign Service 1966	Political Officers		West Point 1959-61	Aspiring				Qualifying		U.S. Pop. 1957
		Military	FSO		Military		FSO				
					Present	Reared	Present	Reared	Present	Reared	
Protestant or nontraditional Christian	69%	71%	73%	65%	61%	73%	51%	72%	56%	63%	66%
Catholic	18	26	8	30	25	22	18	19	23	24	26
Jewish	8	2	11	2	1	1	0	2	7	8	3
Other	3	0	0	2	4	2	5	4	3	3	1
No religion	6	2	8	2	9	2	26	3	11	3	3
Total	100%	100%	100%	100%	100%	100%	100%	100%	100%	100%	100%

NOTE: The data for "West Point (1959-61)" appear in Janowitz, *The Professional Soldier*, p. 98. The "Total Foreign Service (1966)" data are reported by Harr, *The Professional Diplomat*, p. 182.

Religion

thus far have emerged. They are: (1) the great majority of political-policy officers within both the Foreign Service and military establishment describe themselves as Protestant; (2) the extent of Protestant representation, however, is proportional to their number within the United States population; (3) most Protestant officers are affiliated with high-income-educated denominations and relatively few, if any at all, with denominations whose memberships are relatively low-income-educated; and (4) high-income-educated denominations (especially the Episcopal church) are noticeably overrepresented, and low-income-educated denominations (especially Baptists) underrepresented, within both political-policy officer groups. With respect to the military, this religious affiliation pattern bears a resemblance to previous findings contained in the literature. For example, Lovell writes that "Episcopalianism, the core religious faith of the American military profession historically, is slightly overrepresented at West Point, although the percentage affiliation among cadets is not nearly that found among Army top leadership."[4] The religious affiliation of military officers is a subject to which Janowitz also has devoted some attention. The general conclusions derived from his investigation are summarized in the following statement.

> First, the American military elite has been overwhelmingly a Protestant group. Recruitment from rural communities and from older families directly implies such religious affiliation. Second, as the social composition of the military has begun to draw heavily on lower-status groups, the concentration of Catholics has begun to increase, but the lag has been considerable. . . . Future trends are indicated from data on West Point cadet classes of 1959, 1960, and 1961, where the precentage of Catholics has risen to 29. These figures reflect the influx of those from white-collar and working-class background, and may signify an over-representation. . . .
> . . . Fundamentalist sects are wholly unrepresented among the military elite. Is there any special significance in the concentration of Episcopalians among the military elite, a concentration which, until recently, dominated organized military religion?[5]

4. "Professional Socialization of the West Point Cadet," p. 138.
5. *The Professional Soldier*, pp. 97–99. Some of the data upon which the quoted statement is based appear in table 22.

The only point of dispute between our analysis and the statement by Janowitz has to do with his assertion that increased Catholic representation is associated primarily with an "influx of those from white-collar and working-class background." In table 23, we have presented data concerning the religious affiliation, geographical background, and status of father's occupation of both political-military officers and military career aspirants. The finding that very obviously emerges from the latter is that Catholic representation within the Armed Services mainly is associated with increased recruitment from non-southern areas. The reader will recall that the army and navy traditionally (and until rather recently) were very disproportionately composed of persons born and raised in the South. Now note how few political-military officers or military aspirants who are of southern background identify themselves as other than Protestant in their religious affiliation. With respect to the armed services, then, southern predominance implies Protestant predominance. Also evident is the fact that the northeastern and other geographical categories contain far more Catholic political-military officers and military aspirants than does the southern one, even when status of father's occupation is explicitly taken into account. Hence, greater geographical heterogeneity (i.e., a tendency involving less southern orientation) means increased Catholic representation within the military establishment. But we already have argued elsewhere that the former actually is occurring.[6] Consequently, a more persuasive contention than the white-collar and working-class background claim would be that increased Catholic representation largely is associated with a geographic diversity that has not been typical of the armed services for most of its history. In addition, we should comment that Catholics probably are also more likely to pursue a military career today than in the past. Compared with the factors of geographical diversity and greater aspiration, the explanatory potency of "background class" appears minor, if at all relevant.

Our discussion of social origins thus far has suggested that the modal characteristics of both groups of respondents tend to con-

6. See chapter 3.

TABLE 23

Distribution of Political-Military Officers and Military Career Aspirants by Religious Affiliation, Geographical Background, and Status (High or Low) of Father's Occupation

	Northeast				South				Other			
	High		Low		High		Low		High		Low	
	%	N	%	N	%	N	%	N	%	N	%	N
Political-Military Officers												
Catholic	36	5	20	1	11	1	0	0	42	5	15	2
Protestant	50	7	80	4	89	8	100	2	33	4	77	10
Other	13	2	0	0	0	0	0	0	25	3	8	1
	Religion in Which Reared											
Military Career Aspirants												
Catholic	33	9	33	15	3	1	3	1	22	8	33	17
Protestant	52	14	62	28	97	29	97	32	76	28	63	32
Other	15	4	4	2	0	0	0	0	2	1	4	2
	Present Religion											
Catholic	33	9	31	14	7	2	18	6	18	7	37	19
Protestant	44	12	53	24	87	26	79	26	61	23	51	26
Other	22	6	16	7	7	2	3	1	21	8	12	6

stitute an "attribute cluster" that seems to be substantively congruent.[7] By this I mean that the various modal elements identified cohere in such a way so that changing the character of one element from its present to a contrary state would appear to the aware reader to produce dissonant relationships within the set. Such dissonance would occur, for example, if we discovered in this chapter that the overwhelming majority of political-policy officers are Catholic (and not Protestant) after already establishing in the previous one that approximately one-half of our respondents trace their ancestry to Great Britain.

But the question may be raised: Why should this particular attribute cluster be present? On the basis of what data is available, I again submit that the answer lies mainly with the professional-bureaucratic quality of the military establishment and Foreign Service, and the nature of career-choice patterns. With respect to the former, these professional-bureaucratic organizations do not set the achievement of representativeness as an important value that must be attained, but rather seek to staff their political-policy positions with highly educated persons who are disposed to accept responsibilities involving political analysis. But until recently, few families aside from the financially comfortable possessed the means to buy a superior college education for their children. Moreover, the sons of the less privileged who did manage to work their way through college were upwardly mobile and tended to prefer business and academia to the rather unknown and perhaps uncongenial worlds of the military and the Foreign Service. This last remark touches upon the second factor—the subject of career motivation. The important question here is; which social

7. It perhaps is the existence of this feature that enables and even encourages the construction of caricatures. Caricature, of course, is based upon the emphasizing of obvious characteristics of a person or group. Unfortunately, it often is too easy to slip into the mistake of thinking of caricatures as if they were descriptively accurate and, consequently, to speak of caricatured social groups as if they were nearly homogeneous in composition. Our analysis hopefully provides a corrective to the aforementioned tendency while at the same time describing the particular attribute pattern that is predominant.

environment most often provided a normative setting within which the idea of devoting oneself to (executive-administrative) public service was considered to be socially acceptable and even prestigious? The argument, therefore, is that the individuals who gravitated toward the pursuit of a career in the military or Foreign Service and who were able to meet the formal requirements posited by these organizations were more often than not high-income-educated denominational Protestant sons of high-status-occupation fathers who were native-born and of British or other northwest European ancestry because the latter characteristics represent the various facets of a societal subset that provided the necessary normative climate and financial support.[8] In addition, the relatively small size of the two organizations and their political-policy components meant that this rather narrow societal subset could fill most of these organizations' manpower needs. Thus, a number of factors conspired to create and sustain Episcopal-Presbyterian, native-born upper-middle-class predominance.

At the same time, it is clear that this particular pattern of predominance is not immutable. To the contrary, we already have suggested several times that compositional change in the general direction of greater heterogeneity is occurring. The reasons identified that apparently encourage this trend are many and varied. Perhaps the most interesting is that the "elite" military academies and Ivy League schools have themselves substantially broadened their social and religious base. This means that the traditionally predominant societal subset mentioned above will no longer exclusively possess privileged access to (political policy) leadership positions within the military and Foreign Service even if ascriptive promotion practices favoring "elite" alumni continue to be manifest. Although the attribute cluster characteristic of these governmental organizations persists among middle- and upper-level officers (e.g., political-

---

8. One difference we have noted with respect to the organizations as a whole is that the northern-urban part of this societal subset tended to choose the Foreign Service, whereas the southern-rural part opted more often for a military career. We additionally revealed that political-military officers tend not to be southern-rural, but in their geographical background resemble more their Foreign Service counterparts.

policy personnel) who are in their late thirties and forties and were recruited more than a decade or two ago, its extent (and the importance attached to it) is diminishing today and certainly will be less prominent in the future.

The reader will recall that, in the beginning of this chapter, it was stated that we intend to investigate a second aspect of religion—the extent of religious involvement. Our original expectation, as described in chapter 1, was that political-military personnel would be revealed to be significantly more religious than political-FSOs. This proposition rests upon the knowledge that religious involvement is encouraged both at the military academies and within the armed services. Devotion to "duty, honor, and country" is explicitly coupled with devotion to conventional religious principles. This correspondence is forged through the use of such mechanisms as "mandatory" regular attending of church at West Point and Annapolis and, within the military establishment itself, by monthly "character guidance" sessions conducted by chaplains or similar religious leaders. The setting found within the military establishment will thus tend to reinforce what religious impulses an individual may have and induce an initially irreligious officer to become less so. I think it dubious that a climate such as this favoring religious involvement exists and is actively maintained within the Foreign Service. More than likely, the factor of religious involvement is not explicitly joined with the accomplishment of organizational responsibilities and, therefore, is neither encouraged nor discouraged. If the above is in fact true, it would seem that political-FSOs ought to appear to be less religious than their "encouraged" military counterparts, provided of course that each organization's recruits are similar, and personnel who have laterally transferred into or left the organization are not unrepresentative regarding the variable being considered. On the other hand, we should note that similar expectations were voiced with respect to nearly all the attribute variables thus far introduced, expectations that later were not borne out.

Two questions were asked in order to ascertain religious involvement. The first related to how frequently each officer at-

Religion

tended church (regularly, often, or seldom); the second to how religious he perceived himself to be (very religious, somewhat religious, or not religious). Together, these two items are presumed to offer some clues as to the relative religiosity of the two groups of political-policy officers.

The data presented in table 24 are based upon responses to both of the above questions. They indicate that we can with much confidence reject the hypothesis that political-military officers and political-FSOs do not differ with respect to religiosity. Intersample dissimilarity is clear; the proportion of FSOs steadily increases as one moves from high to low religiosity, whereas most of the political-military officers are found within the three categories nearest the high end of the dimension. When all the respondents are divided into high and low religiosity subgroups, we see that about three-quarters of the military, but only one-third of the FSOs, are contained within the former class. In sum, the differences exhibited are dramatic, quite significant, and in the direction which was predicted.

Because variables pertaining to social background often play a prominent part in empirical analyses, there is a great temptation to attempt to account for the above dissimilarity by referring to such features. However, we already know that the political-policy subsystems of the military and Foreign Service do not significantly differ with respect to the social origins (including religious affiliation) of their members. Each organization has been shown to have approximately the same proportion of high-income-educated denominational Protestants, sons of high-status-occupation fathers, and so on. Consequently, we may surmise that these general purpose social status variables will not contribute very much to our understanding of why one group of political officers appears to be more religiously involved than the other. That this is the case is evident from an inspection of the data contained in table 25. We observe that extent of religious involvement (high versus low religiosity) is not significantly related to any of the seven social background variables thus far discussed. This means we cannot

TABLE 24
RELIGIOSITY

Religiosity		Military		FSO		Total	
		%	N	%	N	%	N
High	1	24	14	6	2	17	16
	2	26	15	11	4	20	19
	3	24	14	17	6	21	20
Subtotal		74	43	33	12	59	55
Low	4	12	7	31	11	19	18
	5	14	8	36	13	22	21
Subtotal		26	15	67	24	42	39
Effective Total		100	58	100	36	100	94
Statistics		$\chi^2(1)=15.235/P=.01$ $Gamma=.703/P=.01$					
Not ascertained					1		1
Grand Total			58		37		95

NOTE: The statistical coefficients that are reported in table 24 are the result of a 2 x 2 matrix analysis in which the Religiosity row variable has been dichotomized at the 3/4 cutting point. For the full 5 x 2 matrix, Gamma=.560. Religiosity scores are based upon two items, Church Attendance and Religious Self-description. For each of the latter questions, three responses arranged in an ordinal fashion are possible. The coding matrix employed to yield a Religiosity score for each respondent was the following one:

		Self-description			
Attendance		Very	Some	Not	NA
	Regularly	1	2	3	2
	Often	2	3	4	3
	Seldom	3	4	5	4
	NA	2	3	4	NA

The relationship between Church Attendance (dichotomized between Often and Seldom) and Religious Self-description is: $x2(2)=20.456/P=.01$ and Gamma=.605/P=.01. Church attendance is dichotomized here and in future cases in order to avoid difficulties stemming from its acute bimodal structure. See table 26 for a description of its response distribution.

make the simple argument that one organization's membership is more religious than the other because the former additionally contains, for example, relatively more southerners or sons of low-status-occupation fathers, features associated with intensive religious involvement.

Our effort, moreover, is confounded by a problem that is here encountered for the first time. A person cannot become more

TABLE 25

RELATIONSHIP OF RELIGIOSITY AND CHURCH ATTENDANCE, RELIGIOUS SELF-DESCRIPTION, AND VARIABLES PERTAINING TO SOCIAL ORIGINS

	Statistics	
	$\chi^2=$	Gamma=
Religiosity and:		
Church attendance	53.68*	.976*
Religious self-description	52.93*	1.000*
Place of birth	1.19	
Geographical background	3.85	
Size of hometown	2.25	−.248
Status of father's occupation	1.81	−.293
Educational level	.354	−.125
Religious affiliation	2.52	.448
Denominational status	.167	−.111
The Military only		
Old versus newtimers	.021	−.043
Service affiliation	1.57	
Academy versus nonacademy	7.34*	.849*
Foreign Service only		
New versus oldtimers	.056	−.083
Non-Ivy versus Ivy League	.663	.358

* P = .01; all others: P = NS.

NOTE: For the purposes of comparison and correlation, the variable, "Religious Affiliation," includes only Catholics and Protestants. "Denominational Status" divides Protestant as to whether they are affiliated with a high (Episcopal, Presbyterian, or Congregationalist) or low (all other) status denomination. Graduates of Washington, D.C., area colleges are not included within the "Academy versus Nonacademy" distinction. Note that several variables discussed in chapter 3 (e.g., Ethnic Affiliation, Nativity) are not included here. The reason is that there are no intra-sample differences of any degree regarding these variables and, therefore, any attempt to compute a correlation with a second variable is futile. Also note that here and in the similar tables 29, 34, and 38, "degrees of freedom" varies for the relationships that are cited. This fact needs to be kept in mind when the "significance" figures are considered.

northeastern in regional background or more German in ethnic affiliation. These and similar characteristics by their very nature are immutable; an individual's response to a question concerning these attributes should be the same today as five or twenty years from now. This, of course, is relatively less true regarding religious affiliation and denominational status. But even with respect to these attributes, stability in affiliation rather than change definitely is the rule.[9] This facet is important in the type of pseudolongitudi-

9. An indication of the stability of religious affiliation is provided by an examination of the responses of military and Foreign Service aspirants to two

nal analysis conducted here, for it permits a simplification in interpretation by reducing the number of possible explanations that need to be investigated when differences between data configurations are exhibited. On the other hand, the extent of a person's religiosity is quite susceptible to change. Advancing age or exposure to new ideas and experiences may have a dramatic effect upon the nature of one's attachment to religious principles. Consequently, in addition to the selective effects of recruitment, promotion, lateral transfer, and out-recruitment patterns, we now also have to consider whether the extent of religiosity found among an organization's membership may be influenced by the existence of a particular organizational setting (i.e., the impact of socialization), or even by such an apparently extraneous factor as advancing age.[10]

My guess is that religiosity is not at all related to whether individuals laterally transfer into or leave the organization, and probably is not very relevant either to one's success in being recruited or promoted. In order for religiosity to be a significant criterion for selection, superiors (and peers) whose judgments are necessary in these matters must know the religious involvement of prospective candidates. But how do they come by this information? Are a person's religious activities and beliefs so salient in the military and Foreign Service that they can play such a discriminating role? It could if religious involvement was a feature found in an officer's record as part of his biography or something usually included in evaluations of personnel. But this, of course,

questions mentioned earlier in this chapter: "religion in which reared" and "present religion." Of the 366 respondents who answered the two questions, 77% offered the same answer for both (i.e., no change in affiliation); 15% said they presently had no religion but identified some religious body when asked religion in which reared (many of these students can be expected to revert to the latter after college); and only 8% gave different answers, thereby revealing a change in affiliation.

10. The speculation that follows does not rest upon a firmly established empirical foundation. In order to adequately assess the effects of these various factors, a great deal of data would have to be gathered and sorted. Unfortunately, the amount of information that is available is meager as compared with what is required for satisfactory analysis.

Religion

is not the case. The extent of an officer's religiosity is not explicitly stated anywhere and, hence, is not very visible except, perhaps, to a few close friends. Consequently, it appears unlikely that this factor could serve as a basis for recruitment or promotion within either the military establishment or Foreign Service.

At least two other possibilities remain. First, it may be that the military and Foreign Service initially select recruits from candidate pools that significantly differ with respect to the religiosity of their memberships. Because of impartially administered recruitment procedures, this dissimilarity between aspirants is carried forward and becomes a compositional characteristic that appears whenever the two organizations are compared. The implication here is that no within-organization differences between, for example, aspirants and recruits, or recruits and more senior members, or newtimers and oldtimers will be exhibited. The second theoretical possibility starts with the premise that military and Foreign Service aspirants and recruits are similarly distributed regarding religiosity. The main contention is that the important determinant is the dissimilar socialization to which military officers and FSO's are exposed; either the setting in one case encourages more (or less) religiosity on the part of its members while the other organization's setting has no effect, is indifferent to the religiosity of its membership, or both organizational settings generate change, but in contrary directions. Whichever is the case, interorganization religious involvement differences gradually emerge—differences that are plainly manifested when such middle and high level officers as political-policy personnel are compared. In other words, the expectations here are that: one, no differences between military and Foreign Service aspirants (or recruits) will be exhibited with respect to religiosity; and second, significant differences regarding religiosity will be evident when newtimers and oldtimers within each organization are compared.

The assessment of these two sets of propositions can only be accomplished by indirect means. For example, instead of possessing data that bear directly upon religiosity, we have to be content with information pertaining to its two components, church attendance (table 26) and religious self-description (table 27). However, what data we do have are quite revealing and allow us to develop some inferences. The pertinent data indicate that the differences in church attendance and religious self-description

TABLE 26

CHURCH ATTENDANCE

Church Attendance	Political Officers		Aspiring		Qualifying (1961)	U.S. Pop. (1965)
	Military	FSO	Military	FSO		
Regularly	45%	17%	28%	28%	39%	54%
Often	22	6	35	19	26	19
Seldom	33	77	37	53	35	27
Effective total	100%	100%	100%	100%	100%	100%
Statistics	$\chi^2(2)=18.14$ $P=.01$		$\chi^2(2)=10.99$ $P=.01$			

NOTE: The frequency of church attendance of the "U.S. Population (1965)" is taken from a survey by Louis Harris reported in the *Washington Post*, August 16, 1965, p. A2. In that survey, people were asked: "How often do you go to church?" For purposes of comparison, responses of "more than once a week" and "once a week" were translated as "Regularly"; "twice a month" and "once a month" as "Often"; and "less often" and "never" as "Seldom." The four-wave NORC panel study (the first wave was administered in 1961, the last in 1964) that furnished the data for the "Aspiring" and "Qualifying" populations utilized the following question: "How frequently do you attend religious services?" Six coding categories were used. The first "weekly, almost without exception" was translated as "Regularly." The second, "several times a month," and third, "once a month" were translated as "Often." The "Seldom" designation was reserved for the three remaining entries, "two or three times a year," "once a year," and "never."
The first x^2 determination applied only to political officers; the second to the "Aspiring Population (1965)."

(and religiosity) we find occurring between political-military officers and FSOs are clearly foreshadowed by the existence of similar disparities among the relevant aspirants. We see that military career aspirants attend church more frequently, and more often say they are "very" or "somewhat" religious than do FSO aspirants. This feature lends important support to the first (i.e., prerecruitment) argument, whereas it undermines the contention that organizational socialization is the primary reason for the emergence of interorganization dissimilarities.

The validity of the claim that socialization is the primary determinant is further eroded if we return to table 25 and note that newtimers and oldtimers within both the political-military

TABLE 27
Religious Self-Description

Religious Self-Description	Political Officers		Aspiring (1964)		Qualifying (1961)	U.S. Pop. (1965)
	Military	FSO	Military	FSO		
Very religious	39%	19%	9%	7%	20%	27%
Somewhat religious	46	42	58	36	52	63
Not religious	16	39	33	58	28	8
Effective total	100%	100%	100%	100%	100%	100%
Statistics	$\chi^2(2)=7.43$ $P=.05$ Gamma$=.450$ $P=.01$		$\chi^2(2)=20.55$ $P=.01$			

Note: The "U. S. Population (1965)" data on Religious Self-description were adapted from a survey by Louis Harris, *Washington Post*, August 16, 1965, p. A2. In the survey, people were asked, "Do you feel you are a deeply religious person, only somewhat religious, or hardly religious at all?" The NORC question read as follows: "Please rate yourself on the following dimensions as you really think you are." The five possible responses are very religious, fairly religious, neither, fairly nonreligious, and very nonreligious. The last three answers were translated as "not religious" for purposes of comparison.

and FSO groups do not differ regarding religiosity. The fact that length of service is not related to religiosity implies that increasing exposure to the particular environments found within the military establishment and Foreign Service does not influence officers to change the extent of their religious involvement.[11] On the other hand, our failure to find a difference in religiosity between newtimers and oldtimers is consistent with the prerecruitment argument that the main reason for the existence of disparities in religiosity between military officers and FSOs is the contrasting

---

11. This finding should not be interpreted as decisive. Recall that the personnel whom we have called newtimers have been officers for some time. They are not recruits or even very low-level officers. Hence, our analysis does not fully account for the possibility that relatively "instantaneous socialization" may occur at the recruit or immediately higher authority level. This is one contingency that needs to be mentioned. Another relates to the makeup of our samples; all of our respondents are political-policy officers. Therefore, we do not actually know whether the finding reported above is peculiar to this role-defined subgroup or also is representative of the entire organization's membership.

composition of their respective aspiring populations regarding this factor. Thus, the two pieces of evidence that we do have suggest that the prerecruitment contention probably provides a more accurate interpretation of what actually occurs than does the socialization explanation.

One final question may be raised: Are military officers and FSOs more religious or less religious than the American population? We see from the relevant data contained in tables 26 and 27 that the answer is clear with respect to the Foreign Service. First, FSO aspirants are substantially less religious (i.e., less often attend church and more frequently say they are not religious) than their fellow college students, the qualifying population. Secondly, political-FSOs are shown to be less religious than the United States population in 1965. Furthermore, the latter difference is underlined if we compare our political-FSO respondents, not with the entire nation, but only with those citizens who are of similar age, occupation, education, and religious denomination. A recent Gallup survey asked the following question on seven widely scattered occasions during the year 1967: "Did you, yourself, happen to attend church in the last seven days?" Gallup reports that 46% of those between the ages of 30 and 49, 47% of those who are "professionals and businessmen," 48% of those who have completed college, and 37% of those who identify themselves as being Episcopal, said "yes" to the question (i.e., attend church regularly).[12] By way of contrast, only 17% of the political-FSOs say they attend church regularly.

The relative religiosity of the political-military, on the other hand, is not so clear. The ambiguity here is largely due to the fact that military career aspirants evidently are less religious than their fellow college students, although not to the same degree as

12. *Gallup Opinion Index* (Report No. 31, January, 1968), p. 18. For the year 1965, Gallup reports a lower "church attendance" frequency on the part of the American public than does Louis Harris. The relevant *Gallup Opinion Index* (Report No. 7, December, 1965), p. 12, states that only 44% of the national population answered "yes" to a question similar to the one reproduced in the text, whereas Harris, as indicated in table 26, reports that 54% of his respondents say they attend church regularly.

FSO aspirants. Aside from this rather inexplicable finding, the information available suggests that political-military officers are about as religious as the American public. For example, 45% of the military respondents in our sample report they attend church regularly, whereas 44%, according to Gallup, and 54%, according to Louis Harris, of the United States population say they do. Moreover, the 45% figure cited for the political-military approximates the corresponding percentages reported earlier for the national subpopulations consisting of those persons between the ages of 30 and 49, professionals and businessmen, the college educated, and Episcopalians.[13] In general, then, the various religious involvement patterns displayed by political-military officers do not seem to deviate significantly from what would be anticipated after an inspection of the composition of comparable subgroups of the national population.

Before concluding, let us briefly summarize the findings contained in the second part of this chapter. The question around which our discussion was organized was whether political-military officers are more religious than their counterparts in the Foreign Service. Two related interview items, church attendance and religious self-description, were designed to provide information concerning each respondent's relative religiosity. Subsequent analysis indicated that the religiosity scores of our military respondents were significantly higher than those earned by the political-FSOs. The additional data we were able to gather suggested that this intergovernmental difference more likely than not is the reflection of a disparity manifested even prior to the initial step of recruitment. More specifically, the key element appears to be the unusual "religious" composition of the FSO aspiring population; FSO aspirants were revealed to be significantly less religious than mili-

13. Interpretation is difficult with respect to comparing the "religious self-description" responses of political-military officers and the United States population. The former group exhibits a distribution that is considerably broader than the latter, and, thus, a greater proportion of its membership is contained within each end category of the dimension. Hence, about the only conclusion that can be stated at this time is that the religious self-description data fail to indicate the existence of any consistent deviation concerning the representativeness of the political-military response distribution.

tary aspirants and college students generally. This dissimilarity is perpetuated because the extent of an individual's religiosity apparently is not a feature pertinent to recruitment or promotion, or noticeably altered by the settings found within the two organizations.

The fact that the emergence of religious differences between political-military officers and political-FSOs primarily is due to the prerecruitment factor of self-selection assumes some importance when an attempt is made to explain why students from essentially similar social backgrounds prefer a career in one or the other governmental organization. The reader will recall that the previous chapter closed with the positing of just such a question. Now, we can begin to suggest an answer. Expressing a wish to develop a career in the Foreign Service rather than the military establishment is associated with the extent of an individual's involvement with religion, a personal feature quite unrelated to such social background variables as geographical origins and size of hometown. Assuming an already established interest in seeking a nondomestic, nonelective public service position, a relatively irreligious college student would be more likely than one who is more religious to think of pursuing a career in the Foreign Service rather than the armed services, and vice versa. This is not to say that no other factors are relevant to such a decision. What is being argued is that our analysis has isolated a trait that, other things being equal (i.e., the effects of other factors are random), encourages a student to be more favorably disposed to one governmental organization than the other.

Our concern, of course, is with the consequences that result from the association of religiosity with career choice, at least as it relates to choosing between the Foreign Service or the military. However, the question of why such a relationship should exist is an interesting one. The answer presumably lies with the various perceptions students have of these organizations. For example, an interested investigator would want to know why FSO aspirants are so deviant with respect to religiosity. Harr has shown that half of all FSOs majored in political science (including international politics) or history as undergraduates.[14] Perhaps students who specialize in these subjects are less religious than other students. But this begs the question for we would then have to ask what it is about these particular subjects that is attractive to the relatively irreligious. Or perhaps a career in the Foreign Service frequently is viewed as a "vocation" where one can engage in patriotic and unselfish public service, that is, secular missionary work for idealistically motivated doubters and nonbelievers. These thoughts obviously are speculative in nature, but they do suggest two possible explanations for the sharp deviancy we have observed.

Finally, we may comment that religiosity is the only variable thus far introduced that has been able to distinguish our respondents according to organizational affiliation. In every previous case, the two groups of political-policy officers have exhibited similar distributions. Looking ahead, the ability displayed by the religiosity attribute will become quite important if our often-stated expectation that political-military officers and political-FSOs differ in their political beliefs materializes. In other words, for the first time we are provided with a variable that promises to be useful for resolving the explanation problem we anticipate will develop. But, of course, we hope and, moreover, expect to discover other attribute variables that can play such a role. With this thought in mind, our discussion turns to a consideration of the political orientations of political-policy officers.

14. Harr, *Anatomy of the Foreign Service*, p. 14.

CHAPTER 5

Political Orientation

In this chapter, attention is focused upon the political orientations of political-policy officers within the Departments of State and Defense. The word *orientation* is employed because it conveys more accurately than alternative terms what we intend to investigate. Our purpose is to compare respondents according to what each describes as his characteristic posture with respect to public political issues. Perhaps the two most widely used techniques for arranging individuals as to political orientation are the well-known and much abused liberal-conservative and political party identification (in the United States, Democratic-Republican) continua. The presumption is that knowing where a person locates himself regarding one or both of these dimensions considerably aids the researcher in predicting and understanding that individual's political beliefs and behavior. Most of the important work concerned with this subject has been in the area of electoral behavior.[1] However, more recently some evidence has been gathered that indicates that linkages of this form are also operative with respect to the formation of specifically foreign policy beliefs.[2] This insight

1. See Angus Campbell et al., *The American Voter*.
2. For example, see Milton J. Rosenberg, "Images in Relation to the Policy Process: American Public Opinion on Cold-War Issues," in *International Behavior: A Social-Psychological Analysis*, ed. Herbert C. Kelman, pp. 278–334; Snell Putney and Russell Middleton, "Some Factors Associated with Student Acceptance or Rejection of War," *American Sociological Review* 27(1962):655–67; and Bernard Fensterwald, Jr., "American 'Isolationism' and Expansionism," in *Human Behavior and International Relations*, ed. J. David Singer, pp. 243–58.

Political Orientation

has encouraged us to explicitly include political orientation variables in our analysis.

Before actually beginning our analysis, let us briefly look more closely at these two continua. There is no doubt that party and ideological identification are conceptually and operationally distinct dimensions. At the same time it is equally clear that, among more knowledgeable Americans, the two are quite interrelated empirically. We think it is fair to say that most politically aware Americans perceive the national Democratic party to be more liberal in political matters than the Republican party.[3] Put somewhat differently, the pair-wise identification of Democrats and liberals, and Republicans and conservatives, appears eminently more reasonable than the contrary pairing. Consequently, it generally is expected that individuals who describe themselves as politically conservative will more often identify themselves also as a Republican than as a Democrat. In fact, this turns out to be very much the case with political-military officers and FSOs. Among our respondents, party identification (i.e., Republican, Independent or Democrat) and ideological identification (i.e., conservative, independent, or liberal) are highly interrelated.[4] Moreover, the relationship between the two is so pronounced that it makes a great deal of sense to construct a political orientation index that parsimoniously incorporates these two bits of information about each respondent. This was done, and, as one might expect, the resulting index scores are very strongly related to both party and ideological identification variable scores.[5]

3. See Campbell et al., *The American Voter*, pp. 202–3.
4. $\chi^2(4) = 17.344/P = .01$; and Gamma $= .505/P = .01$. For the questions used in this chapter, see section IIB of the interview schedule in the appendix.
5. The coding matrix employed to yield a political orientation index score for each respondent was the following one:

Party	Ideology			
	Con	Ind	Lib	NA
Rep	1	2	3	2
Ind	2	3	4	3
Dem	3	4	5	4
NA	2	3	4	NA

Two respondents of the 95 who were interviewed said they could not de-

But whether political orientation, or either of its components, is considered, the question of the meaningfulness (i.e., validity, if you like) of such self-described, noncontent designations remains. It should be emphasized that political orientation as the concept is employed here is *not* either logically deduced or empirically drawn from responses to attitudinal-type questions. Quite the contrary, the particular designation a respondent receives is based entirely upon his own assessment as to where he stands relative to others. Consequently, it is quite conceivable that an individual's *self-described* designation may not be appropriate to the actual viewpoints he holds—not appropriate, at least, to the independent, trained observer. On the other hand, because our respondents are politically knowledgeable to an unusual degree, it is very probable that the statements of political orientation expressed by them are quite meaningful.

But, of course, this mainly is conjecture, and one hopes, therefore, to be able to go beyond it to somewhat firmer ground. The following approach provides one method for dealing with the validity problem. Suppose the reader is presented with the following question: Which major political themes in the United States most characteristically divide our population? If such themes, and the various positions that are taken concerning them, can be identified, then we have a means whereby we can determine whether these self-described designations make any sense. Our feeling is that at least two major themes run through much of the literature. They are the relationships of national government to the private economic sector and to the individual citizen. A similar formulation is suggested by Lipset, who, when encountering in his examination of *Political Man* the liberal-conservative ideological dimension, persuasively argues that the term *liberal* in fact contains at least two analytically discriminable components. For example, in his

scribe themselves ideologically; 5 respondents said they could not claim either a partisan or independent "party identification" designation. The relationship between political orientation (dichotomized between 1+2+3 and 4+5) and party identification is: $\chi^2(2) = 41.765/P = .01$; and Gamma $= .942/P = .01$. Between the former and ideological identification, the relationship is: $\chi^2(2) = 62.055/P = .01$; and Gamma $= .979/P = .01$.

discussion of democracy and the lower classes, he states that "the poorer strata everywhere are more liberal or leftist on economic issues; they favor more welfare state measures, higher wages, graduated income taxes, support of trade unions, and so forth. But when liberalism is defined in non-economic terms—as support of civil liberties, internationalism, etc.—the correlation is reversed."[6] In the same vein, Campbell and his coauthors state that

> perhaps no abstraction of this genre has been used more frequently in the past century for political analysis than the concept of a liberal-conservative continuum—the "right" and "left" of a political spectrum. The generality of this dimension makes it a powerful summary tool. Above the flux of specific domestic issues lie a number of broad controversies regarding the appropriate posture of the national government toward other sectors of the social order. . . . Advocacy of increased government activity in matters of social welfare and increased government control in economic production have been the more characteristic "liberal" positions in the recent era, and the positions most vigorously contested by conservative leadership.[7]

Turning first to the economic-oriented theme, it appears that the most efficient way to sum up the difference in posture alluded to above is to say simply that so-called economic conservatives in general favor minimal government intervention and regulation whereas liberals accept increasing government economic involvement as a necessary and inevitable reflection of the changing nature and extent of societal demands. With this broad difference in mind, the political-policy officers were asked to respond to the following question: "Some critics say that the government is too involved in domestic economic affairs. On the other hand, others argue for a more active role for government. How do you feel on

6. Seymour Martin Lipset, *Political Man*, p. 92. Internationalism and other noneconomic foreign policy issues will be discussed in chapter 7.
7. Campbell et al., *The American Voter*, pp. 193, 202. Another example is provided by Schoenberger, who, after examining the verbal responses of New York State Conservative party members in the Rochester area to his interview schedule concludes "that the major political interest of conservatives is in the role, direction and/or activities of the federal government in domestic economic affairs" (Robert A. Schoenberger, "Conservatism, Personality, and Political Extremism," *American Political Science Review* 62[1968]:874).

this issue?" Respondents were coded as to whether they thought government was too involved currently and *less* intervention was desirable, or the balance existing today is *about right*, or *more* government involvement is necessary and/or desirable. Unfortunately, no single question presents itself that as succinctly covers the noneconomic theme as the latter does the economic one. The question chosen thus is less than satisfactory for it only captures one aspect of the complex civil liberties theme: "Do you think American Communists should be allowed to run for and hold public political office?" Respondents here were coded as to whether they thought Communists *should* or *should not* be allowed to participate.

Not surprisingly, the responses of our politically knowledgeable respondents to the latter two questions are very much in keeping with the labels they applied to themselves.[8] More specifically, self-described Democrats and Liberals (i.e., DemLibs) significantly more often than self-described Republicans and Conservatives (i.e., RepCons) say they would permit Communists to participate in the political life of our country and would favor increased government involvement or, at least, are less disturbed by the current level of government intervention into the economy. This finding gives us confidence that some thought and meaning underlies the self-description data which have been gathered.

Now we can turn to the major task of this chapter: ascertaining whether or not political-military officers and FSOs differ with respect to political orientation. From the data presented in table 28, we see that the latter significantly more often than the former describe themselves as leaning toward the DemLib end of the political orientation dimension. The two groups manifest clearly divergent response patterns. More specifically, the number of FSOs found in each category progressively increases as one moves away from the RepCon end, so much so that one extreme category

---

8. The relationship between political orientation and government involvement is: $\chi^2(2) = 11.297/P = .01$; and Gamma $= .517/P = .01$. The relationship between political orientation and civil liberties is: $\chi^2(1) = 5.809/P = .05$; and Gamma $= .474/P = .05$.

TABLE 28
POLITICAL ORIENTATION

ORIENTATION		MILITARY		FSO		TOTAL	
		%	N	%	N	%	N
RepCon	1	7	4	0	0	4	4
	2	21	12	8	3	16	15
	3	45	26	14	5	33	31
Subtotal		72	42	22	8	53	50
DemLib	4	17	10	27	10	21	20
	5	10	6	51	19	26	25
Subtotal		28	16	78	29	47	45
Total		100	58	100	37	100	95
Statistics		$\chi^2(1)=23.376/P=.01$ $Gamma=.810/P=.01$					

is empty and the other contains slightly over one-half of the entire group. The military pattern, on the other hand, resembles an abbreviated "normal" distribution with the middle (and modal) category accounting for nearly one-half of the group and the least populous cells being the extreme ones.

In one sense, the above finding is somewhat surprising. It is not the existence of a substantial divergency, or the direction it takes, that is unexpected but rather the form of the two configurations being compared. In other words, the military configuration "ought" to have been less balanced and more skewed so as to favor the RepCon side. This expectation is based on the argument stated by Janowitz in the only extensive empirical treatment of this subject currently found in the literature. The item he uses in order to identify the political orientation of military officers is the following one: "In domestic politics, do you regard yourself as: conservative, a little on the conservative side, a little on the liberal side, liberal?" Note that, first, there is an explicit restriction to "domestic politics"; second, there is no provision for a nonliberal, nonconservative—i.e., independent—alternative; and third, Janowitz's data when reported will refer to the entire military establishment, not just the subset of political-policy officers. His findings are summarized in the following statement:

> Only a handful of officers (5 percent) from the sample of 576 Army, Navy and Air Force officers on staff duty in the Pentagon in 1954 identified themselves as liberals on an anonymous questionnaire. . . . The extent of conservative perspectives is documented by the full pattern of responses: 21.6 percent identify themselves as conservative, 45.3 percent as a little on the conservative side, and 23.1 percent as a little on the liberal side [with about 5 percent not ascertained].
>
> To measure political attachment to the term "conservative" leaves open the question of what specific content a person attributes to his political commitments. But precisely because these data refer to general identification, they reflect basic orientations. . . .
>
> For the sample as a whole, conservative attitudes increased with higher position in the military hierarchy.[9]

Having knowledge of the above, we were led to expect that the difference in political orientation that was likely to occur would stem from comparing a moderately DemLib oriented FSO group with a predominantly RepCon military contingent. The divergency that developed was foreseen, only its nature was unanticipated. Attempting to investigate why our finding emerged as it did leads naturally into a consideration of the antecedents that give rise to an individual identifying with a particular political orientation and the process leading to the selection of political-military and FSO careers.

As with religiosity, one's first impulse probably is to try to explain the variation regarding political orientation by referring to one or several social background variables. For example, the argument might be made that individuals from the northeastern United States typically are more DemLib than individuals raised elsewhere and that the Foreign Service contains proportionately more of these persons than does the Armed Forces. Consequently, relatively more of the former's membership will describe themselves as DemLib than is true in the case of the latter organization. But this gambit does not lead anywhere because it rests upon two premises that easily are shown to be false. First, we already have established in chapters 3 and 4 that the two samples resemble each

---

9. Janowitz, *The Professional Soldier*, pp. 236–39.

other with respect to these prominent social attributes. Second, we see in table 29 that none of the social background variables are related to political orientation. We therefore are left in very much

TABLE 29

Relationship of Political Orientation
and Variables Pertaining to Social
Origins and Religiosity

	Statistics	
	$\chi^2=$	Gamma=
Orientation and:		
Place of birth	2.870	
Geographical background	.620	
Size of hometown	1.713	.232
Status of father's occupation	.630	.172
Educational level	1.505	.252
Religious affiliation	.289	−.143
Denominational status	.091	.038
The Military only		
Old versus newtimers	.026	.048
Service affiliation	.953	
Academy versus nonacademy	.223	.146
Foreign Service only		
New versus oldtimers	2.285	.574
Non-Ivy versus Ivy League	2.076	−.581
Religiosity	3.962†	.399*

* P = .10; † P = .05; all others: P = NS.

the same position as in the case of religiosity; that is, the observed difference between political-military officers and political-FSOs with respect to political orientation is not at all explained by referring to various prominent social background attributes.

Since the investigation of political orientation thus presented a similar situation to that encountered regarding religiosity, an attempt was made to employ the research strategy utilized earlier. The relevant data that we were able to collect pertains to ideological identification and party preference, the two components of political orientation, and is presented respectively in tables 30 and 31. As in previous situations, serious deficiencies regarding the availability of data limit analysis.

Perhaps the only firm inference that can be drawn concerns the

TABLE 30

POLITICAL IDEOLOGY IDENTIFICATION

Ideology	Total Foreign Service (1)	Political Officers		Military Leaders (4)	Aspiring		Qualifying (7)	U.S. Pop. 1964 (8)
		Military (2)	FSO (3)		Military (5)	FSO (6)		
Conservative	18%	25%	3%	70%	36%	20%	34%	39%
Independent	..	44	22	..	12	16	18	38
Liberal	82	32	76	30	52	64	48	23
Total	100%	100%	100%	100%	100%	100%	100%	100%
ID:2+5=31.5		ID:3+6=17.5		ID:5+7= 6.0			ID:6+8=41.0	
ID:2+7=32.5		ID:3+7=31.5		ID:5+8=29.0			ID:7+8=25.0	
ID:2+8=14.5		ID:3+8=52.5		ID:6+7=16.0				

NOTE: The data for the "Total Foreign Service (1966)" are reported by Harr, *The Professional Diplomat*, p. 183. The "Military Leaders" data are taken from Janowitz, *The Professional Soldier*, table 28, p. 237. Note that Harr and Janowitz did not employ a middle "Independent" category. The "U.S. Population" data are taken from a survey by Louis Harris report in the *New York Post*, June 26, 1967, p. 9.

TABLE 31
POLITICAL PARTY IDENTIFICATION

Party	Political Officers		Aspiring			U.S. Population (1964)	
	Military (1)	FSO (2)	Military (3)	FSO (4)	Qualifying (5)	College Males (6)	Total (7)
Republican	24%	5%	34%	25%	39%	38%	24%
Independent	55	41	29	30	24	25	23
Democrat	21	54	37	45	37	38	51
Total	100%	100%	100%	100%	100%	100%	100%
ID:1+3=26.0		ID:2+4=20.0		ID:3+5= 5.0		ID:4+6=12.5	
ID:1+5=31.0		ID:2+5=34.0		ID:3+6= 4.5		ID:4+7= 7.0	
ID:1+6=30.5		ID:2+6=32.5		ID:3+7=10.0		ID:5+6= 1.5	
ID:1+7=31.0		ID:2+7=20.0		ID:4+5=14.0		ID:5+7=15.0	
						ID:6+7=14.5	

NOTE: The "U.S. Population (1964)" data and tabulations were made available by the Inter-University Consortium for Political Research. The data were originally collected by the University of Michigan Survey Research Center. Neither the Survey Research Center nor the Consortium bears any responsibility for the analysis or interpretations presented here.

relative potency of the prerecruitment stage for explaining the political orientation composition of the political-FSO sample. One observes, first, that political FSOs differ greatly from the U.S. population in the pattern of their ideological identifications (ID:3 + 8 = 52.5). The reader will note also that the qualifying population is considerably more liberal than is the nation (ID:7 + 8 = 25.0), and FSO aspirants somewhat more liberal than college students in general (ID:6 + 7 = 16.0). Juxtaposing the various distributions identified above reveals that the substantial ideological identification unrepresentativeness of political-FSOs (i.e., relative to the entire nation) and, by observation, of the Foreign Service in general is largely accounted for if the prerecruitment element is explicitly taken into consideration (ID:3 + 6 = 17.5 versus ID:3 + 8 = 52.5). In other words, the fact that Foreign Service candidates are college educated *and* aspire to such a career apparently explains a good deal as to why political-FSOs (and the total Foreign Service) appear to be overwhelmingly liberal in ideological identification. This inference is indirectly supported by the finding that political-FSO newtimers and oldtimers do not significantly differ with respect to ideological identification ($x^2[1] = 1.102/P = NS$; Gamma $= .333/P = NS$), party preference ($X^2[2] = 240/P = NS$: Gamma $= .140/P = NS$), or political orientation (see table 29). In addition, one can see in table 31 that FSO aspirants tend to be somewhat less Republican than college students in general (ID:4 + 5 = 14.0), a feature that, in direction at least, is consistent with the predilections of political-FSOs. Finally, we may add that the political socialization and related literature pertaining to political orientation lends strong support to the notion that party preferences and ideological identifications are developed in the teens and exhibit a great deal of stability thereafter.[10] Stability rather than change, then, seems to be rule here. This conclusion is reinforced by the experience of

---

10. For example, see Herbert Hyman, *Political Socialization*; Richard E. Dawson, "Political Socialization," in *Political Science Annual: An International Review*. Vol. 1, ed. James A. Robinson, pp. 27 ff.; and Campbell et al., *The American Voter*.

our respondents. Twenty-four of the 36 FSOs (or 67%) who stated a party preference said they always had identified with the party they now preferred. Of the twelve who had changed, about one-half said the switch had occurred previous to their entering the Foreign Service. In other words, approximately 30 of 36 FSOs (or 83%) had the same party preference when they entered the Foreign Service as they now have. Incidentally, of the twelve FSOs who did alter their party preference, all but one changed in the direction of the Democratic party. The existence of such stability is important because it undermines the counterargument which could be made that change as a result of socialization actually is occurring, but its effect is being offset in our analysis by the contrary influence of another factor, for example, the impact of advancing age. The action of such a contrary influence obviously would make it difficult to detect the effects of postrecruitment experiences when the method used here of comparing newtimers and oldtimers is applied. In sum, while one cannot definitely affirm the prerecruitment inference, the information that is available lends support to this rather than alternative explanations. Nevertheless, the fact that some portion of the observed difference still is not accounted for (e.g., note that political FSOs are somewhat more liberal and Democratic in their identifications than FSO aspirants) suggests that recruitment bias and/or postrecruitment practices and experiences may have some minor effects.

A similar, but less firm, inference concerning the relative potency of prerecruitment factors seems feasible also with respect to political-military officers. Like political-FSOs, political-military newtimers and oldtimers do not significantly differ with respect to political orientation (see table 29), ideological identification ($x^2[2] = 3.555/P = NS$; Gamma $= .220/P = NS$), or party preference ($x^2[2] = 1.409/P = NS$; Gamma $= .266/P = NS$). Moreover, political-military officers demonstrated an even greater tendency toward stability in party identification. Forty-six of 56 (or 83%) never have changed their preference. However, of those who did change, nearly all did so after joining the military, with six switching toward a Democratic association and five becoming

Republicans.[11] At this point, the reader may recall the statement made by Janowitz reproduced earlier in this chapter that "conservative attitudes increased with higher position in the military hierarchy." This conclusion at first glance seems to support the organizational socialization position and contradict our inference. But first glances can be deceiving. Several other interpretations of the same data are equally reasonable. For example, one may argue that the greater conservatism of senior- relative to middle-grade military officers is a reflection of the difference in age between the members of the two levels (i.e., with advancing age, individuals tend to become more conservative) and/or is one manifestation of a long-term trend toward liberalism (i.e., in the last century, each generation has been more liberal than the one that preceded it) and/or is a result of the fact that an increasing number of military officers are college graduates (i.e., the changing nature of warfare requires the armed forces to increasingly seek out college graduates, a group that is more liberal than those who did not continue their education beyond high school). Any one of these factors can be responsible for the data structure described by Janowitz, even where further exposure to the organization has no effect with respect to changing political orientations. Hence, we think it fair to say that Janowitz's data, as it stands, neither supports nor is contrary to the inference developed above.

One interesting and surprising finding that emerges from an inspection of table 30 is that military career aspirants are no more conservative than college students generally. The choosing of a military career has been commonly associated with the holding of politically conservative tendencies. For example, recall Huntington's persuasive linking of military doctrine and conservative realism in his study *The Soldier and the State*.[12] The validity of this association is reinforced through data reported by Janowitz (partially reproduced in table 30 as column 4) that indicate the

---

11. Those political-FSOs and political-military officers who had shifted their party identification were asked to recall the reasons that underlay their decision to change. The reasons that emerged were diverse in nature, with no single one enjoying any observable saliency.

12. Pp. 93–94.

Political Orientation

willingness of military officers "to identify themselves as conservatives."[13] We do not have an explanation for the above finding other than to suggest that one consequence of the "new technology" and so-called cold war, particularly their impact upon the character and prestige of the military profession, may have been to make the choosing of a military career attractive to individuals who do not consider themselves to be conservative.

Perhaps the most salient feature contained in tables 30 and 31 is the predilection political-military officers show for the independent alternative. Slightly less than one-half of the respondents surveyed did not wish to identify themselves as either liberal or conservative; more than one-half similarly answered the "party identification" question. This pattern quite obviously suggests the continuing existence within the military establishment of a genuine commitment to nonpartisanship. The maintenance of the nonpartisan tradition may be encouraged by the fact that no influence pattern exists that is sufficiently consistent and strong to pull (or push) military officers in one or the other direction. Certainly the pro–Defense Department voting record of congressional Democrats (relative to their Republican colleagues) over the last four decades[14] ought to have made a deep impression. Yet, during this same period, the Democratic party was and continues to be more identified with liberal political positions than the Republican. This single contradiction should make it difficult for military officers to say, even if they wanted to, whether in general they are Democrats or Republicans. One implication that may possibly be drawn from the above is that a substantial relaxation of the nonpartisan tradition, if it were to occur, would not dramatically alter the balance between self-described Democrats and Republicans within the military establishment. The past record and ideological associations of the two major parties should prevent the development of an overwhelming trend toward one or the other, that is, as long as both continue to behave in a manner consistent with

---

13. *The Professional Soldier*, pp. 236–41. His findings are summarized in an earlier part of this chapter.
14. Huntington, *The Common Defense*, pp. 251–67.

recent historical experience. But, because of the slight liberal leanings of political-military officers, this prediction may not be as appropriate for that group as for the entire military. Among such officers, there would probably be less resistance toward Democratic party identifications than would obtain among the more conservative nonpolitical-policy military officers. Thus, we would anticipate a relatively growing Democratic representation among political-military officers if the force of nonpartisanship should diminish.

A final point needs to be made before this chapter is concluded. It concerns the analogy between political orientation and religiosity. If the reader will return to table 29, he will observe that these two attributes are significantly related. This is not entirely surprising since it already has been revealed that political-military and FSOs differ with respect to both variables. Another common feature pertains to the similarity of the analyses undertaken in this and the second part of the previous chapter. Both times the variables of interest represented the combination of two highly related items. In each case, they easily were able to distinguish respondents on the basis of their organizational affiliation, a feat no other variable so far has accomplished. Both religiosity and political orientation were found not to be associated with a number of social background features. Moreover, what evidence we have been able to collect suggests that the most persuasive interpretation for the divergent responses exhibited by political-military officers and FSOs regarding political orientation and religiosity directs attention to the characteristics of those individuals who initially present themselves as candidates for recruitment to each organization rather than the possible effects of such factors as the existence of selective recruitment procedures maintained by the institutions or organizational socialization consequent to entrance. This is not to say that the latter is completely unimportant. On the contrary, we are not excluding the possibility that such factors may have some, though *relatively minor*, influence. Second, and equally important, although recruitment practices and increasing exposure to the "value and attitudinal environment" existing

Political Orientation

within the institutions may not result in a *change* in religiosity or political orientation, they may serve to *perpetuate* already existing inclinations. Hence, they assuredly should not be dismissed as irrelevant, especially since the data necessary for a thorough examination of all such issues are presently not available and probably will continue to be lacking in the future (e.g., access problems are difficult to overcome).

The support given to the prerecruitment explanation in this chapter adds credence to our explanation of why individuals coming from essentially similar social backgrounds end up in different organizations. We can now amend our previously stated conclusion to read as follows: expressing a wish to develop a career in the Foreign Service rather than military establishment is associated with the extent of an individual's involvement with religion *and* his political orientation, personal features quite unrelated to such social background variables as geographical origins and size of hometown.

We certainly do not believe that these two attributes exhaust the list of those variables related to career choice or the formation of political beliefs. It is quite possible that, in addition to these characteristics, some aspect of the individual's psychological makeup, perhaps the manner in which he relates to, and evaluates, people and information, also may be relevant. It is to such attributes that attention is now turned.

CHAPTER 6
Cognitive Style

Military officers as distinguished from their civilian counterparts frequently are believed to possess a set of attributes and/or attitudes that are usually collectively depicted by the term *military mind*. In spite of both the ambiguity surrounding this label, and the lack of evidence regarding its validity, the concept of the military mind continues to enjoy some currency in the literature and mass media. But what is meant by the term *a military mind*? Several scholars have addressed themselves to this question. For example, in their study of the role of the military in foreign policy, Sapin and Snyder, after citing several typical interpretations, state:

> The most serious criticisms of the military mind appear to be of alleged tendencies toward (a) rigidity in thought and problem analysis—the rejection of new ideas and reliance on tradition rather than lessons learned from recent experience; (b) inadequate weighing of nonmilitary factors in military problems, and inability to understand complex politico-military relationships; (c) an authoritarian approach to most social issues and situations, accompanied by disrespect for and disregard of civilian authority; (d) insulation from nonmilitary knowledge and anything beyond what is narrowly defined as militarily relevant; and (e) judgment of policy goals and techniques primarily in terms of military force and military strategy.[1]

In a similar vein, Huntington comments:

> The military mind may be approached from three viewpoints: (1) its ability or quality; (2) its attributes or characteristics; and (3) its attitudes or substance. . . .

1. Sapin and Snyder, *Role of the Military in American Foreign Policy*, p. 20.

Cognitive Style

The second approach holds that the uniqueness of the military mind lies in certain mental attributes or qualities which constitute a military personality. Military and civilian writers generally seem to agree that the military mind is disciplined, rigid, logical, scientific; it is not flexible, tolerant, intuitive, emotional.[2]

From the above statements, it would appear that claims with respect to the existence of a military mind proceed from assumptions concerning at least two conceptually and operationally distinct but supposedly related aspects: one involving the peculiar character of the cognitive style of military officers, the other involving their attitudinal positions. The issue of concern in the latter case is with the content or substance of expressed beliefs and opinions and with whether the military as an organizationally identifiable group can be relatively cleanly separated attitudinally from similar but nonmilitary social groups—that their positions on politically relevant matters are in nature (i.e., direction and degree) unique and consequently set them apart from others. The chapter following the present one will be devoted to an inquiry into this aspect of the military mind proposition.

The former aspect concerns those alleged tendencies of the military mind that Sapin and Snyder have called "rigidity in thought and problem analysis" and "an authoritarian approach," and also the "attributes or characteristics" viewpoint cited by Huntington. What seems to be at issue here is the relative ability (or rather inability) of military officers to satisfactorily process novel information. In other words, the indictment is directed not at *what* (i.e., ideological content) military officers believe, but *how* (i.e., char-

---

2. Huntington, *The Soldier and the State*, pp. 59–60. In yet another analysis, Lyons says that "if the 'military mind' is a type, it is not typical; it is a model produced by a particular set of career demands, but not exemplified by anyone who has lived under the demands. . . . Nevertheless, there is a military mind and all military men, to one degree or another, possess it. It is a mind that is used to order and predictability, that insists on decisions being made, that cannot tolerate procrastination, that is comfortable in the manageable world of a military post and often unconsciously makes over any other setting—the home, the office, even the presidency of the United States—with the same characteristics of punctuality, rank and simplicity" ("The Military Mind," p. 19).

acter trait) they believe.[3] The words that seem especially relevant within this context are ones such as *rigid, intolerant, disciplined, dogmatic*. In each case, the feeling conveyed is that of an unusual resistance to change of a person's beliefs (i.e., the maintenance of "will") when confronted with nonreinforcing and/or contrary information. Obviously, such structural characteristics may typically be associated with the holding of certain political beliefs. But, of course, this is an empirical question and precisely the one that will be investigated in chapter 8.

Put another way, all of us at one time or another have encountered an individual whom, after an exchange of viewpoints, we thought to be rigid, dogmatic, and so on. The question is raised, What was it about him that encouraged this perception? It might have been the particular positions taken by him during the discussion. On the other hand, it was quite possibly the manner in which he treated opposing arguments. He was defensive, unyielding even where evidence was presented which clearly demonstrated the incorrectness of his position, unwilling or unable to consider the merit of a point of view expressed by a person known to be of a different persuasion, and capable of taking a "don't confuse me with the facts" approach. This posture is thought unreasonable precisely because the person's belief system, or some part of it, implicitly has been withdrawn from the process of "becoming." Beliefs, or the belief system itself, have hardened to such an extent that, relative to other examples, they are locked at a certain stage of development; locked with respect to the influence of what usually is regarded as legitimate input. Hence, the effective reception and utilization of information is impaired. When an individual's cognitions characteristically are of such a nature, he is referred to, in conventional terms, as intolerant, rigid, and closed-minded,

---

3. "To study the organization of belief systems, we find it necessary to concern ourselves with the *structure* rather than the *content* of beliefs . . . it is not so much *what* you believe that counts, but *how* you believe" (Milton Rokeach, *The Open and Closed Mind: Investigations into the Nature of Belief Systems and Personality Systems*, p. 6). As will become increasingly apparent, the approach and methods employed in the research reported in this chapter lean very heavily upon the work of Rokeach and his associates.

rather than tolerant, flexible, and open-minded. Rokeach describes this structural feature in the following way:

> This leads us to suggest a basic characteristic that defines the extent to which a person's system is open or closed; namely, the extent to which the person can receive, evaluate, and act on relevant information received from the outside on its own intrinsic merits unencumbered by irrelevant factors in the situation arising from within the person or from the outside. Examples of irrelevant internal pressures that interfere with the realistic reception of information are unrelated habits, beliefs, and perceptual cues, irrational ego motives, power needs, the need for self-aggrandizement, the need to allay anxiety, and so forth. By irrelevant external pressures we have in mind most particularly the pressures of reward and punishment arising from external authority; for example, as exerted by parents, peers, other authority figures, reference groups, social and institutional norms, and cultural norms.[4]

It should be noted that the concept being discussed here, "cognitive style," may easily and erroneously be interchanged with personality. The two are not strictly synonymous. Cognitive style is an analytical construct that denotes a tendency of an individual to respond in a characteristic manner. The question of distinguishing rigid persons from those who are not, the open-minded from the closed-minded, focuses attention upon a pattern of cognitive functioning that is relatively enduring and applies to a variety of social events and ideas. The polar terms employed are meant to represent ideal types; no single individual is expected to have a belief system that is completely open or completely closed. "Personality" similarly may be depicted as a general-response disposition. Yet, it is broader in scope than cognitive style because "to talk about personality implies a comprehensive understanding of the life development of an individual's emotions."[5] A study of person-

---

4. Ibid., p. 57. "Conceptually, dogmatism is a stylistic attribute, relatively free from specific belief prescriptions. Through a structurally closed system of beliefs and disbeliefs, the highly dogmatic person defends himself against anxiety by reliance on authority and sharp, categorical rejection of beliefs not consonant with his established values" (John P. Kirscht and Ronald C. Dillehay, *Dimensions of Authoritarianism*, p. 46).

5. Morris Janowitz and Dwaine Marvick, "Authoritarianism and Political Behavior," *Public Opinion Quarterly* 17(1953):185.

ality, then, ought to include a developmental dimension, and be concerned with such things as needs and motives. Cognitive style is a middle-level construct that is less inclusive than this.

At this point, it might also do well to introduce another distinction that until now has gone unnoticed. Reference has been made to the fact that individuals differ as to the extent to which their belief system, or some individual belief that they hold, is susceptible to change when confronted with novel information. The distinction to be made is addressed to the level of analysis employed, whether it is the system level (i.e., the belief system qua system) or subsystem level (i.e., the particular component parts—beliefs—of which the belief system is composed). Rokeach and his associates describe this distinction, and its implications, in the following way:

> We have said that at first glance rigid and dogmatic thinking appear to be synonymous: they both refer to resistance to change. On second thought, however, we see a possibly legitimate distinction between them: the first refers to the resistance to change of *single* beliefs (or set of habits), and the second refers to the resistance to change of *systems* of beliefs. . . .
> Thus, the referent of dogmatic thinking seems to be a total cognitive configuration of ideas and beliefs organized into a relatively closed system; rigidity, on the other hand, points to difficulties in overcoming single sets of beliefs encountered in attacking, solving, or learning specific tasks or problems. . . . Thus, rigid thinking should be expected to lead to difficulties in thinking analytically.
> On the other hand, to the extent a person is said to be characteristically dogmatic or closed in his thinking, the preservation of his total system will be at stake rather than the preservation of a particular belief in his system.[6]

Two character traits are thought to be involved: one relating to system resistance to change and concerning problem-solving difficulties at the synthesis level; the other relating to change in specific beliefs and concerning analytical problem-solving difficulties. The authors consequently endeavored to ascertain whether any empirical evidence could be generated to support this conceptual differentiation. To identify the former trait, a "Dogmatism Scale" (open versus closed belief systems) consisting of a battery of balanced items representing a variety of content was developed. The

---

6. Rokeach, *The Open and Closed Mind*, p. 183.

Gough-Sanford Rigidity Scale was employed in order to tap the latter trait. The Dogmatism and Rigidity Scales were then administered to a number of college students. Following this, the subjects were asked to participate in a problem-solving experiment that required, for successful completion, the accomplishment of tasks relating to both analysis and synthesis. The pattern of difficulties encountered by the subjects, whether it was of an analytical or synthetical nature, then was examined in view of scores they also received on the two scales. The findings generally lent "empirical support to the theoretical distinction drawn between dogmatic and rigid thinking. . . . All the conclusions above imply that dogmatic and rigid thinking are *discriminable* processes. In fact, in the various groups we have studied the correlations found between the Dogmatism and Rigidity Scales range from .37 to .55; and the correlation in this study between analysis and synthesis of thinking is around .45, suggesting that rigidity and dogmatism in the personality, and the ability to analyze and the ability to synthesize, tend to go together."[7]

The "military mind" stereotype does not make this distinction. Emphasizing not the discrimination of the two traits by their correlation, it argues that military officers are both more rigid *and* dogmatic without ever distinguishing between the two. In other words, the designation *military mind* refers to one end segment of a multivariate dimension that contains components pertaining to the content *and* structure of belief systems. Included within the latter category are the related yet distinguishable characteristics of dogmatism and rigidity. In order to assess whether the military in fact are more "doctrinaire" (i.e., dogmatic *and* rigid) than FSOs, these two critical elements will need to be combined into a single indicator of cognitive style. A first step toward the achievement of this end entailed administering the Gough-Sanford Rigidity Scale and a shortened form of the Dogmatism Scale developed by Rokeach and his associates to those officers comprising the political-military and political-FSO samples.[8]

7. Ibid., p. 193.
8. The Gough-Sanford Rigidity Scale appears in Rokeach, *The Open and Closed Mind*, pp. 418–19. The shortened form of the Dogmatism Scale

The officers were asked to indicate their answers according to a six-alternative Likert-type continuum ranging from "I agree very much" to "I disagree very much." Positive scores were coded either 7,6, or 5 depending upon intensity of agreement; negative scores were coded either 1, 2, or 3 depending upon intensity of disagreement (e.g., "I agree very much" received a score of 7 whereas "I disagree very much" received a score of 1). In those cases where individuals found it impossible to opt for one of the six alternatives, and generally were pro-con, or neutral in orientation, a score of 4 was assigned. This circumstance occurred only twice.

Rokeach's method for scoring individuals with respect to these two traits was simply to develop a total score for each subject through a procedure of summing the scores obtained on all the items in the two sets. However, an initial perusal of the response patterns of our two samples revealed that a strongly skewed distribution of responses is exhibited in approximately one-fourth of the items. In those cases, one or two response alternatives, out of the possible six, accounted for 80% or more of the total number of responses. In addition, these unusually popular alternatives without exception tended to be the more extreme ones in terms of the intensity dimension.

Items falling within this situation, although often expressing contrasting content, generally appear to include several kinds of questions. One group consists of statements that are structurally almost black or white and fairly unsophisticated in nature, qualities that in every case resulted in overwhelming rejection (e.g., items D-Dogmatism-5, D6, D9, D12, and R-Rigidity-9). Some others are politically oriented and appear, at least to these populations, to connote naïveté, (e.g., items D7 and D18). Another group of questions, ones that enjoyed unusual response agreement, relate somewhat to career-bureaucratic imperatives; that is, FSOs and military officers by the nature of their position must be able to

contains twenty items and was developed from Rokeach's forty-item Dogmatism Scale by Professors Troldahl and Powell (see Verling C. Troldahl and Frederick A. Powell, "A Short-Form Dogmatism Scale for Use in Field Studies," *Social Forces* 44[December, 1965]:211–14). Both scales appear in the interview schedule in the appendix.

Cognitive Style

adjust to new situations and places (e.g., rotation is an institutionalized way of life), be prompt ("crisis is normal" is the often remarked motto), and defer to the judgment of superiors (e.g., items D16, R20, and R22).

Subsequently, a Guttman scale analysis was performed on those items showing a relatively varied response distribution. This procedure yielded a five-item dogmatism scale and a ten-item rigidity scale. Total scores were then determined for each individual for each of the derived scales (i.e., those yielded by the Guttman analysis) and also for the two original scale sets themselves, by summing the scores made on those specific items included within them. The intercorrelation of the various scales, and respective reproducibility levels, is indicated in table 32.

TABLE 32
Intercorrelation Matrix of Dogmatism and Rigidity Scales

Scale	Derived Dogmatism	Original Dogmatism	Derived Rigidity	Reproducibility Level
Derived Dogmatism	...	...	...	84%
Original Dogmatism	.750	...	...	...
Derived Rigidity	.310	.320	...	84%
Original Rigidity	.420	.468	.883	...

Note: The statistic employed in table 32 is Pearson's product-moment correlation coefficient.

First, Rokeach's claim that dogmatism and rigidity are conceptually distinguishable though probably empirically related characteristics is reinforced by our findings. Here, as in his studies, a moderately strong correlation emerges when the two are compared (i.e., $r = .468$ and $r = .310$). Second, the two derived scales are revealed to be highly related to their respective original scales (i.e., $r = .750$ and $r = .883$). Third, although the reproducibility levels achieved are not completely satisfactory (84% versus the conventional and rather arbitrary 90% threshold), they are sufficiently great so that the derived scales can be considered to be unidimensional. These three features of the data taken together suggest that the derived scales (hereafter, simply dogmatism and rigidity scales) actually distinguish our respondents along the lines that are intended.

The next step toward the development of a cognitive style index entailed organizing the raw scores received by individuals on the dogmatism and rigidity scales into 8 ordered ranks of approximately equal number.[9] An 8 × 8 matrix was then developed through the juxtaposition of the scale distributions. Each officer consequently was assigned a summary index score depending upon his location within the matrix (i.e., according to the particular intersection of his dogmatism and rigidity scale scores).[10] These index scores are meant to indicate how doctrinaire (i.e., dogmatic *and* rigid) the individual officer is relative to all the other respondents.

It is now possible to proceed directly to the question of whether political-military officers in fact are more doctrinaire than their counterparts in the State Department. The data needed to answer this query appear in table 33. For purposes of correlation, the two eight-class distributions are dichotomized. The reader can observe that the military sample contains a significantly higher proportion of doctrinaire respondents than does the FSO one. Less than one-quarter of the latter fall within the "high doctrinaire" category compared with 60% of the military. Hence, we have established that the structural or stylistic aspect of the military mind hypothesis has some validity, at least with respect to the comparison of military and nonmilitary political-policy staff officers.[11]

9. Here, and throughout this study, no rearrangement of raw data is made unless it is clear through examination that such an alteration does not change the character of the data in any significant way.
10. Starting with the upper-lefthand corner of the dogmatism-rigidity matrix: The first three diagonals were coded as a 1 for the cognitive style index; diagonals 4 and 5 as 2; diagonal 6 as 3; diagonal 7 as 4; diagonal 8 as 5; diagonals 9 and 10 as 6; diagonals 11, 12, and 13 as 7; and diagonals 14 and 15 as 8. This coding scheme was used because it resulted in the eight cognitive style ranks containing an approximately equal number of respondents.
11. Similar significant differences between political-military and politi-

TABLE 33
COGNITIVE STYLE

DOCTRINAIRE	MILITARY		FSO		TOTAL	
	%	N	%	N	%	N
High	14	8	6	2	11	10
	17	10	8	3	14	13
	16	9	3	1	11	10
	14	8	6	2	11	10
Subtotal	60	35	22	8	46	43
	16	9	6	2	12	11
	12	7	19	7	15	14
	3	2	33	12	15	14
Low	9	5	19	7	13	12
Subtotal	40	23	78	28	54	51
Effective Total	100	58	100	36	100	94
Statistics	$\chi^2(1) = 13.007/P = .01$ Gamma $= .684/P = .01$					
Not Ascertained				1		
Grand Total		58		37		

Those few authors who have seriously considered this question and admitted the possibility that military officers may be relatively more doctrinaire or something similar, appear to try to explain such a situation by referring to the impact of what we have called organizational socialization. For example, Sapin comments that

cal-FSOs are obtained for the two components of cognitive style, dogmatism ($\chi^2[1] = 9.441/P = .01$ and Gamma $= .596/P = .01$) and rigidity ($\chi^2[1] = 4.028/P = .05$ and Gamma $= .411/P = .05$).

It should be pointed out that "The Authoritarian Personality" literature has been legitimately criticized for not satisfactorily taking into account the possible impact of education and intelligence. The sampling strategy employed here to a large extent has reduced the relevance of such objections to this study. It already has been shown that nearly all of our respondents are college graduates. In addition, all have undergone extensive in-service training and have continually taken on vital responsibilities. Given these facts, it seems very reasonable to assume that the two samples do not differ significantly regarding the intelligence of their members, no matter how one attempts to measure this quality.

some credence is still given to the concept of the "'military mind,' the notion that a lengthy period of professional service in one of the armed forces tends to produce a frame of mind narrow and rigid in thought patterns, one that oversimplifies problems and their solutions, is somewhat authoritarian in procedures and values, insensitive to the nonmilitary factors in situations, inclined to use force—in sum, not completely compatible with basic democratic values."[12] Lyons, in his discussion of the military mind, explicitly argues that "the military is largely a product of the military system, the repetitious training, the requirements of obedience, the instilling of assured responses to known stimuli, and the development of trust through a respect for position and hierarchy. The system, in turn, is essentially determined by the demands of combat."[13]

Since neither of the authors presents data that allow for a test of the socialization postulate, the reader is left wondering whether the postrecruitment stage actually is primary in the development of military minds. Moreover, the argument presented by Lyons is not very convincing. It may be true that the military "system" is as he describes and its nature "essentially determined by the demands of combat." But does this relationship confirm that "the military [mind] is largely a product of the military system." Of course not. For one thing, it is reasonable to propose that the aspirants who represent themselves as candidates for recruitment to the institution are aware of the institution's nature and have selected themselves with this information explicitly in mind. Furthermore, it also may be that the institution's recruiters tend to accept candidates who are like them. Thus, we see that Lyons's description of the military, even if completely accurate, does not exclude the possibility that the military mind exhibited by officers may be more fully explained by the prerecruitment or recruitment hypotheses than by the postrecruitment one. We are not in a position here to definitively choose between these three alternatives. Neverthe-

12. Burton M. Sapin, *The Making of United States Foreign Policy*, p. 140.
13. "The Military Mind," p. 19.

less, it is possible to present some evidence pertinent to the question. First, there is the data provided by our respondents that are presented in table 34. The reader will immediately observe that

TABLE 34

RELATIONSHIP OF COGNITIVE STYLE AND VARIABLES PERTAINING TO SOCIAL ORIGINS, RELIGIOSITY, AND POLITICAL ORIENTATION

	Statistics	
	$\chi^2 =$	Gamma $=$
Cognitive style and:		
Dogmatism	46.282‡	.941‡
Rigidity	26.047‡	.830‡
Place of birth	.236	
Geographical background	.718	
Size of hometown	1.249	.203
Status of father's occupation	.008	.020
Educational level	.016	.026
Religious affiliation	.496*	.192
Denominational status	3.265	.467
The Military only		
Old versus newtimers	1.038	.268
Service affiliation	3.384	
Academy versus nonacademy	.000	.003
Foreign Service only		
New versus oldtimers	.890	.250
Non-Ivy versus Ivy League	.226	.222
Religiosity	13.227‡	.697‡
Political orientation	6.464†	.495†

* $P = .10$; † $P = .05$; ‡ $P = .01$; all others: $P = $ NS.

political-military and political-FSO newtimers and oldtimers do not differ with respect to cognitive style or, in fact, with respect to either of the latter's two components, dogmatism and rigidity.[14] If socialization were operative and "producing military minds,"

14. The relevant coefficients are: $\chi^2(1) = .000/P = $ NS and Gamma $= .015/P = $ NS for the military regarding dogmatism; $\chi^2(1) = 1.66/P = $ NS and Gamma $= .333/P = $ NS for the military regarding rigidity; $\chi^2(1) = .290/P = $ NS and Gamma $= .200/P = $ NS for the FSOs regarding dogmatism; and $\chi^2(1) = .048/P = $ NS and Gamma $= .077/P = $ NS for the FSOs regarding rigidity.

one would expect to see a noticeable divergence when the distributions of the two subgroups are compared. But these findings, though important, do not by themselves settle the question. To reiterate a point made in the previous chapter, such results do not exclude the possibility that the effects of organizational socialization are being offset by the contrary influence of other factors. Let us suppose for sake of argument that prolonged exposure to the military system actually does have a tendency to "produce military minds." For this effect to be countered so that it would not be detected in a "newtimer versus oldtimer" analysis, other factors must be tending to develop a condition whereby oldtimers would be less doctrinaire than their younger colleagues if socialization did not occur. The effect of advancing age seems an unlikely prospect for, if anything, we would expect this factor to generate just the opposite condition from that proposed. Another possibility is that each generation is more doctrinaire than the one that preceded it. A trend of this type would act to cancel out the opposing effect produced by socialization. Such a situation, however, seems as unlikely as the first, and for a similar reason—if anything, each succeeding generation seems less, not more doctrinaire. A third possibility stems from the fact that the military is increasingly seeking and recruiting individuals who are college graduates. If college students currently and historically are more doctrinaire than non-college persons, then the effects of socialization again would not be evident. But, once more, the reverse seems more plausible; college students probably are relatively less doctrinaire.

A final possibility is that socialization is actually occurring, but its impact is relatively instantaneous rather than continual. By *instantaneous* we mean a situation where the effect generated by organizational socialization has an impact immediately following recruitment. After this initial period, further exposure to the organization does not result in an officer becoming more (or less) doctrinaire; the environment maintained within the formal institution, though, may act to sustain the temperament emerging from the initial exposure. Since even those whom we have called newtimers have been members of their services for at least several years, our analysis may not be sensitive enough to fully take into account the possible influence of instantaneous socialization.

Unfortunately, we were unable to find other studies that directly deal with this question, studies where dogmatism or rigidity scales were administered to recruits, relevant career aspirants, a cross section of the college (qualifying) population, or the nation. The best we can do is cite two investigations from "the authoritarian personality" literature in which the by now classic F[ascism]-Scale was administered to military personnel. In one, French and Ernest submitted the F-Scale's items to 186 men undergoing air force basic training. They state that "the authors of the scale assume that it is measuring a basic and stable personality syndrome and also that it is sufficiently indirect so that it won't be 'faked'." One of the hypotheses that French and Ernest test is whether "F-Scale scores will tend to remain stable over a period of military training." They report that their "results tend to confirm Hypothesis III that F-Scores will remain stable over a period of military training."[15] Another hypothesis they test is whether "the F-Scale can identify those men who will be more likely to express an intention of making a career of the service." Here they conclude that "although the F-career intention correlations are in the expected direction, they are too low to be considered confirmation of the hypothesis." This finding is ambivalent in its meaning because, as the authors of the study immediately point out, "possibly men who accept the military way of life because it is authoritarian may shift readily to another authoritarian environment, if that is a ready alternative, while those who accept it for relevant reasons will tend to remain."[16] In other words, one also has to assess whether so-called authoritarians have available alternative institutions to which they can turn and become members. Unfortunately, French and Ernest's investigation was not designed to explore this question.

In another research effort, Campbell and McCormack ask the

---

15. Elizabeth G. French and Raymond R. Ernest, "The Relation between Authoritarianism and Acceptance of Military Ideology," *Journal of Personality* 24(1955):182, 185.

16. Ibid., pp. 182, 187.

question "Does military experience lead to authoritarian and superior-oriented attitudes?" The respondents in this investigation were air force cadets and their instructors. The conclusion arrived at by Campbell and McCormack is that "longer experience in the Air Force has not led to increased authoritarianism. . . . Air Force cadets and their instructors, who are of the lower officer ranks, are clearly more authoritarian and superior-oriented on all three measures than the sample of college men of comparable age. Furthermore, these differences must be primarily a matter of recruitment of the Air Force personnel from the more authoritarian segments of the population, inasmuch as military indoctrination and experience seem to have no such effect."[17]

A final piece of circumstantial evidence is provided by Bengt Abrahamsson in his review of some studies dealing with the Swedish military.

> For the military profession, it has been shown that self-selective processes in officer recruitment tend to over-represent people with conservative and authoritarian attitudes. Some findings in a study by Erikson indicate that individuals with high proneness towards becoming officers are more conservative than comparable groups of people not striving towards the military profession. Korpi shows that men who go to cadet school and become regular officers are clearly more conservative than those who do not; this holds also when the father's social class is kept constant.

This conclusion is, of course, entirely consistent with the findings contained in the previous chapter. Abrahamsson goes on to say that "there is also a clear relationship between choice of the military profession and authoritarianism. . . . The differences cannot be explained by educational or intelligence factors, since the relationship between authoritarianism and attendance at cadet schools holds even when the sample is split up according to these variables."[18]

    17. Donald T. Campbell and Thelma H. McCormack, "Military Experiences and Attitudes toward Authority," *American Journal of Sociology* 62(1957):487.
    18. Bengt Abrahamsson, "Military Professionalization and Estimates on the Probability of War," in *Military Profession and Military Regimes: Commitments and Conflicts*, ed. Jacques van Doorn. Pp. 39–40.

The empirical findings of these investigations are by no means conclusive. For one thing, the French and Ernest study pertains to enlisted men, not officers. Far more serious is the fact that since the F-Scale rather than dogmatism (or rigidity) scale was employed, the findings reported above at best can only be considered evidence of an analogous type. There is no doubt that the concepts of authoritarianism and dogmatism have much in common. In fact, it has been said that "Rokeach developed the theory of dogmatism as part of his interpretation and extension of authoritarianism."[19] Nevertheless, there are obvious differences between the two. Most conspicuous is the fact that the F in F-Scale refers to fascism. This symbolizes a connection between cognitive structure and content features that exists within the concept of authoritarianism that Rokeach has recognized and, to reiterate, explicitly rejected. Dogmatism does not imply right-wing or any other political belief system. Yet, the fact that exposure to military experience twice was discovered not to be related to increasing authoritarianism is impressive, and entirely consistent with the lack of intra-sample differences with respect to dogmatism and rigidity found here. If one attempted to summarize what the above studies suggest, he would have to admit that on balance they diminish further the credibility of the postrecruitment socialization hypothesis and, additionally, somewhat undermine the alternative argument that recruitment bias manifested by the institution is the most potent factor. The latter claim is implied by the Swedish study, which argues that there is "a clear relationship between *choice* of the military profession and authoritarianism." Consequently, the prerecruitment hypothesis once again appears to be relatively the most persuasive.

Finally, let us return to table 34. If the reader peruses the table's contents, he will observe two things in addition to the finding that newtimers and oldtimers do not differ with respect to cognitive style: one, that cognitive style is significantly related to religiosity and political orientation; and two, that doctrinaire and nondoc-

---

19. Kirscht and Dillehay, *Dimensions of Authoritarianism*, p. 11.

trinaire officers generally do not differ with respect to their social origins.

The second finding is somewhat surprising in spite of the fact that the lack of relationship between cognitive style and social background clearly parallels the pattern that emerged when the latter and the two variables of religiosity and political orientation were analyzed. For example, many very persuasive-sounding hypotheses quickly come to mind when cognitive style (or something similar like authoritarianism) and such features as geographical origins and size of hometown are juxtaposed. On the other hand, the evidence we present undermines the credibility of such inferences. In addition, we also may cite a study done by DiRenzo, who administered a shortened version of the dogmatism scale to a sample of Italian parliamentarians and another control sample of Italian nonpoliticians. He found, just as we do, that social background features are not associated with dogmatism. More specifically, he states that "significant relationships are found between various degrees of religious practice and dogmatism. . . . The lowest dogmatism mean (1.73) in the political sample was derived from non-believers, whereas respondents professing Catholicism yielded means in the various categories of religious practice that average 7.33—clearly a marked discrepancy. . . . With the exception of religious practice, our data show no relationship between dogmatism and social background factors. These include age, educational level, parliamentary experience, and the geographic region of constituency."[20] Thus, we must conclude that those features that pertain to social background are not related to either religiosity, political orientation, or cognitive style. Knowing an officer's social origins will not tell you anything significant about how religious, DemLib, or doctrinaire he is. If any one of these attributes, or some combination of them, is critically associated with the formation of international political beliefs, then we can anticipate that social background variables will not be very relevant to an investigation of the latter either.

20. Gordon J. DiRenzo, "Professional Politicians and Personality Structures," *American Journal of Sociology* 73(1967):221–22.

But what of the association of religiosity, political orientation, and cognitive style? It already has been demonstrated in tables 29 and 34 that the three are significantly interrelated. Other empirical analyses may be cited that lend support to the validity of this pattern. The reader will note that DiRenzo finds that, among Italians, dogmatism and religious practice are related. Moreover, the tendency that DiRenzo explicitly identifies (i.e., for Catholics to be more dogmatic than nonbelievers) also is reported by Rokeach in one of the many investigations included in *The Open and Closed Mind*.[21] Similar associations between the related concept of authoritarianism, and religiosity and political orientation are revealed by Kirscht and Dillehay in their critical review of the authoritarian personality literature.[22] What we seem confronted with, then, is the existence of an attribute cluster consisting of the three interrelated variables of religiosity, political orientation, and cognitive style.[23] Concretely, this means that officers who described themselves as RepCons, more often than DemLibs, were revealed also to be relatively more religious and more doctrinaire.

This condition represents one aspect of the bifurcation that is manifest between the variables thus far introduced in our analysis. On the one hand, there are the social background features discussed in chapter 3 and the first part of chapter 4. We showed that political-military officers and political-FSOs did not differ with respect to these variables. On the other hand, the attributes of religiosity, political orientation, and cognitive style were successful in distinguishing our respondents according to their organizational

21. P. 351.
22. *Dimensions of Authoritarianism*, especially pp. 69–71, 131–34.
23. Incidentally, the existence of such an empirically revealed cluster lends additional (though again, indirect) support to the prerecruitment hypothesis regarding cognitive style. The argument here would take the following path: the prerecruitment hypothesis appeared to be the most defensible when religiosity and political orientation were analyzed; religiosity and political orientation now are shown to be significantly related to cognitive style; hence, prerecruitment probably is more relevant here, too, than the alternative hypotheses of recruitment bias and postrecruitment socialization in explaining why there is a difference in composition between our military and FSO samples concerning cognitive style.

affiliation. More specifically, political-military officers were revealed to be more religious, RepCon, and doctrinaire than their FSO counterparts. We suggested that the most persuasive explanation for this pattern seemed to be the prerecruitment hypothesis, that is, that individuals who present themselves as candidates for recruitment to the two governmental institutions already incorporate to a large extent the differences we find to exist between the political-policy officers of the Departments of State and Defense. Furthermore, none of these three variables appears to be associated with social background features. The division between the two variable-subsets, social background on the one hand and religiosity–political orientation–cognitive style on the other, thus is quite clear. Also clear is the fact that the relative importance of the two subsets will vary depending upon whether political-military officers and political-FSOs express similar or dissimilar political beliefs. It is precisely to this query that we now turn our attention.

CHAPTER 7

Foreign Policy Beliefs

In the initial part of the previous chapter, two aspects of the "military mind" hypothesis were distinguished: one aspect pertained to the structure of belief systems (i.e., *how* people believe), the other to the content of belief systems (i.e., *what* people believe). Until now, only the former aspect of the "military mind" has been considered. Here, attention is turned to the complimentary task of ascertaining whether significant attitudinal divergencies exist between political-military officers and political FSOs.

Before continuing, it should be noted that the terms *belief, attitude,* and *opinion* will be used interchangeably in the present discussion (i.e., mainly for stylistic relief), even though possible subtleties of meaning may thereby be obscured. The general meaning conveyed by the three words, the element which they appear to share, is their association with the act of choosing. Berelson and Steiner similarly comment with respect to these words: "These terms do not have fixed meanings in the literature, but in general they refer to a person's preference for one or another side of a controversial matter in the public domain—a political issue, a religious issue, a moral position, an aesthetic taste, a certain practice. . . ."[1] In other words, although the terms may differ according to comprehensiveness and/or intensity, they all have in common the notion of "selection among alternatives," and this is the basic quality to which their usage in this study refers.

---

1. Bernard R. Berelson and Gary A. Steiner, *Human Behavior: An Inventory of Scientific Findings,* p. 557.

One problem in any investigation of opinions is the relevance of the latter to a particular population; that is, how salient are the controversial matters to the individuals whose answers are being ascertained? Another problem concerns the amount of information upon which the preference rests. In the present case, these two issues are not pressing ones; for it can be reasonably assumed that the officers constituting the two samples, as a direct result of the specific nature of their roles and corresponding responsibilities, are unusually well informed and interested regarding matters of a political nature.

To return at this time to the question of the political beliefs of Foreign Service and military officers, it is common to suppose that the latter take a harder line toward internationally oriented political issues than do FSOs. But what does this label convey? In order to respond to this query, let us first assume we have before us a relevant set of political issues: A, B, and C. Second, let us posit that only two positions can be taken with respect to each of these issues: A_1 and A_2, B_1 and B_2, and C_1 and C_2. Now, at least two things seem to be implied when a term such as *hard-line* is used. The first involves the explicit identification and representation of one of an issue's various positions as hard-line. For example, because of its particular nature, position A_1 (and not A_2) may commonly be accepted as a typical hard-line response. Note that *hard-line*, as the term's usage is interpreted here, has no reality aside from the act of preferring A_1 to A_2. The employment of hard-line rather than another label is arbitrary. Thus, the reader is free to substitute a different term if he feels it more appropriately conveys the essence of the contrast between A_1 and A_2. The important point, consequently, is not really the suitability of the label hard-line but rather the "defining" relationship that is implied between it and the specific preferences of individuals.

Something else appears to be implied when the term *hard-line* is used. Its intended meaning seems broader than merely the representation of a number of specific positions (e.g., A_1, B_1, and C_1). It also alludes to the prospect of the positions A_1, B_1, and C_1 being related; that individuals who choose A_1 probably will additionally choose B_1 and C_1. The term *hard-line* consequently refers to a constellation of content-specific attitudinal preferences that are presumed to cohere. Put somewhat differently, a hard-line belief system may be depicted as a content-specific

> configuration of ideas and attitudes in which the elements are bound together by some form of constraint or functional interdependence. In the static case, "constraint" may be taken to mean the success we would have in predicting, given initial knowledge that an individual holds a specific attitude, that he holds certain further ideas and attitudes. . . . In the dynamic case, "constraint" or "interdependence" refers to the probability that a change in the perceived status (truth, desirability, and so forth) of one idea-element would *psychologically* require, from the point of view of the actor, some compensating change(s) in the status of idea-elements elsewhere in the configuration.[2]

It should be clear to the reader that, strictly speaking, an individual does not express a "belief system." On the contrary, the respondent only expresses preferences regarding the questions put to him. It is the analyst who infers some pattern and imposes structure upon the responses which are given. The identification of a belief system, therefore, is something the analyst derives through the utilization of statistical and other means. Only through such a methodology can a person's belief system come to be characterized as hard-line. Of course, an especially knowledgeable person,

---

2. Philip E. Converse, "The Nature of Belief Systems in Mass Publics," in *Ideology and Discontent*, ed. David E. Apter, pp. 207–8. An earlier description of what here is called "belief system" took the following form: "We speak of an 'attitude structure' when two or more beliefs or opinions held by an individual are in some way or another functionally related. . . . In most attitude studies, functional relationships are presumed to exist where it is found that knowledge of a person's belief on one issue helps to predict his belief on some other issues" (Campbell et al., *The American Voter*, pp. 189, 191). A similar position is taken by Giovanni Sartori, "Politics, Ideology, and Belief Systems," *American Political Science Review* 63(1969):398–411. Somewhat similar conceptualizations are provided by Boulding in his depiction of *image* as "the total cognitive, affective, and evaluative structure of the behavioral unit, or its internal view of itself and its universe" (Kenneth E. Boulding, "National Images and International Systems," *Journal of Conflict Resolution* 3[1959]:120–21); and by D'Amato when he speaks of "psychological constructs" (Anthony A. D'Amato, "Psychological Constructs in Foreign Policy Prediction, *Journal of Conflict Resolution* 11[1967]:295–96).

through introspection, may reach a similar realization and become cognizant of the fact that the beliefs he holds are not isolated entities. The relatively few individuals who have achieved this level of sophistication are aware of the systemic nature of their political thinking.[3]

The recognition that individual beliefs may cohere so as to form a system can be useful for a variety of reasons, both to the respondent and to the analyst. Converse suggests that the "idea-organization which leads to constraint permits [an individual] to locate and make sense of a wider range of information from a particular domain than he would find possible without such organization. . . . The psychological economies provided by such yardsticks for actors are paralleled by economies for analysts and theoreticians who wish to describe events in the system parsimoniously. Indeed, the search for adequate over-arching dimensions on which large arrays of events may be simply understood is a critical part of synthetic description."[4] Note that Converse sees belief systems as being critical both to the need of individuals to make sense of their environment and to the investigator who is trying to describe the cognitive functionings and activities of people. Rokeach assumes "that all belief-disbelief systems serve two powerful and conflicting sets of motives at the same time: the need for a cognitive framework to know and to understand and the need to ward off threatening aspects of reality."[5] D'Amato in his discussion of the term *psychological construct* indicates that his partiality for this rather than alternative terms, such as world view or conceptual system, stems from the fact that "it suggests an abstract *struc*ture for *constru*ing environment."[6] The word *construing* is popularly used as denoting the activity of explaining, deducing, inferring, or interpreting the meaning of some action, statement, idea, and so forth. Finally, we may cite Holsti, who says that a belief system

---

3. See Converse, "The Nature of Belief Systems," pp. 213 ff., for a discussion of the relationship between level of information and constraint within belief systems.
4. Ibid., p. 214.
5. Rokeach, *The Open and Closed Mind*, p. 67.
6. "Psychological Constructs in Foreign Policy Prediction," p. 295.

"may be thought of as a set of lenses through which information concerning the physical and social environment is received. It orients the individual to his environment, defining it for him and identifying for him its salient characteristics. . . . In addition to organizing perceptions into a meaningful guide for behavior, the belief system has the function of the establishment of goals and the ordering of preferences."[7] In sum, belief system or nearly equivalent constructs such as attitude structure appear to provide people with the opportunity to better manage their environment through enhancing their ability to understand (i.e., analyze, interpret, and evaluate) and learn. In addition, the employment of terms such as hard-line belief system, *if used carefully*, enable a researcher to economically summarize the diverse beliefs of an individual.

The hard-line label has been and continues to be utilized in order to describe in a parsimonious way what are thought to be the peculiar political beliefs of military officers. But has this designation been carefully applied or not? Has it been firmly established that this designation is justified? And, furthermore, has the meaning of the designation been clarified and explicitly stated? We have argued that in order for such a label to be usefully applied, the employer of it must first accomplish two things: initially he must explicitly identify as hard-line specific positions regarding some relevant set of political issues; and second, he must demonstrate that the positions are functionally related. Only then can he be in a position to assess or use the terms hard-line or military mind. Therefore, let us retrace our steps and begin with the necessary task of operationalizing "hard-line."

Fortunately, our work is simplified because several attempts have already been made to classify foreign policy political beliefs. One notable contribution is Levine's effort to distinguish, in *The Arms Debate*, what he calls "schools of thought."

> By the first criterion, major purpose of recommendation, arms-policy schools in the United States can be grouped into three classes: (1) those whose main objective . . . is to decrease the probability of war, particu-

7. Ole R. Holsti, "The Belief System and National Images: A Case Study," *Journal of Conflict Resolution* 6(1962):245.

larly thermonuclear war; (2) those whose primary objective is to stem and/or reverse the advance of Communism; and (3) those, in some sense in the middle, who can be best characterized by the fact that they do not fit comfortably into either of the other two groups because their recommendations do not appear to put one of these two objectives clearly above the other. . . . The three classes according to this simplified categorization should be labeled primarily anti-war, primarily anti-communist, and "middle."[8]

Evidently Levine feels that two perspectives essentially underlie, and consequently influence, current American thinking about international political-military problems; one is primarily concerned with the idea of war and its prevention, the other with communism and the prevention of its expansion.[9] Furthermore, these contrasting viewpoints are believed to share in a rough way the two opposite end segments of a single dimension. Much of Levine's book is involved with illustrating how these schools of thought differ in their values (i.e., concerning peace, freedom, power, and time) and analyses (i.e., concerning war, opponent, power, allies and neutrals, and ourselves).[10] Note that the "identifications" yielded by his analysis (i.e., the positions associated with each school) are not empirically determined; they are the result merely of Levine's reasoning. Yet Levine's study is of benefit in two important ways: first, by suggesting which of an almost endless number of political issues are significant for investigation, he has furnished us with a list of variables from which we can select those we feel are especially pertinent to our analysis; and second, by endeavoring to organize political positions in terms of

8. Robert A. Levine, *The Arms Debate*, pp. 45–46.

9. Brown contends that "to prevent the spread of international Communism and to prevent the outbreak of a Third World War" are the two major objectives of United States foreign policy as defined by American decision-makers (Seyom Brown, *The Faces of Power: Constancy and Change in United States Foreign Policy from Truman to Johnson*, pp. 7–14).

10. For discussion purposes, Levine subsequently breaks down each of the general topics (i.e., war, opponent, power, and so on) into several more specific issues. For example, the "analysis of war" includes references to the causes of war, escalation of limited wars, the effects of arms races, and so forth. Since nine topics are mentioned under the headings of "values" and "analyses," the number of issues that eventually are introduced is quite large.

three schools of thought, he has suggested which specific positions should cohere.

Lovell, in an exercise similar to Levine's, identifies three "strategic perspectives" that he calls the "pacifist," "pragmatic," and "absolutist" approaches.[11] To readers already acquainted with the literature concerning the political thinking of American military officers, the latter two approaches should be very familiar ones. Lovell has endeavored to first systematize and then elaborate, through the addition of the pacifist approach, the scheme initially worked out by Janowitz in *The Professional Soldier*.[12] Following Janowitz, Lovell has distinguished the three approaches according to such issues as Communist intentions, motivation of neutrals, preferred United States political-military strategy, and so forth. The articulation of these three strategic perspectives contributes to our analysis in the same way as Levine's does.

Unfortunately, neither Levine nor Janowitz-Lovell take the step of ascertaining whether the constituent parts of what they respectively have called schools of thought and strategic perspectives actually cluster. By this, we mean to direct attention to the fact that the belief systems they depict take the form they do because the authors presume that the patterns they describe are reasonable or natural. The positions making up the patterns are associated because it is thought that they ought to be associated. The implicit rationale employed is similar to what Converse has called "logical sources of constraint."[13] The authors seem almost to be saying that, by their very nature, position A_1 logically implies (or should imply?) position B_1; that is why they are grouped. But this does not mean, and cannot be interpreted to mean, that these two positions are actually empirically related. This is an entirely different question and one we are concerned with.[14]

11. "The Professional Socialization of the West Point Cadet," p. 127.
12. Pp. 283–344.
13. "The Nature of Belief Systems," p. 209.
14. It should be pointed out that Levine never intended to pursue such an empirical objective. His valuable book is an intellectual-logical effort designed "to identify the policy alternatives being offered by the various schools

This is not all that Levine and Janowitz-Lovell share. If the reader were to juxtapose their typologies, he immediately would be struck by the substantial correspondence that exists between the two categorizations. The "anti-communism school of thought," as it is described by Levine, does not appear to be noticeably dissimilar to what Janowitz-Lovell have called the "absolutist" approach. A similar correspondence is manifested between the middle school and pragmatic approach, and the antiwar school and pacifist approach. The correspondence not only proceeds from an affinity that is strongly conveyed by the titles themselves (e.g., antiwar and pacifist), but also from an examination of the specific positions presumed to separate each classification scheme's three categories. Let us try to summarize this conformity in viewpoint by organizing the numerous specific issues introduced by Levine and Janowitz-Lovell into three broad attitudinal dimensions: anti-Communism; Arms Control and/or Disarmament (hereafter, ACD); and Nonalignment. A perusal of these authors' analyses reveals that the perspective of both the anti-communism school and the absolutist approach generally is portrayed as being vigorously anti-Communist, deeply unsympathetic to ACD proposals, and genuinely suspicious of the motives of states who claim to be trying to pursue a nonaligned policy with respect to the so-called cold war. The antiwar school and pacifist approach reveal a similar overlap, but of course with very dissimilar viewpoints involved.

The fact that the literature's two major efforts to distinguish internationally oriented political belief systems yield such a conformity is remarkable. Also quite remarkable is the likeness between their depiction of the "anti-Communism–absolutism" perspective and what is popularly conceived of as "hard-line." It behooves us to take advantage of this resemblance, and we do by explicitly

of thought and to understand the reasoning which lies behind these offerings" (*The Arms Debate*, p. 4). No attempt was made to explore whether any individual actually displays a belief system that in form resembles one of the schools of thought. Within this context, D'Amato ("Psychological Constructs in Foreign Policy Prediction") goes further than either Levine or Janowitz-Lovell when he distinguishes "four foreign-policy constructs." Especially useful is his discussion of the construct he calls "hawk-dove."

equating hard-line with anti-Communism–absolutism. In other words, for the purposes of this analysis we will identify as hard-line beliefs those idea-elements that are characterized by vigorous anti-Communism, opposition to the pursuit of ACD, and distrust of the motivations of nonaligned states. This will be the yardstick used to judge whether or not a respondent possesses hard-line beliefs. Of course, we will go farther and also attempt to empirically determine whether these hard-line beliefs cluster so as to form a system.

One obvious question however remains to be answered: What are the indicators that allow the analyst to distinguish respondents' positions with respect to these three dimensions? Let us attempt to respond to this query by taking each dimension in turn. Our strategy regarding the anti-Communism dimension was to initially break it down into four parts. (See figure 2, p. 164 for a visual representation of the approach used here.) The first part related to the *saliency* of anti-Communism relative to other international political issues. The reader will recall that both Levine and Brown explicitly argue that Communist expansion and the possible outbreak of a major war are the most critical contemporary foreign policy problems. Lovell implicitly accepts this formulation when he contrasts the "absolutist" (e.g., described as believing that the Communists are intent on world domination) and "pacifist" approaches. Our interest here was in discovering the relative prominence a respondent would give to the anti-Communism issue when asked to identify "the most important international political issues in this generation."[15]

15. The exact items used are presented in the interview schedule in the appendix. Since open-ended questions were employed, more than one issue may be mentioned and recorded. A list of all the comments expressed by each respondent, therefore, was assembled. Each entry subsequently was examined as to whether in nature it was anti-Communist (e.g., winning the cold war, containing Communism), antiwar (e.g., peace, disarmament), or neither of these two (e.g., population explosion). The numerous entries then were grouped according to their respective designations (e.g., anti-Communism, and so on). The response of each individual consequently was coded on the basis of the designation ascribed to his particular remarks. On many occasions, an individual's response contained comments that included more than

The second component of the anti-Communism dimension involves the degree of *apprehension* that the individual expresses when he is asked to assess Soviet foreign policy goals and means. The idea to use such an item resulted from the fact that both Levine and Lovell devote great attention to this matter. Lovell states that the "pacifist," "pragmatic," and "absolutist" approaches view "Communist intentions" respectively as "defensive-potential friends," "expansionistic," and "intent on world domination."[16] Levine explains that the anti-war school perceives the USSR as "becoming consolidationalist in order to conserve its successes," with the middle school taking the position that the "USSR is still carefully aggressive in the short run but perhaps it may change in the long," and the anti-Communists arguing that the "USSR is implacably aggressive and out to bury us, with no sign of change."[17] Some confusion is created here by Levine's failure to separate two analytically distinguishable elements. One aspect of his formulation refers to the alleged *aggressiveness* of the USSR's *methods*; the other refers to the *scope* of its policy *ends*. Quite obviously, one may perceive another as timid, but as having grandiose plans. Our respondents, however, tend to associate these two qualities. Those officers who saw the Communists as intent on world domination, for example, also tended more often than others to see them as implacably aggressive. Thus, it makes a good deal of sense to incorporate both these aspects into a single summary indicator of apprehension concerning the Soviet Union. We did this by developing a "mini-index" that enables us to represent by a single score where any respondent stands with respect to these two related, yet dis-

one designation. In such an event, the relative importance given to the problem by the respondent was determined by the following criteria: order of presentation, amount of time spent discussing the problem, and, if relevant, the probability assigned regarding the occurrence of the phenomenon. Here as with all the open-ended questions, to encourage correct assessment, two individuals, working separately but using the same procedures, coded each response. Respondents subsequently were distinguished according to whether their response was: (1) exclusively anti-Communist (31% of all the respondents); (2) a mix of anti-Communism and either antiwar or other problems (28%); or (3) exclusively antiwar or other problems (41%).

16. "The Professional Socialization of the West Point Cadet," p. 127.
17. *The Arms Debate,* p. 213.

criminable, subitems. Consequently, a relatively apprehensive respondent is one who tends to perceive the Soviet Union as *aggressively* pursuing their unchanging goal of *world domination*.

The third component pertains to the respondent's perception of the internal nature of the Communist community of states, whether or not he sees that community as constituting a *monolithic* bloc. Much of the discussion concerning this subject has revolved around the use of the term *Soviet Bloc*. Some people contend that this term still has substantial meaning as a shorthand label descriptive of the very real enemy in the very real cold war. If the existence of genuine differences among the members of the alleged bloc (i.e., differences not manufactured by the Communist leaders themselves in order to confuse and mislead the Free World) is at all admitted, they are thought to be minor ones essentially concerning specific tactical problems rather than questions concerning objectives. The more enthusiastic proponents of this viewpoint might take this argument one step further and talk in terms of a single Communist conspiracy. At the other end, there is the viewpoint that the Soviet community is a thoroughly fragmented one, divided by national, political, and economic interests and emotions. The term Soviet Bloc hence is conceived of here as symbolic of a perspective that unfortunately fails to comprehend this fact, with the term itself acting to obscure the reality and significance of these divisions. Thus, the idea of Soviet monolithicity is considered to be something left over from a previous period, a relic whose meaningfulness was doubtful even then. We are not interested in which of these opposing perceptions is correct, but rather with ascertaining the sympathies of our respondents regarding this issue. Two related questions were asked in order to achieve this aim: the first related to the possible existence of differences within the Soviet community; the second, to the possible seriousness of these differences. Again a mini-index was constructed to allow the responses to these two questions to be represented by a single score. For example, those respondents who were assigned a "high monolithicity" score were inclined to deprecate the existence and seriousness of intra–Soviet community differences.

The fourth and final component concerns the cold war's *impact* on American values, institutions, and ways of thinking. This item was inspired in part by Levine's comment that the antiwar school charges "we are in danger of being dominated by militaristic psychology [and] the political power of the military." On the other hand, the anti-Communist school is described as believing that "the relation of the political forces within the U.S. to arms policy is so tenuous as to require no analysis."[18] Our concern is somewhat broader than merely the role of the military. We are interested in ascertaining what our respondents feel are the major domestic effects of the cold war competition. On the basis of their responses, respondents were distinguished according to whether they primarily thought the impact of the cold war was beneficial (e.g., encouraged interest in science and politics, stimulated the economy and technological innovation) or detrimental (e.g., encouraged right-wing-oriented political aberrations such as McCarthyism or adverse psychological reactions such as the present anxiety and/or alienation of our youth).

The anti-Communism dimension, then, has four component parts. For the sake of brevity, we can refer to them as: salient, apprehensive, monolithic, and impact. Further analysis of our respondent's answers to the relevant interview items revealed, as one might expect, that these components are functionally interdependent.[19] This is another way of saying that those respondents for whom the problem of Communism was relatively *salient* also exhibited comparatively high *apprehension* regarding Soviet goals and means, perceived the Soviet community of states as *monolothic*, and saw the *impact* of the cold war on America as being, on balance, beneficial. On the other hand, those respondents who gave relatively unusual prominence to the "war prevention" theme also were inclined to be less apprehensive about Soviet goals and means and so on.

At this point, an anti-Communism scale was constructed that satisfactorily incorporated the information collected concerning

18. Ibid., p. 215.
19. All the pair-wise combinations among the four components yielded statistically significant correlation coefficients.

Foreign Policy Beliefs

each respondent's viewpoint on each of the four component items.[20] Because there are just four items present, the anti-Communism scale provides a maximum of five classes within which the respondents may fall. The respondents who were revealed to be "vigorously anti-Communist" are those who exhibit a relatively high saliency with respect to the problem area of Communism, high apprehension regarding Soviet goals and means, and so on. This extreme category captured 13 (or 14%) of the 95 respondents. The adjacent category contained 27 (or 28%) of the respondents. The middle category was the most numerous, claiming 28 officers (or 30%). The next category contained 20 respondents (or 21%). The final and other extreme (i.e., non-anti-Communist) category was the most sparse, containing only 7 officers (or 7%).[21]

Let us now move on to a discussion of the second dimension. Both Levine and Lovell devote some attention to the issue of ACD. The fact that the end segments of their typologies are called respectively the anti-war school and pacifist approach implicitly underscores the significance of this subject. Five items were used in order to ascertain where a respondent stood with respect to ACD. The first asked whether ACD was a question *worth* discussing. The second involved how much *attention* ACD proposals should get relative to other foreign policy concerns. The third called for an evaluation of the *performance* of the United States regarding the pursuit of ACD. The fourth asked for the respondent's opinion on the United States–Soviet Union *treaty* to ban nuclear testing in the atmosphere. The fifth and last attempted to assess the respondent's feeling about the United States further *pursuing* ACD agreements with the Soviet Union. A perusal of the responses to

---

20. The scale was developed through the utilization of standard Guttmann analysis techniques. The range of "yes" votes varies from a high of 76% for the "apprehension" item to a low of 31% for the "saliency" one. The scale's reproducibility level turned out to be .910.

21. This anti-Communism variable will be dichotomized at a cutting point that distinguishes the first two and the last three categories whenever it and another variable are intercorrelated. This transformation results from the attempt to attain adequate representation for each matrix cell so that statistical analysis can be performed.

these items revealed that the third (i.e., *performance*) failed to generate any real difference of opinion. About 90% of the officers within both samples said that the amount of attention the United States has been giving to ACD is "about right"; very few thought the United States either deficient or excessive in this area. The diverse pattern of responses achieved on the four other items, however, permitted the construction of an ACD scale.[22] Upon examining the distribution of ACD scale scores, we found that the "most unsympathetic to ACD" category contained 16 (or 17%) of the 95 officers. The adjacent category accounted for another 15 officers (or 16%). Twenty-five officers (or 26%) were included in the middle and neutral position. The next category consisted of 15 officers (or 16%). The fifth and "most sympathetic to ACD" category contained the remaining 24 officers (or 25%).[23]

The third and last dimension we will introduce pertains to the subject of nonalignment. The "motivation of neutrals" is one of the five issues that Lovell uses to distinguish his three "strategic perspectives." The following distinctions are made by Lovell: according to the "absolutist" viewpoint, neutrals "desire to get something for nothing [and are] potential enemies"; according to the "pragmatic" viewpoint, neutrals do not have the capacity "to make a commitment [but are] potential allies"; and according to the "pacifist" viewpoint, neutrals "desire to promote world stability."[24] Similarly, Levine sees a growing empathy for neutrals as one moves from the anti-Communism to the antiwar end of the spectrum.[25] It seemed worthwhile to follow the lead of Lovell and Levine, and

22. The scale's reproducibility level turned out to be .931. The range of "yes" votes varied from a high of 75% for the "worth" item to a low of 39% for the "pursuit" one.

23. For the reason cited in footnote 21, it will be necessary in statistical analysis to dichotomize this distribution between the first three and the last two categories.

24. "The Professional Socialization of the West Point Cadet," p. 127. Regarding the use of the term *neutral*, a more descriptive word and one that the author personally prefers, is *nonaligned*. Third-party states, strictly speaking, are not neutral. They may take sides in a particular dispute, even though they are not associated with either camp.

25. *The Arms Debate*, p. 215.

Foreign Policy Beliefs

attempt to discern our respondents' reaction to the term *nonaligned*. We therefore asked: "Many countries present themselves as being nonaligned with respect to the cold war; what generally is your attitude toward these nations and such a foreign policy?" This question is very broad, and was meant to be. What is of interest here is not the eliciting of particular views toward particular countries, but rather assessing the general tone of the individual's remarks as he responds to the open-ended item. Corresponding to this aim, three general code categories are utilized: supportive; pro-con; and unsupportive. Typical of the first are comments such as "we would do the same if in their position," "the United States in the past has often pursued such a policy," and "nothing wrong with it as long as they are genuinely neutral." A sampling of unsupportive responses included answers like "most of them are Communists or Communist sympathizers," "they want to get something for nothing by playing off both sides," and some comments that if stated here would only be censored. It turned out that 33 (or 35%) of the 95 respondents expressed essentially unsupportive comments. Another 16 officers (or 17%) had pro-con responses. The remaining 46 (or 48%) were supportive.[26]

Now that the three dimensions have been introduced, we can proceed to the very critical task of ascertaining whether or not they are functionally interdependent. We anticipate that they will cohere, that respondents who are vigorously anti-Communist will also be unsympathetic to ACD *and* unsupportive with respect to nonalignment. But, to reiterate, this is not a premise but rather a hypothesis to be explored. The data pertinent to a test of this hypothesis are presented in table 35. We see that, consistent with our expectations, the three dimensions are related and in the direction we predicted (e.g., note the positive Gamma coefficients). In other words, a sufficient degree of constraint is evident between the idea-elements of anti-Communism, ACD, and nonalignment so as to allow one to think about them as forming a coherent for-

---

26. For the reason cited in footnote 21, it will be necessary in statistical analysis to dichotomize this distribution between the first two and third categories.

TABLE 35

Relationship between Anti-Communism, ACD, Nonalignment, and Foreign Policy Belief System

	ACD	Nonalignment	Belief System
Anti-Communism	$\chi^2(1)=3.488/P=.10$ Gamma$=.385/P=.10$	$\chi^2(1)=3.299/P=.10$ Gamma$=.366/P=.10$	$\chi^2(1)=31.775/P=.01$ Gamma$=.889/P=.01$
ACD		$\chi^2(1)=4.558/P=.05$ Gamma$=.427/P=.05$	$\chi^2(1)=33.980/P=.01$ Gamma$=.887/P=.01$
Nonalignment			$\chi^2(1)=36.603/P=.01$ Gamma$=.897/P=.01$

eign policy–oriented belief system. Having established this, we can go on to construct a belief system index that will incorporate the information gathered about each respondent's stance on these three dimensions. Such an index was developed and every respondent subsequently assigned a summary belief system score.[27] The coefficients appearing in the last column of table 35 indicate that the "belief system" scores the respondents received are strongly associated with their relative positions on the three dimensions.[28]

Thus, the two tasks we set for ourselves have been satisfactorily accomplished. First, specific operationalized beliefs (i.e., particular positions regarding relevant political issues) have been explicitly identified as hard-line. Second, these beliefs have been shown to form a coherent foreign policy belief system. These steps are diagrammed in figure 2. The reader will note that three distinct levels of generality are involved.[29] At the lowest level are found the individual question items—elements that are quite object-specific in nature. The next level contains the three dimensions of anti-Communism, ACD, and nonalignment. We view each of the latter as representing a cluster of content-related, object-specific beliefs involving some relatively broad political issue. The third and highest level of generality is represented by the foreign policy belief system. Here we have the existence of a condition of interdependence between dimensions representing relatively diverse issues.

27. The belief system index was constructed in the following way. The cutting points described in previous footnotes were used to dichotomize the three distributions into "yes" and "no" subgroups. The "yes" subgroup each time was identified as the hard-line position. Every respondent then was assigned a summary score depending on now many "yes" scores he accumulated. Hence, a belief system score of 3 indicates that the respondent expresses a hard-line view on all of the dimensions; a score of 2, that he twice took a hard-line position and once did not; and so forth.

28. For the reason cited in footnote 21 above, it will be necessary in statistical analysis to dichotomize the four-class "belief system" distribution between the first two and last two categories. See table 37 for the presentation of the entire "belief system" distribution yielded by the index.

29. For discussions of the idea of differing levels of generality between systems and attitudes, see William A. Scott, "Rationality and Non-Rationality of International Attitudes," *Journaal of Conflict Resolution* 2(1958):10–11; and Hans Jurgen Eysenck, *The Psychology of Politics*, pp. 107–13.

FIGURE 2
THE CONSTRUCTION OF THE FOREIGN POLICY BELIEF SYSTEM

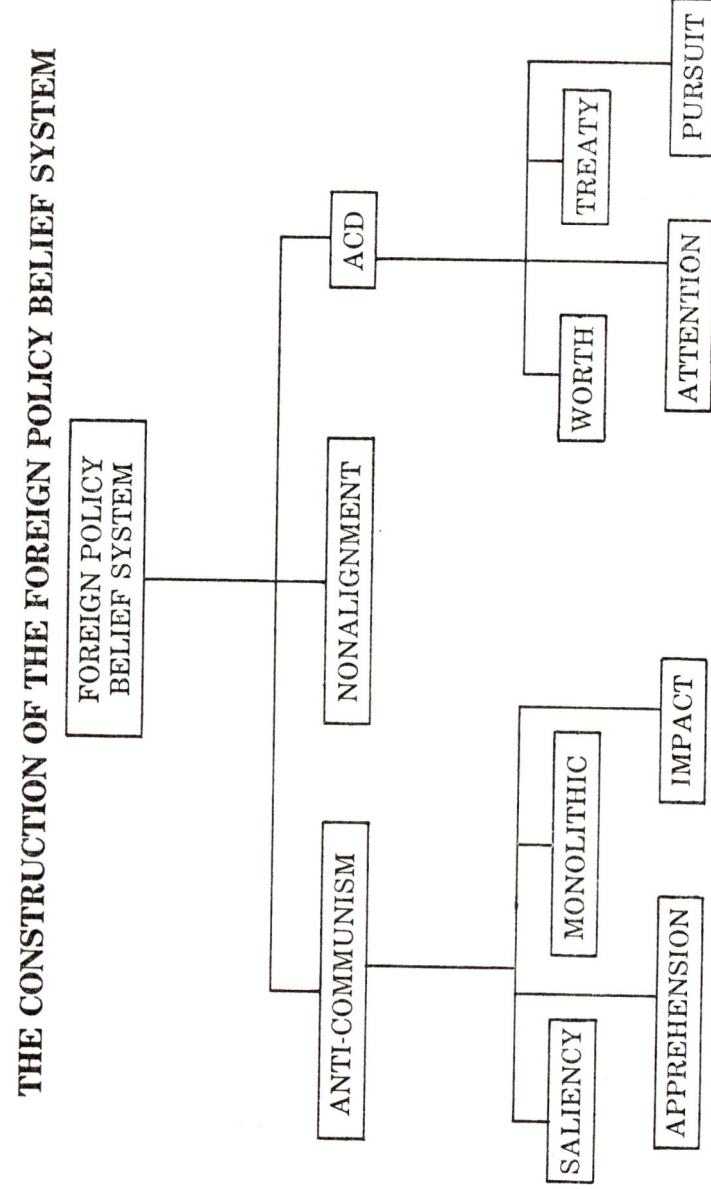

Foreign Policy Beliefs

Our construction does not go beyond this point. Needless to say, higher levels of generality are possible. A *foreign policy* belief system may only be one part of a more general *political* belief system, which itself may only be one part of a more general *cognitive* system, and so forth. For example, the data presented in table 36 suggest that what is called the "foreign policy belief system"

TABLE 36

RELATIONSHIP BETWEEN BELIEFS PERTAINING TO FOREIGN POLICY, GOVERNMENT INVOLVEMENT IN THE ECONOMY, AND CIVIL LIBERTIES

	Government Involvement	Civil Liberties
Foreign Policy	$\chi^2(2)=7.375/P=.05$ Gamma$=.392/P=.05$	$\chi^2(1)=11.756/P=.01$ Gamma$=.634/P=.01$
Government Involvement		$\chi^2(2)=5.323/P=.10$ Gamma$=.370/P=.05$

may indeed be an aspect of a more general "political belief system," at least with respect to our respondents. Once again, variables relating to "government involvement in domestic economic affairs" and "civil liberties" are introduced. The reader will note that these two domestic attitudes and foreign policy beliefs are related. More concretely, those respondents whose beliefs may be described as hard-line also are inclined to favor less government involvement in the economy *and* believe Communists should not be allowed to participate in the American political process.[30] This association is not unexpected given the identity of our respondents. By this last statement we mean again to call explicit attention to the fact that

---

30. We recognize that use of the last item may be somewhat unfair since it partially refers to feelings about Communism—a subject incorporated within the foreign policy belief system. On the other hand, one may be very hostile to Communism but at the same time be very committed to the full exercise of civil liberties within the United States. He may see the existence of such freedoms as the essential difference between "us" and "them," and additionally the best way to counteract any internal influence "they" may try to achieve (e.g., through the "marketplace of ideas" the true and undesirable character of Communism will be exposed).

the political-policy officers interviewed for this study do not represent a "public" or mass population where interest and information about political issues tend to be relatively low. Such deficiencies have been demonstrated to coincide with the failure of domestic and foreign policy beliefs to cohere.[31] On the contrary, our respondents are an elite group characterized by unusual political sophistication. It is because of this that one may anticipate they will manifest belief systems which can incorporate viewpoints on quite a variety of political issues.[32]

The point now has been reached where we can address ourselves to the main task of this chapter—to test the proposition that political-military officers are more hard-line in their foreign policy beliefs than are their counterparts in the Foreign Service. Certainly, the "military mind" concept contends that such a divergence is real. A similar expectation may be deduced from Huntington's description of the "professional military man."

> The military man normally views with alarm the potency and immediacy of the security threats to the state. As Lord Salisbury once remarked: "If you believe the doctors, nothing is wholesome: if you believe the theologians, nothing is innocent: if you believe the soldiers, nothing is safe." The military man recognizes the continuing character of threats to the state, but he also stresses the urgency of the current danger. . . .
> The concern of military men with the dangers to national security leads them to urge the enlarging and strengthening of the military forces available to protect the security of the state.[33]

31. For example, see Converse, "The Nature of Belief Systems," pp. 227–31; also, Campbell et al., *The American Voter*, pp. 194–209; and V. O. Key, Jr., *Public Opinion and American Democracy*, pp. 154–63.

32. Converse ("The Nature of Belief Systems") argues that, in general, the range of a person's belief system will directly vary according to his level of sophistication. For a similar finding, also see Herbert McClosky, *Political Inquiry: The Nature and Uses of Survey Research*, pp. 109–20. McClosky sets out to examine the "personality and attitude correlates of foreign policy orientation." Like so many other analysts, he unfortunately restricts his attention to a consideration of the "isolationist-nonisolationist distinction." I feel that this research focus is not nearly as relevant today as the distinguishing of viewpoints concerning such important issues as Communism, ACD, and nonalignment.

33. *The Soldier and the State*, pp. 66–67.

Another illustration involving the political thinking of military officers is provided by Lyons in his reporting of some remarks made by Senator Fulbright.

> In the summer of 1961, Senator J. W. Fulbright attacked the participation of a large number of military officers in the activities of right wing political groups. In his memorandum on the "propaganda activities of military personnel," the Senator asserted that "the philosophy of the [right wing] programs is representative of a substantial element of military thought and has great appeal to the military mind."[34]

A further comment on the relative viewpoints of military and Foreign Service officers is offered by the contrasting contentions of Horowitz, and Monsen and Cannon. The first author states that "there is no question that the State Department . . . has become the focus of disarmament and settlement in this country."[35] Monsen and Cannon report that "the military has been very skeptical about the ending of atomic tests [and that] they believe that this type of curb on the military could endanger United States' security."[36]

Our findings on the question of the relative political beliefs of military officers and FSOs are presented in table 37. The reader will observe that previously stated expectations are confirmed–political-military officers are revealed to be significantly more hard-line than political-FSOs. One-quarter of the former group are contained within the most extreme hard-line category. Another 43% are included within the adjacent moderate hard-line category. This distribution contrasts sharply with that of the FSO where nearly three-fourths of the respondents are found within the two non-hard-line classes. Needless to say, analogous dissimilarities between the two samples are manifest regarding the three dimensions of political belief, that is, anti-Communism, ACD, and non-

34. "The Military Mind," p. 19.
35. Irving Louis Horowitz, *The War Game: Studies of the New Civilian Militarists*, p. 31.
36. R. Joseph Monsen, Jr., and Mark W. Cannon, *The Makers of Public Policy: American Power Groups and Their Ideologies*, p. 295.

TABLE 37

FOREIGN POLICY BELIEFS

BELIEF	MILITARY		FSO		TOTAL
	%	N	%	N	%
Hard-line	26	15	8	3	19
	43	25	22	8	35
	19	11	38	14	26
Non-hard-line	12	7	32	12	20
Total	100%	58	100%	37	100%
Statistics	$\chi^2(3)=14.500/P=.01$ Gamma$=.544/P=.01$				

alignment.[37] In sum, our findings lend empirical support to the contention that political-military officers and political-FSOs may be distinguished attitudinally, and that the direction of the differences between them consists of the military manifesting a more hard-line perspective (i.e., one with anti-Communism–absolutist idea-elements) than FSOs.

Having stated this conclusion, we immediately are confronted with the obvious query: Why does this difference emerge? The sources of the revealed divergence in political belief no doubt are varied. It indeed would be surprising if a single factor could account for all, or nearly all, of the attitudinal diversity we have uncovered. We could, of course, speculate about which variables might be relevant and which probably are unimportant. But such a discussion would not begin to settle the issue. Consequently, let us take another road and proceed directly to an empirical investigation of the question.

37. Respectively: $\chi^2(1) = 3.808/P = .10$ and Gamma $= .405/P = 10$; $\chi^2(1) = 8.4585/P = .01$ and Gamma $= .559/P = .01$; and $\chi^2(1) = 6.561/P = .01$ and Gamma $= .503/P = .05$.

CHAPTER 8

Why Political-Military Officers and Political-FSOs Differ with Respect to Foreign Policy Beliefs

Why are political-military officers more hard-line than political-FSOs. One way to respond to this question is to try to ascertain what else is different about these two groups of officers and to see if that other feature (or features) is significantly related to the manifesting of a hard-line belief system. The establishment of such a relationship may permit us to argue that the divergence in belief we have uncovered is due to some attribute difference occurring among the members of the two organizations, and if such compositional variations did not exist, attitudinal dissimilarities of the type we have found would not be evident. It was the anticipation of such a search for possible correlates of foreign policy beliefs that led us to consider the variables introduced in chapters 3–6. To reiterate a point made earlier, it is our feeling, based upon an examination of the literature, that either social background characteristics, religiosity, political orientation, or cognitive style, or some combination of these attributes, is linked with the articulation of political beliefs. Previous analysis has shown that variables of the first type are not related to any of the other three, and that the latter are highly interrelated, so that religious officers tend also to be RepCon and doctrinaire. Furthermore, political-military officers and political-FSOs differ regarding their religiosity, political orientation, and cognitive style, whereas they do not with respect to social background characteristics. With these empirical findings in mind, let us now see which of the above attributes are related to foreign policy beliefs.

The data presented in table 38 reveal that none of the social background variables is associated with foreign policy beliefs. Knowing an officer's place of birth, geographical origins, and so on does not help us to understand why his beliefs are hard-line rather

TABLE 38

RELATIONSHIP OF FOREIGN POLICY BELIEFS AND VARIABLES PERTAINING TO SOCIAL ORIGINS, RELIGIOSITY, POLITICAL ORIENTATION, AND COGNITIVE STYLE

	STATISTICS	
	$\chi^2=$	Gamma=
Beliefs and:		
Place of birth	2.020	
Geographical background	.728	
Size of hometown	1.760	.218
Status of father's occupation	.037	.043
Educational level	.048	.046
Religious affiliation	.000	.000
Denominational status	1.146	.287
The Military only		
Old versus newtimers	3.535*	.500*
Service affiliation	2.485	
Academy versus nonacademy ...	.021	−.045
Foreign Service only		
New versus oldtimers	.064	.091
Non-Ivy versus Ivy League	.276	.212
Religiosity	8.007†	.544†
Political orientation	11.301†	.618†
Cognitive style	12.983†	.661†

* $P = .10$; † $P = .01$; all others: $P = NS$.

than non-hard-line. This circumstance—together with the fact that social background attributes additionally are not related to religiosity, political orientation, and cognitive style, variables which now are observed to be significantly associated with foreign policy beliefs—enables us to eliminate them from further consideration. Apparently social background characteristics are not relevant to our subject.[1]

1. "The variables which have little or no effect on defence and foreign

The above has an important implication for the effect of changes in social composition. In recent decades, some emphasis has been given to broadening the geographical and class base of the military establishment and Foreign Service. For example, the desire to increase the proportion of new FSOs coming from other than the northeastern United States has been an important part of several reorganization plans submitted to the Foreign Service. The question is raised whether greater social heterogeneity would result in these organizations subsequently exhibiting different attitudinal profiles. Our analysis indicates that such a shift in belief is improbable, at least with respect to the political-policy parts of Defense and the Foreign Service. In other words, "democratization" in the form of organizational membership becoming more representative regarding social origins should not lead to their membership also becoming significantly more or less hard-line, an aspect of what we previously have called "interest representativeness."

Other important information provided by table 38 is contained in the last three correlations reported. The reader will observe that religiosity, political orientation, and cognitive style are strongly related to the manifesting of foreign policy beliefs. Moreover, the positive Gamma coefficients indicate that the direction of each of the relationships is as we expected: religious, RepCon, and doctrinaire officers tend also to be hard-line. Thus, the data suggest that if the political-policy parts of Defense and State had similar proportions of religious, RepCon, and doctrinaire officers, they additionally would exhibit more similar foreign policy belief profiles. Put somewhat differently, the fact that the military sample contains relatively more religious, RepCon, and doctrinaire individuals means it will also contain relatively more hard-liners.

This is shown to be the case when the relationship between the

policy attitudes are: age, sex, income, social status, military experience and personal suffering as a result of war, place of residence (big city, small town or country), economic concerns about disarmament, ethnic origin (French or English-Canadian)" (Jerome Laulight, "Canadian Foreign Policy Attitudes: Some Major Conclisions," *International Social Science Journal* 17 [1965]:482). Also see Putney and Middleton, "Some Factors Associated with Student Acceptance or Rejection of War," pp. 660–61.

variables of organizational affiliation and foreign policy belief is examined after respondents are divided into two subgroups according to whether they are or are not predominantly religious-RepCon-doctrinaire (i.e., those officers who possess either two or all three of these three related attributes). Subsequent analysis reveals that no relationship is evident between organizational affiliation and foreign policy belief when only predominantly nonreligious-DemLib-nondoctrinaire respondents are considered, whereas among members of the other subgroup, the probability that a relationship exists is not especially high.[2] These results derived from the attempt to control for the effects of religiosity, political orientation, and cognitive style should be compared with the dramatic intersample difference indicated in table 37.

The relationship we have uncovered between religiosity, political orientation, cognitive style, and political beliefs is not surprising, for it is, in general, consistent with analogous findings reported elsewhere. For example, Rokeach, in a section of his book entitled "Ideological Content versus Ideological Structure," states the following conclusion:

> When we view all the findings presented in this chapter, they indicate that we have on the whole succeeded in our aims to formulate and to measure general authoritarianism and intolerance. Nevertheless, the data also stubbornly suggest that people to the right of center are somewhat more prone to authoritarianism and intolerance than people to the left of center. The dogmatism scores show slight but consistent positive correlations with conservatism. So do the opinionation scores. Also, the dogmatism scores correlate more highly with right than with left opinionation.[3]

In his study of the "Authoritarian Personality and Foreign Policy," Levinson reports as follows:

> There is a gradually accumulating body of evidence concerning the kinds of personal characteristics that tend to be associated with preference for a strongly nationalistic viewpoint. . . .
> The individual's approach to the external, social world will in significant

2. The respective coefficients are $\chi^2(1) = 1.221/P = $ NS, and, when corrected for continuity, $\chi^2(1) = 3.459/P = .10$.
3. *The Open and Closed Mind*, pp. 125–26.

degree reflect his approach to himself—his self-conceptions, character traits, modes of dealing with inner conflict, and the like. A corollary hypothesis in the present case is that an autocratic approach to problems of social orization will most often be found within an authoritarian personality structure. . . . The general conclusion that seems warranted by the various clinical, survey, and other studies is that personal authoritarianism constitutes an important inner source (though by no means the only source) of the disposition toward nationalism and related ideologies. . . . Various political and religious groupings were found to differ in their average degree of nationalism. The Republicans had a significantly higher (more nationalistic) mean score than the Democrats or the independents. . . . In the case of religious attendance (regardless of affiliation), those who attend service weekly had [a] mean of 36.2 [a relatively high nationalistic score]; those who attend occasionally, 30.9; and the non-attenders, 25.3. Findings of this sort have been obtained in a large number of surveys which used various types of items and scales.[4]

Conclusions generally similar in nature to our results also are presented by Rosenberg in his examination of American public opinion on cold-war issues. He says that the "self-avowed liberal-conservative" variable is significantly connected with "the degree to which most hard-line items are accepted or rejected. In all these comparisons the self-designated liberals are more questioning and rejecting of the Cold-War consensus. . . . There can be little question that ten to fifteen years of exposure to containment and deterrence ideology have provided the authoritarian with a presently stable channelling of his character-based needs toward the goal of victory in the Cold War and toward a stance that disdains conciliation and disarmament as a kind of cowardly yielding."[5]

4. Daniel J. Levinson, "Authoritarian Personality and Foreign Policy," in *War: Studies from Psychology, Sociology, and Anthropology*, eds. Leon Bramson and George W. Goethals, pp. 140–43. Another form of association between personality structure and political viewpoint is proposed in a succinctly stated remark attributed to Herman Kahn: "People tend to see the Russians in terms of their personalities; a bureaucratic rigid type would see them as bureaucratic and rigid and an aggressive person would see them as aggressive. . . . You might sum it up by saying the right wing has an enemy, I have an opponent and the peace movement has a misguided friend" (Arthur Herzog, *The War-Peace Establishment*, p. 81).

5. "Images in Relation to the Policy Process," pp. 320, 327. Rosenberg also states that ideological identification (i.e., what he calls self-avowed liberals versus conservatives) is a considerably more potent predictor of cold-

In a later statement on the same theme, Rosenberg also adds "that 'religiosity' in general is associated with the hard-line approach. Churchgoers, self-described believers, whatever their denomination, are more hard-line than those who are detached from religious institutions."[6] Numerous other studies may be cited which offer evidence that supports the pattern of interrelationships described above.[7]

Establishing that religiosity, political orientation, and cognitive style are significantly related to foreign policy beliefs certainly is critical to understanding why political-military officers are more hard-line than political-FSOs. Yet this is not all we wish to know. We additionally want to ascertain the relative predictive potency of these three attributes. More concretely, if we had to predict whether an officer is or is not hard-line and we could be provided with only one bit of information about him, should we choose to know if he is or is not religious, or what his political orientation is, or how doctrinaire he is? Put somewhat differently, we are asking how powerful these three attribute variables relatively are as predictors of foreign policy belief. Needless to say, unraveling and identifying their respective predictive potencies can be a knotty problem.

---

war beliefs than is party identification: "A close examination of recent studies on Cold-War attitudes reveals only a few differences between Democrats and Republicans and these are of a rather limited and unimpressive order" (pp. 318–19). A secondary analysis of our data showed it to support this proposition. For our respondents, ideological identification is strongly associated with foreign policy beliefs (P = .01 for both χ^2 and Gamma), whereas party identification is not (P very slightly exceeded .10 with respect to Gamma and approached .25 with respect to χ^2).

6. "Attitude Change and Foreign Policy in the Cold War Era," p. 157.

7. Among them are Putney and Middleton, "Some Factors Associated with Student Acceptance or Rejection of War"; Bjorn Christiansen, *Attitudes towards Foreign Affairs as a Function of Personality*; Charles D. Farris, "Selected Attitudes on Foreign Affairs as Correlates of Authoritarianism and Political Anomie," *Journal of Politics* 22(1960):50–67; Peter Blau, "Orientation of College Students toward International Relations," *American Journal of Sociology* 59(1953):205–14; and Howard Leventhal, Robert L. Jacobs, and Nijole Z. Kudirka, "Authoritarianism, Ideology, and Political Candidate Choice," *Journal of Abnormal and Social Psychology* 69(1964):539–49.

If the reader will consult table 39, he will observe that the specific predictive powers of religiosity, political orientation, and cogni-

TABLE 39

RELATIVE POWER OF RELIGIOSITY, POLITICAL ORIENTATION AND COGNITIVE STYLE WITH RESPECT TO PREDICTING FOREIGN POLICY BELIEFS

Symbols: R—Religiosity
P—Political Orientation
C—Cognitive Style
B—Foreign Policy Belief

$\text{Lambda}_{B \cdot P} = .262$ $\text{Lambda}_{B \cdot RP} = .349$
$_{B \cdot P} = .302$ $_{B \cdot RC} = .372$
$_{B \cdot C} = .302$ $_{B \cdot PC} = .326$
$\text{Lambda}_{B \cdot RPC} = .372$

NOTE: The statistic used in this table, Lambda, was introduced by Goodman and Kruskal, "Measures of Association for Cross Classifications," pp. 732–64. "Lambda" is an "index of predictive association" that "shows the proportional reduction in the probability of error afforded by specifying Aj. If the information about the A category does not reduce the probability of error at all, the index is zero, and one can say that there is no predictive association. On the other hand, if the index is 1.00 no error is made given the Aj classification" (William L. Hays, *Statistics for Psychologists*, p. 608).

tive style are substantial and approximately equal in degree. Each of the three considerably reduces the probability of error with respect to predicting whether officers are or are not hard-line. Equally interesting is the rather small incremental increase in predictive power that is achieved when pairs of predictor variables are considered. This is especially true with respect to political orientation and cognitive style. They are nearly as effective individually as when they are combined with one of the other two. Moreover, we see that all three taken together give us hardly more information than any pair of them.

This pattern suggests that religiosity, political orientation, and cognitive style have some quality in common, a quality that is associated with the possession of a hard-line viewpoint. Each of the three interrelated attributes appears to reflect a different aspect of that fundamental quality. Together, religiosity, political orientation, and cognitive style form an "attribute set" (or status set if you prefer) that is critical to understanding (and predicting) the varying foreign policy beliefs of political-military officers and political-FSOs.

At this point, we should warn that it is not our intention to argue that the three components of this attribute set are the only or even the major determiners of foreign policy belief. On the contrary, our analysis has succeeded only in uncovering several of many possible predictors of belief. Much unexplained variance obviously still exists. Yet the degree to which probability of predictive error is reduced by referring to religiosity, political orientation, and cognitive style gives us confidence that important correlates of foreign policy belief have been identified.

The above findings permit us to comment about the likelihood of officers who exhibit hard-line beliefs changing to the contrary viewpoint, and vice versa. This question is similar to the one raised many times in earlier chapters concerning the possible impact of socialization. If socialization effects were operating—that is, if exposure to one or both organizational structures is influencing belief—we would expect to observe differences in attitude between the various ranks within each institution (e.g., between what we have called newtimers and oldtimers). Furthermore, it seems reasonable to suppose that attitudinal change occurring under the influence of socialization should be in the direction of making one's belief more consistent with those prevailing within the organization. Since a hard-line opinion climate is evident within the military group, socialization, if operating, should result in the oldtimer stratum containing a relatively greater percentage of hard-line officers (and also being more attitudinally homogeneous) than the newtimer one. For the same reason, the opposite trend should be evident if socialization were occurring within the non-hard-line dominated Foreign Service.[8]

Let us briefly review now the evidence available concerning

8. The return to a point made earlier, the impact of selective promotion, if operating in a way so that its effects are contrary to that of socialization, could obscure the influence of the latter in our analysis. But this circumstance seems very unlikely for reasons already mentioned. The existence of biased promotion practices would, if anything, reinforce differences between the newtimer and oldtimer groups, not reduce or eliminate them.

whether or not the attitudes of officers are likely to change with continued membership in their respective organizations. Looking first at table 38, we see that no variation in foreign policy beliefs is evident among the FSOs. Within both the newtimer and oldtimer groups, the non-hard-line viewpoint is dominant. In the case of political-military officers, the possibility that oldtimers actually are relatively more hard-line than newtimers is barely supported by the relevant data ($P = .10$).

The significant relationships existing between religiosity, political orientation, cognitive style, and foreign policy beliefs revealed earlier are also relevant to the question of "socialization effects." The reader will recall that we concluded at the end of chapters 4, 5, and 6 that prerecruitment is the primary (though certainly not exclusive) reason for the military and Foreign Service manifesting divergent distributions regarding these attributes. For example, nearly all the officers reported that they had not changed their party or ideological identifications since entering their respective organizations. But now we also know that religiosity, political orientation, and cognitive style have considerable "power" with respect to predicting whether an officer is or is not hard-line. The query is then posed: Is it likely that the foreign policy beliefs of political-military officers and political-FSOs will undergo noticeable change when powerful predictors of it exhibit such stability in commitment? It seems far more reasonable to suppose that religiosity, political orientation, cognitive style, *and* foreign policy belief all exhibit stability.

Another and important piece of evidence is furnished by Lovell in his study, "The Professional Socialization of the West Point Cadet." He interviewed students of various classes at West Point and Dartmouth, trying to ascertain whether the military academy has a critical impact upon the strategic perspectives and professional orientations of cadets. The three strategic perspectives he conceptualized, pacifist, pragmatic, and absolutist, were partially described in the previous chapter. His findings in general support our inferences concerning the relative potency of the prerecruitment and socialization hypotheses in accounting for the political beliefs of military officers. West Point and Dartmouth students were revealed to differ substantially in their strategic perspectives, with the former group more often tending toward the absolutist approach.[9] Lovell's remarks regarding the influence of the academy upon the viewpoints of cadets are also pertinent.

> There were many reasons to question the idea of the military academy as a total institution with a comprehensive impact of implanting traditional military values on its student body, although this idea may have been more applicable in the past. The empirical results of this study clearly do not support a conclusion of comprehensive impact.
> During an academy education, the cadet experiences only slight changes in his orientation toward his professional role and in the perspectives with which he views the use of force in international relations. Even more important, there is no single attitude pattern on these matters, either at the beginning or at the end of his four-year education.[10]

The pattern described by Lovell is consistent with our analysis in deemphasizing the relative importance of postrecruitment features as an explanation for the attitudinal distributions which have been uncovered. A more persuasive case can be made for the proposition that Defense and the Foreign Service, because of the types of organization they are, attract different types of individuals. People will seek out and attempt to join organizations with "belief climates" compatible with their own. Consequently, the military establishment will tend to appeal to religious-RepCon-doctrinaire individuals whose political beliefs are hard-line, because its mission and character is understood and acknowledged by prospective candidates. Thus, it is not so much a matter of "roles influencing beliefs" as "people with certain beliefs seeking out certain roles.[11]

---

9. An interesting side aspect regarding the selection of Dartmouth for the purposes of comparison is that this Ivy League school is precisely the type of educational institution that can be expected to contribute a disproportionate number of candidates to the Foreign Service.

10. P. 120.

11. Abrahamsson, in "Military Professionalization and Estimates on the Probability of War," after reviewing Lovell's study and other research contributions concludes that "from the recruitment base consisting of young men there are flows of applicants to the military profession and to other occupa-

To summarize, then, relatively more political-military officers than political-FSOs are hard-line in their international political thinking in part as a consequence of the political-policy part of Defense containing relatively more individuals who are religious-RepCon-doctrinaire, attributes that are critically associated with the expression of foreign policy belief. The primary reason that the military group contains more officers who are religious-Rep Con-doctrinaire appears to be prerecruitment features rather than recruitment or postrecruitment ones. The fact that most newcomers already have attitudes compatible with the organization's dominant belief structure makes it unlikely that many of them will change their beliefs while still an officer. Consequently, the political-policy subsystem of Defense should remain more hard-line than its corresponding part within the Foreign Service.

tions. The flows are primarily the products of self-selective processes; together with the selection employed in the screening process this leads to a predominance of individuals with attitudes congenial to the military normative system among the actually recruited (conservatism rather than radicalism, authoritarianism rather than egalitarianism, activist rather than pacifist outlook, etc." (p. 42).

CHAPTER 9

A Brief Summary and Implications for Future Research

As stated in chapter 1, the primary substantive focus of this study is the question of whether officials occupying positions within the political-policy parts of the Departments of State and Defense have similar or dissimilar foreign policy beliefs. Subsequent analysis revealed that the political viewpoints of the members of the two organizations actually are dissimilar; that is, significantly more political-military officers than political-FSO respondents could be described as having a hard-line perspective. This empirical finding is quite consistent with popularly held stereotypical notions as typified by the use of the term military mind.

An effort additionally was made to ascertain why political-military officers and political-FSOs differ with respect to their foreign policy beliefs. In brief, the sources of the attitudinal divergency were traced to the fact that military respondents tended to be also more religious, RepCon, and doctrinaire than their counterparts in the State Department, and that the three attributes of religiosity, political orientation, and cognitive style are associated with whether an officer does or does not manifest a hard-line perspective. This pattern of interrelationships emerged in spite of the fact that the members of these two groups were shown to possess essentially similar social backgrounds.

Secondary analysis indicated that the observed intersample differences are primarily the result of applicant self-selection and other forces occurring prior to recruitment. In all likelihood, each

Summary and Implications

organization recruits from a candidate pool that is already biased. Qualified religious-RepCon-doctrinaire and hard-line individuals in disproportionate number are attracted to the military establishment probably because of the ethos with which that service is identified; for the same reason, a different sort of person is attracted to the Foreign Service. Hence, neither the military establishment nor the Foreign Service needs to rely very much upon recruitment and promotion procedures that actively seek to filter out officers with deviant political views. Nor is it necessary for them to undertake widespread indoctrination of their officers in order to "bring them around" to the "right attitude."

In sum, the data provided suggest that the prerecruitment stage is the most critical of the three filter stages. The greatest differentiation of people appears to take place at this point in the process.[1] In order for an individual to present himself as a candidate for recruitment, he must satisfy certain objective requirements (i.e., recruitment rules) set by the organization (e.g., level of formal education achieved) and want to become one of its members. The objective requirements that are stated will eliminate immediately a good part of the general population from consideration because they appear not to possess the credentials necessary for candidate eligibility. The second aspect pertaining to self-selection (i.e., the motivation criterion) additionally will limit the number of persons who actually will present themselves as candidates. In other places, we have asserted that the ethos of an organization probably has an important influence upon self-selection by making the organization attractive to some (i.e., these persons perceive the organization's ethos and their own as compatible) and not attractive to others. This means, for instance, that few individuals who are not religious-RepCon-doctrinaire and hard-line will wish to become military careerists.[2] Consequently,

---

1. Unfortunately, we are not in a position to specify quantitative "transition functions" for each of the stages within the process model. The best we can do are ordinal-like statements of the "more than" and "less than" variety.

2. Once again, this does not mean that each and every individual who is religious-RepCon-doctrinaire and hard-line wants to pursue a military

the composition of the political-policy parts of State and Defense is both the product of differentiation occurring at several successive stages of a discernible selection process and, at the same time, affects the composition of what we have called the aspiring population, that very critical group of persons who say they wish to, and are qualified to, pursue a career in the Foreign Service or Defense Department.

At least three questions for future research are suggested by our discussion. The first and perhaps easiest to deal with is the historical question that directs attention at the relationship between the foreign policy beliefs (and cognitive style, etc.) of our respondents and the beliefs of their predecessors and successors. The analysis described here is essentially cross-sectional in design and thus does not directly concern itself with this issue. On the other hand, through the selective use of retrospective questions and the device of dividing the two samples into so-called newtimer and oldtimer subgroups, evidence of a quasi-longitudinal nature is generated. This indirect approach has yielded results which suggest that the general difference in belief observed to exist between State and Defense Department political-policy officers is to an important extent self-perpetuating. The condition of self-perpetuation is strongly implied by the feedback pattern suggested in the influence of the present characteristics of the organization upon "career choice." Therefore, we expect that if one or the other of our samples is compared with either its predecessor or successor group regarding the variables discussed in this book, no significant difference between them would be revealed. There is little doubt that the likelihood of uncovering a contrary finding would increase

career. Other influences in addition to mere perceived compatibility of political views, and so on, are necessary before an individual is sufficiently motivated to actually want to become an applicant. Moreover, there are many alternative nongovernmental institutions (e.g., the police) that probably are also attractive to religious-RepCon-doctrinaire and hard-line individuals. Unfortunately, we are not in a position to specify which individuals with the above attributes will attempt to pursue a military (or Foreign Service) career and which will join functionally equivalent institutions. Again we state, however, that our self-imposed task primarily consists of identifying the consequences of such career choices.

Summary and Implications

as our respondents are compared with groups increasingly further removed in time from their own.[3] What we then would wish to know is the attrition rate concerning the propensity of each organization to perpetuate its ethos. In other words, how far into the past or future do we have to go before significant differences are found to exist between our respondents and a political-policy officer group of another era with whom they are being compared? Moreover, it would be interesting to attempt to identify those factors that might undermine continuity of foreign policy beliefs between successive groups of political-policy officers within State or Defense.

In addition to such historically oriented research, cross-cultural investigation is required. All our respondents are American officials. We do not know, and cannot know on the basis only of the data we have collected, whether findings similar to those contained in this book would emerge if replication of this study were undertaken in another nation-state; i.e., if non-American political-military officers and political-FSOs or personnel with analogous positions, are compared according to their foreign policy beliefs, cognitive style, and so on. Of further interest is the interrelationship of social background, religiosity, political orientation, and belief variables within other national contexts. It obviously cannot be assumed that the pattern described here also is valid elsewhere.[4]

The third and final question for future research is the relationship between beliefs and behavior. Quite obviously, the utility of the findings contained in this book is enhanced to the degree to which beliefs and behavior are in fact linked. In chapter 1 we stated that our analysis supposes such an association and, as Smith put it, that *"expressed* opinions are, after all, a form of behavior, and opinions *held* are but one type of behavioral disposition." A simi-

---

3. In practical terms, this suggests research of an on-going type that compares present officers with future ones as they are recruited and promoted.

4. See Donald D. Searing, "The Comparative Study of Elite Socialization," *Comparative Political Studies* 1(1969):471–500, for a provocative beginning effort to research these questions.

lar position is taken by Edinger and Searing when they affirm that "while attitudinal and behavioral dimensions are not necessarily identical or equivalent—other variables, such as situational factors may intervene—elite attitudes undoubtedly represent an important component of elite behavior."[5] Evidence to support the claim that political beliefs and behavior are associated among elite members of the polity is provided by James A. Robinson who, in his study *Congress and Foreign Policy-Making*, finds "the correlation between answers received to this one attitudinal question [concerning disposition toward recent American foreign policy] and the votes of the same Congressman on the 27 Senate and 19 House roll calls on foreign policy issues in the 85th Congress was 0.41 (significant at the 0.01 level of analysis). This correlation between attitudes (what Congressmen told us in the interview) and behavior (how they voted on a real issue) should probably be regarded as a rather high one."[6] Moreover, experimental evidence is available that also suggests that political beliefs and behavior are linked. For example, Lutzker conducted a study in which the general hypothesis was whether "performance in an experimental situation in which both cooperation and competition were possible could be predicted on the basis of the subjects' views regarding international cooperation. It was predicted that the subjects who were internationalistically oriented would tend to be cooperative, whereas isolationists would tend to be competitive." He reports

5. Lewis J. Edinger and Donald D. Searing, "Social Background in Elite Analysis: A Methodological Inquiry," *American Political Science Review* 61(1967):428.
6. James A. Robinson, *Congress and Foreign Policy-Making*, rev. ed., p. 160. Robinson adds that "the general topic of the relation of attitude to behavior is surprisingly largely unexplored. While there have been many roll-call studies of legislative behavior, there have been fewer studies of attempts to relate attitude to behavior in legislative situations." McClosky reached a similar conclusion regarding "political inquiry" generally: "Surveys are repeatedly used to measure beliefs (political and others), but the relation of beliefs to action has received little attention. Although beliefs are unquestionably important clues to how people act, they are not perfect indicators of action, and the exact connection between the two must therefore be explored if we are to achieve a more scientific understanding of politics" (*Political Inquiry*, pp. 50–51).

that "a scale of political opinions can be used to predict behavior in a decision-making situation. . . . Evidence has been presented here to show that internationalists differ from isolationists in at least two important ways: (1) they are more cooperative, and (2) they are more reluctant to abandon efforts at cooperation."[7] On the other hand, after an extensive overview of the psychology literature, Wicker states a somewhat contrary conclusion. He finds that "taken as a whole, these studies suggest that it is considerably more likely that attitudes will be unrelated or only slightly related to overt behaviors than that attitudes will be closely related to actions."[8]

If beliefs and behavior in fact are significantly correlated, then our findings suggest that the organizational composition of foreign policy "decisional units" that include military officers and FSOs must be taken into consideration when the behavioral outcomes of such interactions are examined. However, it would be misleading, of course, to think that the relationship between object-oriented beliefs and behavior is direct and simple. The linkage between the two no doubt is about as complex as the linkage between belief and its various antecedents. For one thing, the correlation between beliefs and behavior may be affected by the confounding effects of "situation." For example, particular occasions may exist that would strongly encourage one to suppress "personal philosophy" and act upon other grounds (e.g., role prescriptions). In such a case, the observed correlation between object-oriented beliefs and behavior would approach zero. Yet it seems fair to suppose that instances of the latter type—or the contrary, where the two are nearly perfectly correlated—are relatively rare in practice and, more often than not, that behavior is the result of the joint influence of both situation and object-oriented attitudes.[9]

7. Daniel R. Lutzker, "Internationalism as a Predictor of Cooperative Behavior," *Journal of Conflict Resolution* 4(1960):429–30.

8. Allan W. Wicker, "Attitude versus Actions: The Relationship of Verbal and Overt Behavioral Responses to Attitude Objects," *Journal of Social Issues* 25(Autumn, 1969):65.

9. See Milton Rokeach, *Beliefs, Attitudes, and Values: A Theory of Or-*

If this is true, then the really critical question is the one that asks how varying attitudes regarding object and situation, individually and simultaneously, affect behavior.

With answers to this and the other research questions identified earlier, we feel scholars will have begun to understand and predict the foreign policy behavior of international political actors.

ganization and Change, especially chapters 6 and 7. For a related discussion concerning "actor dispensability"—that is, the question of "under what circumstances . . . do different actors (placed in common situations) vary in their behavior and under what circumstances is behavior uniform?"—see Fred I. Greenstein, "The Impact of Personality on Politics: An Attempt to Clear Away Underbrush," American Political Science Review 61(1967):635 ff. In another article, Greenstein conceptualizes the relationship between beliefs, situational circumstances, and behavior in the following way: "Politics . . . is a matter of human behavior, and behavior—in the familiar formulation of Lewin and others—is a function of both the environmental situations in which actors find themselves and the personal psychological predispositions they bring to those situations" ("Personality and Politics: Problems of Evidence, Inference, and Conceptualization," American Behavioral Scientist 11[1967]:39). For further discussion of the relationship between beliefs and behavior, see Martin Fishbein, "The Relationships between Beliefs, Attitudes, and Behavior," in Shel Feldman, ed., Cognitive Consistency: Motivational Antecedents and Behavioral Consequents, pp. 199–223; and McClosky, Political Inquiry, pp. 50–52.

APPENDIX

Interview Schedule

I. The first group of questions concerns your views about the nature of international political relations. First of all:
   A. What do you consider to be the most important international political issues in this generation?
   B. For many years statesmen and negotiators from both the East and West have been offering alternative schemes for arms control and disarmament.
      1. First of all, do you think arms control and disarmament are questions worth discussing?
      2. Relative to other foreign policy concerns, how much attention should these proposals get?
      3. Do you think arms control and disarmament are currently receiving the proper amount of attention from the United States government, or should they get more attention, or less attention?
      4. The United States and Russia recently concluded a bilateral agreement banning nuclear testing in the atmosphere. Do you approve or disapprove of this East-West agreement?
      5. What is your feeling about further arms control agreements between the United States and Russia?
   C. Many countries present themselves as being nonaligned with respect to the cold war; what generally is your attitude toward these nations and such a foreign policy?
   D. There has been much discussion concerning the extent to which the Soviet Union, China, and the eastern European countries differ on matters of strategy and ideology.
      1. Do you think genuine differences exist?
      2. How serious are they to the future of the Soviet community?
   E. What do you believe to be the primary foreign policy goal of the Soviet Union: in other words, what are they really after?

F. Which of the following statements most closely represents your viewpoint: The U.S.S.R. in its general international strategy can be primarily characterized as (1) becoming a consolidationist "have" power aiming primarily at maintaining its current holdings; (2) tending toward being a consolidationist power but still aggressive on those few occasions when the risks are low; (3) generally aggressive, but in the process of becoming less so; (4) aggressive, but may change in the future; or (5) implacably aggressive with little sign of change.

G. What influence, if any, do you think the cold war has had on the values, institutions, and ways of thinking of Americans concerning matters other than foreign policy and international politics?

H. Do you think American Communists should be allowed to run for and hold public political office?

I. Some critics say that the government is too involved in domestic economic affairs. On the other hand, others argue for a more active role for government. How do you feel on this issue?

II. The second group of questions is designed to furnish information about your background and career.

A. Personal data:
1. *By observation*:
    a) Sex of respondent.
    b) Race of respondent.
2. What is your date of birth?
3. Where were you born? *If born in United States,* Which state?
4. *Not asked of Negroes or foreign born*: Were both of your parents born in this country?
    a) *If answer is no*: Which country was your father born in? Which country was your mother born in?
    b) *If answer is yes*: Do you remember what country your family came from originally on your father's side?
5. What kind of work did your father do for a living while you were growing up?
6. What part of the United States did you grow up in? Which state or states?
7. Were you brought up mostly on a farm, in a town, in a small city, in a large city, or on a military installation?
8. Did you finish college?
    a) *If answer is yes*:
        (1) What college or academies did you attend?
        (2) Where is it (are they) located?
        (3) Do you have a college degree?
            (a) What degree(s) did you receive?

Appendix

        (b) At what college(s) did you get your degree(s)?
     (4) What were your major fields of study in college?
  b) *If answer is no*: How many years of schooling did you complete?
9. Is your church preference Protestant, Catholic, Jewish, or other (specify)?
  a) *If Protestant*: What church is that?
  b) *If some church preference*: Would you say that you go to church regularly, often, or seldom?
     (1) How religious, then, would you say you are?

B. Political orientation data.
1. Generally speaking, do you usually think of yourself as a Republican, a Democrat, an independent, or what?
  a) *If Republican or Democrat*:
     (1) Would you call yourself a strong Republican (or Democrat) or a not very strong Republican (or Democrat)?
        1. Strong Democrat
        7. Strong Republican
        2. Not very strong Democrat
        6. Not very strong Republican
     (2) Was there ever a time when you thought of yourself as a Republican (or Democrat) rather than a Democrat (or Republican)?
        1. Yes, a Democrat   2. Yes, a Republican
        5. No, never. *Skip to question II.B.2.*
        (a) *If answer is yes* (i.e., 1 or 2, not 5):
           i) When did you change?
           ii) What was the main thing that made you change?
  b) *If independent or other*:
     (1) Do you think of yourself as closer to the Republican or Democrat party?
        3. Yes, Democrat   5. Yes, Republican
        4. No, neither
        (a) *If answer is no* (i.e., 4, not 3 or 5): Was there ever a time when you thought of yourself as a Democrat or Republican? Which party was that?
           1. Yes, Democrat   2. Yes, Republican
           5. No, never. *Skip to question II.B.2.*
        (b) *If closer to Democrats or Republicans* (i.e.,

3 or 5, not 4): Was there ever a time when you thought of yourself as closer to the Republican (or Democrat) party instead of the Democrat (or Republican) party?
1. Yes, Democrat   2. Yes, Republican
5. No, never. *Skip to question II.B.2.*
(c) *If answer is yes to either (a) or (b)* (i.e., 1 or 2, not 5):
  i) When did you change?
  ii) What was the main thing that made you change?

2. Do you remember when you were growing up whether your father was very much interested in politics, somewhat interested, or didn't he pay much attention to it?
3. Did he think of himself mostly as a Democrat, as a Republican, or what? Specify.
4. Now how about your mother? When you were growing up was she very much interested in politics, somewhat interested, or didn't she pay much attention to it?
5. Did she think of herself mostly as a Democrat, as a Republican, or what? Specify.
6. Did you ever discuss politics with your friends or other relatives?
7. Did they mostly think of themselves as Democrats, Republicans, or what? Specify.
8. Generally speaking, do you usually think of yourself as a liberal, conservative, or independent?
   a) *If liberal or conservative:*
     (1) Would you call yourself a strong liberal (or conservative) or not a very strong liberal (or conservative)?
       1. Strong liberal
       7. Strong conservative
       2. Not very strong liberal
       6. Not very strong conservative
     (2) Was there ever a time when you thought of yourself as a liberal (or conservative) rather than a conservative (or liberal)?
       1. Yes, a liberal   2. Yes, a conservative
       5. No, never. *Skip to Question II.C.1.*
       (a) *If answer is yes* (i.e., 1 or 2, not 5):
         i) When did you change?
         ii) What was the main thing that made you change?

Appendix

    b) *If independent or other*:
       (1) Do you think of yourself as closer to liberals or conservatives?
          3. Yes, liberal   5. Yes, conservative
          4. No, neither
        (a) *If answer is no* (i.e., 4 not 3 or 5): Was there ever a time when you thought of yourself as a liberal or conservative? Which one was that?
          1. Yes, liberal   2. Yes, conservative
          5. No, never. *Skip to question II.C.1.*
        (b) *If closer to liberals or conservatives* (i.e., 3 or 5, not 4): Was there ever a time when you thought of yourself as closer to the liberal (or conservative) instead of the conservative (or liberal)?
          1. Yes, liberal   2. Yes, conservative
          5. No, never. *Skip to question II.C.1.*
        (c) *If answer is yes to either (a) or (b)* (i.e., 1 or 2, not 5):
          i) When did you change?
          ii) What was the main thing that made you change?

C. Career data.
    1. What is your current rank in the service?
    2. How long have you been an officer in the service?
    3. What is your current assignment or position in the service?
    4. How satisfied are you with your career choice?

III. The final group of questions concerns your personal philosophy and ways of doing things. I am going to read some statements people have made as their opinion on several topics, including their own characteristics. *Respondent receives cue card with the following information*:

Agree	*Disagree*
1. Agree a little.	1. Disagree a little.
2. Agree on the whole.	2. Disagree on the whole.
3. Agree very much.	3. Disagree very much.

We want your *personal* opinion of each statement. When I read each one, first tell me whether, in general, you agree or disagree with it; then tell me a number—1, 2, or 3—to indicate how strongly you agree or disagree with it.

A. Dogmatism Scale.
    1. Even though freedom of speech for all groups is a worthwhile goal, it is unfortunately necessary to restrict the freedom of certain political groups.

2. The highest form of government is a democracy and the highest form of democracy is a government run by those who are most intelligent.
3. The main thing in life is for a person to want to do something important.
4. Most people just don't know what's good for them.
5. Most of the ideas which get printed nowadays aren't worth the paper they are printed on.
6. The *present* is all too often full of unhappiness. It is only the *future* that counts.
7. To compromise with our political opponents is dangerous because it usually leads to the betrayal of our own side.
8. Most people just don't give a "damn" for others.
9. There are two kinds of people in this world: those who are for the truth and those who are against the truth.
10. In this complicated world of ours the only way we can know what's going on is to rely on leaders or experts who can be trusted.
11. My blood boils whenever a person stubbornly refuses to admit he's wrong.
12. Of all the different philosophies that exist in this world there is probably only one that is correct.
13. I'd like it if I could find someone who would tell me how to solve my personal problems.
14. It is only when a person devotes himself to an ideal or cause that life becomes meaningful.
15. Man on his own is a helpless and miserable creature.
16. It is often desirable to reserve judgment about what's going on until one has had a chance to hear the opinions of those one respects.
17. It is better to be a dead hero than to be a live coward.
18. The United States and Russia have just about nothing in common.
19. In a discussion I often find it necessary to repeat myself several times to make sure I am being understood.
20. While I don't like to admit this even to myself, my secret ambition is to become a great man, like Einstein or Beethoven or Shakespeare.

B. Rigidity Scale.
1. I prefer to stop and think before I act even on trifling matters.
2. I am a methodical person in whatever I do.
3. I prefer work that requires a great deal of attention to detail.
4. I often become so wrapped up in something I am doing that I find it difficult to turn my attention to other matters.

5. I often find myself thinking of the same tunes or phrases for days at a time.
6. I am always careful about my manner of dress.
7. I try to follow a program of life based on duty.
8. I have a work and study schedule that I follow carefully.
9. There is usually only one best way to solve most problems.
10. I always put on and take off my clothes in the same order.
11. I always finish tasks I start, even if they are not very important.
12. I usually check more than once to be sure that I have locked a door, put out the light, or something of the sort.
13. I think it is usually wise to do things in a conventional way.
14. I find it easy to stick to a certain schedule, once I have started it.
15. I usually find that my own way of attacking a problem is best, even though it doesn't always seem to work in the beginning.
16. I dislike to change my plans in the midst of an undertaking.
17. I have never done anything dangerous for the thrill of it.
18. I never miss going to church.
19. I usually maintain my own opinions even though many other people may have a different point of view.
20. I believe that promptness is a very important personality characteristic.
21. I am often the last person to give up trying to do a thing.
22. I do not enjoy having to adapt myself to new and unusual situations.

BIBLIOGRAPHY

Abrahamsson, Bengt. "Military Professionalization and Estimates on the Probability of War." In *Military Profession and Military Regimes: Commitments and Conflicts*, ed. Jacques van Doorn. The Hague: Mouton and Co., 1969. Pp. 35–51.

Abrams, Philip. "The Late Profession of Arms: A Study of Ambiguous Goals and Deteriorating Means in Britain," *European Journal of Sociology* 6(1965): 238–61.

Andrzejewski, Stanislau. *Military Organization and Society*. London: Routledge and Kegan Paul, 1954.

Argyris, Chris. *Some Causes of Organizational Ineffectiveness within the Department of State*. Washington, D.C.: Department of State, 1966.

Baldwin, Hanson. "The Military Move In," *Harper's Magazine* 195 (December, 1947): 481–89.

Barnes, William, and John Heath Morgan. *The Foreign Service of the United States: Origins, Development, and Functions*. Washington, D.C.: U.S. Government Printing Office, 1961.

Barnett, Correlli. "The Education of Military Elites." In *Governing Elites: Studies in Training and Selection*, edited by Rupert Wilkinson. New York: Oxford University Press, 1969. Pp. 193–214.

Belknap, George, and Angus Campbell. "Political Party Identification and Attitudes toward Foreign Policy," *Political Science Quarterly* 15(Winter, 1951–52): 601–23.

Berelson, Bernard R., and Gary A. Steiner. *Human Behavior: An Inventory of Scientific Findings*. New York: Harcourt, Brace and World, 1964.

Berelson, Bernard R., Paul F. Lazarsfeld, and William N. McPhee. *Voting: A Study of Opinion Formation in a Presidential Campaign*. Chicago: University of Chicago Press, 1954.

Blau, Peter. "Orientation of College Students toward International Relations," *American Journal of Sociology* 59(1953):205–14.

Bogue, Donald J. *The Population of the United States.* Glencoe, Ill.: The Free Press of Glencoe, 1959.

Boulding, Kenneth E. "National Images and International Systems," *Journal of Conflict Resolution* 3(June, 1959):120–31.

Brown, MacAllister, and John W. Masland. "Some Evidence on the 'Military Mind'." Unpublished manuscript, Dartmouth College, June, 1958.

Brown, Seyom. *The Faces of Power: Constancy and Change in United States Foreign Policy from Truman to Johnson.* New York: Columbia University Press, 1968.

Campbell, Angus, Philip E. Converse, Warren E. Miller, and Donald E. Stokes. *The American Voter.* New York: John Wiley and Sons, 1960.

Campbell, Donald T., and Thelma H. McCormack. "Military Experiences and Attitudes toward Authority," *American Journal of Sociology* 62(March, 1957):482–90.

Childs, J. Rives. *American Foreign Service.* New York: Henry Holt and Co., 1948.

Christiansen, Bjorn. *Attitudes towards Foreign Affairs as a Function of Personality.* Oslo: Oslo University Press, 1959.

Converse, Philip E. "The Nature of Belief Systems in Mass Publics." In *Ideology and Discontent*, edited by David E. Apter. New York: Free Press of Glencoe, 1964. Pp. 206–61.

Corson, John J., and Paul R. Shale. *Men near the Top.* Baltimore: Johns Hopkins Press, 1966.

D'Amato, Anthony A. "Psychological Constructs in Foreign Policy Prediction," *Journal of Conflict Resolution* 11(September, 1967): 294–311.

Davis, James A. *Undergraduate Career Decisions.* Chicago: Aldine Publishing Company, 1965.

Dawson, Richard E. "Political Socialization." In *Political Science Annual: An International Review*, edited by James A. Robinson. Indianapolis: The Bobbs-Merrill Co., 1966. 1:1–84.

Deutsch, Karl W. "External Influences on the Internal Behavior of States." In *Approaches to Comparative and International Politics*, edited by R. Barry Farrell. Evanston: Northwestern University Press, 1966. Pp. 5–26.

Deutsch, Karl W., Lewis J. Edinger, Roy C. Macridis, and Richard L. Merritt. *France, Germany and the Western Alliance: A Study of Elite Attitudes on European Integration and World Politics.* New York: Charles Scribner's Sons, 1967.

DiRenzo, Gordon J. "Professional Politicians and Personality Structures," *American Journal of Sociology* 73(September, 1967): 217–25.

Bibliography

Dobie, J. Frank. "Samples of the Military Mind," *Harper's Magazine* 193 (December, 1946):529–36.

Dornbusch, Sanford M. "The Military Academy as an Assimilating Institution," *Social Forces* 33(May, 1955):316–21.

Edinger, Lewis J. "Military Leaders and Foreign Policy-Making," *American Political Science Review* 57(June, 1963):392–405.

Edinger, Lewis J., and Donald D. Searing. "Social Background in Elite Analysis: A Methodological Inquiry," *American Political Science Review* 61(June, 1967):428–45.

Elder, Robert Ellsworth. *The Policy Machine: The Department of State and American Foreign Policy.* Syracuse: Syracuse University Press, 1960.

Eysenck, Hans Jurgen. *The Psychology of Politics.* New York: Frederick A. Praeger, 1955.

Farris, Charles D. "Selected Attitudes on Foreign Affairs as Correlates of Authoritarianism and Political Anomie," *Journal of Politics* 22(February, 1960):50–67.

Feld, Maury D. "Professionalism, Nationalism, and the Alienation of the Military." Paper presented to the Working Group on Armed Forces and Society at the Sixth Congress of Sociology, Evian, September, 1966.

Fensterwald, Bernard, Jr., "American 'Isolationism' and Expansionism." In *Human Behavior and International Politics,* edited by J. David Singer. Chicago: Rand McNally & Co., 1965. Pp. 243–58.

Fielder, Frances, and Godfrey Harris. *The Quest for Foreign Affairs Officers: Their Recruitment and Selection.* New York: Carnegie Endowment for International Peace, 1966.

Finer, S. E. *The Man on Horseback: The Role of the Military in Politics.* London: Pall Mall Press, 1962.

Fishbein, Martin. "The Relationships between Beliefs, Attitudes, and Behavior." In *Cognitive Consistency: Motivational Antecedents and Behavioral Consequents,* edited by Shel Feldman. New York: Academic Press, 1966. Pp. 199–223.

French, Elizabeth G., and Raymond R. Ernest. "The Relation between Authoritarianism and Acceptance of Military Ideology," *Journal of Personality* 24(December, 1955):181–91.

Gallup Opinion Index, Report Number 7. Princeton, N.J.: American Institute of Public Opinion, December, 1965.

Gallup Opinion Index, Report Number 31. Princeton, N.J.: American Institute of Public Opinion, January, 1968.

Galtung, Johan. "Social Position, Party Identification and Foreign Policy Orientation: A Norwegian Case Study." In *Domestic Sources of Foreign Policy,* edited by James N. Rosenau. New York: Free Press, 1967. Pp. 161–93.

Ginsburgh, Colonel Robert N. "The Challenge to Military Professionalism," *Foreign Affairs* 42(January, 1964):255–68.

Gladstone, Arthur I. "The Possibility of Predicting Reactions to International Events," *Journal of Social Issues* 11(1955):21–28.

Gladstone, Authur I., and Martha A. Taylor. "Threat-Related Attitudes and Reactions to Communications about International Events," *Journal of Conflict Resolution* 2(March, 1958):17–28.

Goodman, Leo A., and William H. Kruskal. "Measures of Association for Cross Classifications," *Journal of the American Statistical Association* 94(1954):732–64.

Greenstein, Fred I. "Personality and Politics: Problems of Evidence, Inference, and Conceptualization," *American Behavioral Scientist* 11(November-December, 1967): 38–53.

——. *Personality and Politics: Problems of Evidence, Inference, and Conceptualization*. Chicago: Markham Publishing Co., 1969.

——. "The Impact of Personality on Politics: An Attempt to Clear Away Underbrush," *American Political Science Review* 61(September, 1967): 629–41.

Hammond, Paul Y. "Foreign Policy-Making and Administrative Politics," *World Politics* 17(July, 1965):656–71.

Harr, John E. *The Anatomy of the Foreign Service: A Statistical Profile*. New York: Carnegie Endowment for International Peace, Foreign Affairs Personnel Study No. 4, 1965.

——. *The Development of Careers in the Foreign Service*. New York: Carnegie Endowment for International Peace, Foreign Affairs Personnel Study No. 3, 1965.

——. *The Professional Diplomat*. Princeton: Princeton University Press, 1969.

Harris (Louis) Survey Report. "On Church Attendance" and "On Perceived Religious Commitment," *Washington Post*, August 16, 1965, p. A2.

Harris (Louis) Survey Report. "On Political Philosophy," *New York Post*, June 26, 1967, p. 9.

Haviland, H. Field. *The Formulation and Administration of United States Foreign Policy*. Washington, D.C.: The Brookings Institution, 1960.

Hays, William L. *Statistics for Psychologists*. New York: Holt, Rinehart and Winston, 1963.

Herzog, Arthur. *The War-Peace Establishment*. New York: Harper and Row, 1963.

Hickman, Martin B., and Neil Hollander. "Undergraduate Origin as a Factor in Elite Recruitment and Mobility: The Foreign Service—A Case Study," *Western Political Quarterly* 19(June, 1966):337–53.

Bibliography

Holsti, Ole R. "The Belief System and National Images: A Case Study," *Journal of Conflict Resolution* 6(1962):244–52.

Horowitz, Irving Louis. *The War Game: Studies of the New Civilian Militarists*. New York: Ballantine Books, 1963.

Howard, Michael. *Soldiers and Governments: Nine Studies in Civil-Military Relations*. London: Eyre and Spottiswoode, 1957.

Huntington, Samuel P., ed. *Changing Patterns of Military Politics*. New York: Free Press of Glencoe, 1962.

———. "Interservice Competition and the Political Roles of the Armed Services," *American Political Science* 55(March, 1961):40–52.

———. *The Common Defense: Strategic Programs in National Politics*. New York: Columbia University Press, 1961.

———. *The Soldier and the State: The Theory and Politics of Civil-Military Relations*. Cambridge, Mass.: Belknap Press of the Harvard University Press, 1957.

Hyman, Herbert. *Political Socialization*. Glencoe, Ill.: Free Press, 1959.

Ilchman, Warren F. *Professional Diplomacy in the United States: 1779–1939*. Chicago: University of Chicago Press, 1961.

Janowitz, Morris. "Armed Forces in Western Europe: Uniformity and Diversity," *European Journal of Sociology* 6(1965):225–37.

———. "Military Elites and the Study of War," *Journal of Conflict Resolution* 1(March, 1957):9–18.

———, ed. *The New Military*. New York: Russell Sage Foundation, 1964.

———. *The Professional Soldier: A Social and Political Portrait*. New York: Free Press of Glencoe, 1960.

Janowitz, Morris, and Dwaine Marvick. "Authoritarianism and Political Behavior," *Public Opinion Quarterly* 17(1953):185–201.

Janowitz, Morris, in collaboration with Lt. Col. Roger Little. *Sociology and the Military Establishment*. Rev. ed. New York: Russell Sage Foundation, 1965.

Jensen, Lloyd. "United States Elites and Their Perceptions of the Determinants of Foreign Policy Behavior." Paper delivered at the Midwest Political Science Association meeting, April 28–30, 1966.

———. "American Foreign Policy Elites and the Prediction of International Events," *International Peace Research Society Papers* 5(1966):199–209.

Key, V. O., Jr. *Public Opinion and American Democracy*. New York: Alfred A. Knopf, 1967.

Kilpatrick, Franklin P., Milton C. Cummings, Jr., and M. Kent Jennings. *The Image of the Federal Service*. Washington, D.C.: The Brookings Institution, 1964.

Kingsley, J. Donald. *Representative Bureaucracy.* Yellow Springs, Ohio: Antioch Press, 1944.

Kintner, William R. *Forging a New Sword: A Study of the Department of Defense.* New York: Harper & Bros., 1958.

Kirscht, John P., and Ronald C. Dillehay. *Dimensions of Authoritarianism.* Lexington: University of Kentucky Press, 1967.

Kjellberg, Francesco. "Some Cultural Aspects of the Military Profession," *European Journal of Sociology* 6(1965):283–93.

Lang, Kurt. "Military Organizations." In *Handbook of Organizations*, edited by James G. March. Chicago: Rand McNally and Co., 1965. Pp. 838–78.

———. "Technology and Career Management in the Military Establishment." In *The New Military*, edited by Morris Janowitz. New York: Russell Sage Foundation, 1964. Pp. 39–81.

Laulicht, Jerome. "Canadian Foreign Policy Attitudes: Some Major Conclusions," *International Social Science Journal* 17(1965):472–86.

Leventhal, Howard, Robert L. Jacobs, and Nijole Z. Kudirka. "Authoritarianism, Ideology, and Political Candidate Choice," *Journal of Abnormal and Social Psychology* 69(1964):539–49.

Levine, Robert A. *The Arms Debate.* Cambridge, Mass.: Harvard University Press, 1963.

Levinson, Daniel J. "Authoritarian Personality and Foreign Policy." In *War: Studies from Psychology, Sociology and Anthropology*, edited by Leon Bramson and George W. Goethalls. New York: Basic Books, Inc., 1964. Pp. 133–46.

Lipset, Seymour Martin. *Political Man.* Garden City, N.Y.: Doubleday and Co., Anchor Books Edition, 1963.

Lovell, John. "The Professional Socialization of the West Point Cadet." In *The New Military*, edited by Morris Janowitz. New York: Russell Sage Foundation, 1964. Pp. 119–57.

Lutzker, Daniel R. "Internationalism as a Predictor of Cooperative Behavior," *Journal of Conflict Resolution* 4(1960):426–30.

Lyons, Gene M. "The Military Mind," *Bulletin of the Atomic Scientists* 19(November, 1963):19–22.

———. "The New Civil-Military Relations," *American Political Science Review* 55(March, 1961):53–63.

Lyons, Gene M., and John W. Masland. *Education and Military Leadership.* Princeton: Princeton University Press, 1959.

McCamy, James L. *The Administration of American Foreign Affairs.* New York: Alfred Knopf, 1950.

———. *Conduct of the New Diplomacy.* New York: Harper and Row, 1964.

McCamy, James L. and Alessandro Corradini. "The People of the State Department and Foreign Service," *American Political Science Review* 48(December, 1954):1067–82.

McClosky, Herbert. *Political Inquiry: The Nature and Uses of Survey Research.* New York: The Macmillon Co., 1969.

———. "Personality and Attitude Correlates of Foreign Policy Orientation." In *Domestic Sources of Foreign Policy*, edited by James N. Rosenau. New York: Free Press, 1967. Pp. 51–109.

Mackinnon, William J., and Richard Centers. "Authoritarianism and Internationalism," *Public Opinion Quarterly* 20(Winter, 1956–57): 621–30.

Marquand, John P. "Inquiry into the Military Mind," *New York Times Magazine*, March 30, 1952, pp. 53 ff.

Masland, John W., and Laurence I. Radway. *Soldiers and Scholars.* Princeton: Princeton University Press, 1957.

Matthews, Donald R. *The Social Background of Political Decision-Makers.* New York: Random House, 1954.

Millis, Walter. "Puzzle of the 'Military Mind'," *New York Times Magazine*, November 18, 1962, pp. 142 ff.

Modelski, George. *A Theory of Foreign Policy.* New York: Frederick A. Praeger, 1902.

Monsen, R. Joseph, Jr., and Mark W. Cannon. *The Makers of Public Policy: American Power Groups and Their Ideologies.* New York: McGraw-Hill Book Co., 1965.

Mosher, Frederick C. *Democracy and the Public Service.* New York: Oxford University Press, 1968.

Ogburn, Charlton, Jr. "The Flow of Policy-Making in the Department of State." In *The Formulation and Administration of United States Foreign Policy*, edited by H. Field Haviland. Washington, D.C.: Brookings Institution, 1960. Appendix C, pp. 172–77.

Porter, John. *The Vertical Mosaic.* Toronto: The University of Toronto Press, 1965.

Pruitt, Dean G. *Problem Solving in the Department of State.* The Social Science Foundation and Department of International Relations Monograph Series in World Affairs, No. 2. Denver, Colo.: University of Denver, 1964–65.

Putney, Snell, and Russell Middleton. "Some Factors Associated with Student Acceptance or Rejection of War," *American Sociological Review* 27(1962): 655–67.

Queener, L. "The Development of Internationalist Attitudes," *Journal of Social Psychology* 29(1949):221–36, 237–52; 30(1949):105–126.

Razzell, P. E. "Social Origins of Officers in the Indian and British Home Army: 1758–1962," *British Journal of Sociology* 14(September, 1963): 248–60.

Robinson, James A. *Congress and Foreign Policy-Making.* Rev. ed. Homewood, Ill.: The Dorsey Press, 1967.

Robinson, James A., and Richard C. Snyder. "Decision-Making in International Politics." In *International Behavior: A Social-Psychological Analysis*, edited by Herbert C. Kelman. New York: Holt, Rinehart and Winston, 1965. Pp. 435–63.

Rokeach, Milton. *Beliefs, Attitudes and Values: A Theory of Organization and Change.* San Francisco: Jossey-Bass, Inc., 1969.

———. *The Open and Closed Mind: Investigations into the Nature of Belief Systems and Personality Systems.* New York: Basic Books, Inc., 1960.

Rosenberg, Milton J. "Attitude Change and Foreign Policy in the Cold War Era." In *Domestic Sources of Foreign Policy*, edited by James N. Rosenau. New York: Free Press, 1967. Pp. 111–59.

———. "Images in Relation to the Policy Process: American Public Opinion on Cold-War Issues." In *International Behavior: A Social-Psychological Analysis*, edited by Herbert C. Kelman. New York: Holt, Rinehart and Winston, 1965. Pp. 278–334.

Rosenberg, Morris. "Misanthropy and Attitudes toward International Affairs," *Journal of Conflict Resolution* 1(December, 1957):340–45.

Rossow, Robert. "The Professionalization of the New Diplomacy," *World Politics* 14(July, 1962):561–75.

Sapin, Burton M. *The Making of United States Foreign Policy.* New York: Frederick A. Praeger, 1966.

———. "The Organization and Procedures of the National Security Council Mechanism." In *The Formulation and Administration of United States Foreign Policy*, edited by H. Field Haviland. Washington, D.C.: Brookings Institution, 1960. Appendix B, pp. 162–71.

Sapin, Burton M., and Richard C. Snyder. *The Role of the Military in American Foreign Policy.* Garden City, N.Y.: Doubleday and Co., 1954.

Schoenberger, Robert A. "Conservatism, Personality and Political Extremism," *American Political Science Review* 62(September, 1968):868–77.

Scott, William A. "Psychological and Social Correlates of International Images." In *International Behavior: A Social Psychological Analysis*, edited by Herbert C. Kelman. New York: Holt, Rinehart and Winston, 1965. Pp. 71–103.

———. "International Ideology and Interpersonal Ideology," *Public Opinion Quarterly* 24(1960):419–35.

Bibliography

———. "Correlates of International Attitudes," *Public Opinion Quarterly* 22 (Winter, 1958-59): 464–72.

———. "Rationality and Non-Rationality of International Attitudes," *Journal of Conflict Resolution* 2(March, 1958):8–16.

Searing, Donald D. "The Comparative Study of Elite Socialization," *Comparative Political Studies* 1(January, 1969):471–500.

———. "Two Theories of Elite Consensus: Tests with West German Data." Paper presented to the 66th American Political Science Association meeting in Los Angeles, California, September 8–12, 1970.

Segal, David R. "Selective Promotion in Officer Cohorts," *Sociological Quarterly* 8(Spring, 1967):199–206.

———. *Selection of General Officers in the United States Armed Forces*. University of Chicago Center for Social Organization Studies, Working Paper No. 43. Chicago: University of Chicago, 1964.

Seligman, Lester G. "Opportunity, Risk, Selection and Decision-Making: A Model of Political Recruitments." Paper presented at the 66th American Political Science Association meeting in Los Angeles, California, September 8–12, 1970.

Siegelman, Marvin, and Robert F. Peck. "Personality Patterns Related to Occupation Roles," *Genetic Psychology Monographs* 61(1960):291–349.

Simpson, Smith. *Anatomy of the State Department*. Boston: Houghton Mifflin Co., 1967.

Smith, Earl E. T. *The Fourth Floor: An Account of the Castro Communist Revolution*. New York: Random House, 1962.

Smith, M. Brewster. "Opinions, Personality, and Political Behavior," *American Political Science Review* 52(March, 1958):1–17.

Snyder, Richard C., H. W. Bruck, and Burton M. Sapin, eds. *Foreign Policy Decision-Making: An Approach to the Study of International Politics*. New York: Free Press of Glencoe, 1962.

Snyder, Richard C., and James A. Robinson. *National and International Decision-Making*. The Institute for International Order, Program of Research No. 4. New York, 1961.

Stanley, David T. *The Higher Civil Service*. Washington, D.C.: Brookings Institution, 1964.

Stanley, David T., Dean E. Mann, and Jameson W. Doig. *Men Who Govern*. Washington, D.C.: Brookings Institution, 1967.

Stanley, Timothy W. *American Defense and National Security*. Washington, D.C.: Public Affairs Press, 1956.

Steiner, Zara S. *Present Problems of the Foreign Service*. Princeton: Center of International Studies, 1961.

———. *The State Department and the Foreign Service: The Wriston Report— Four Years Later.* Center for International Studies Policy Memorandum No. 16. Princeton: Center for International Studies, 1958.

Subramaniam, V. "Representative Bureaucracy: A Reassessment," *American Political Science Review* 61(December, 1967):1010–19.

Troldahl, Verling C., and Fredric A. Powell. "A Short-Form Dogmatism Scale for Use in Field Studies," *Social Forces* 44(December, 1965):211–14.

U.S. Department of Commerce. *Statistical Abstract of the United States.* Washington, D.C.: U.S. Government Printing Office, 1964, 1965, 1966.

U.S. Department of State. *Toward a Stronger Foreign Service: Report of the Secretary of State's Committee on Personnel.* Department of State Publication 5458. Washington, D.C.: U.S. Government Printing Office, June, 1954.

Van Doorn, Jacques. "The Officer Corps: A Fusion of Profession and Organization," *British Journal of Sociology* 6(1965):262–82.

Van Riper, Paul P. *History of the United States Civil Service.* Evanston, Ill.: Row, Peterson and Co., 1958.

Van Riper, Paul P., and Darab B. Unwalla. "Voting Patterns among High-Ranking Military Officers," *Political Science Quarterly* 80(March, 1965): 48–61.

Walther, Regis. *Orientations and Behavioral Styles of Foreign Service Officers.* Carnegie Endowment for International Peace, Foreign Affairs Personnel Study No. 5. New York: Carnegie Endowment for International Peace, 1965.

Warner, W. Lloyd, Paul P. Van Riper, Norman H. Martin, and Orvis F. Collins. *The American Federal Executive.* New Haven: Yale University Press, 1963.

Wicker, Allan W. "Attitudes versus Actions: The Relationship of Verbal and Overt Behavioral Responses to Attitude Objects," *Journal of Social Issues* 25(Autumn, 1969):41–78.

Willick, Daniel H. *The Recruitment and Promotion of Foreign Service Officers.* University of Chicago Center for Social Organization Studies, Working Paper No. 58. Chicago: University of Chicago, February, 1966.

Wise, Captain Arthur E. *A Comparison of New Cadets at USMA with Entering Freshmen at Other Colleges.* West Point: Office of Research, United States Military Academy, March, 1969.

Worchel, Philip. "Social Ideology and Reactions to International Events," *Journal of Conflict Resolution* 11(December, 1967): 414–30.

Wright, Quincy. "The Military and Foreign Policy." In *Civil-Military Relationships in American Life,* edited by Jerome G. Kerwin. Chicago: University of Chicago Press, 1948. Pp. 116–36.

Zald, Mayer N., and William Simon. "Career Opportunities and Commitments among Officers." In *The New Military*, edited by Morris Janowitz. New York: Russell Sage Foundation, 1964. Pp. 257–85.

INDEX

Abrahamsson, Bengt, 142
Age, 30–31
Air Force, International Affairs Division of, 26–27
Annapolis. See U.S. Naval Academy
Anticommunism, 11, 154–55; and arms control and/or disarmament, and nonalignment, 161–63; dimensions of, 155–59
Arms control and/or disarmament (ACD), 11, 154–55; and anticommunism, and non-alignment, 161-63; dimensions of, 159–60
Army, International Policy Division of, 26–27
Attitudes. See Beliefs; Beliefs, foreign policy
Authoritarianism. See Cognitive style

Beliefs, 147; and behavior, 14–15, 183–86; system of, 149–51, 174–75
Beliefs, foreign policy, 11, 151–55; and behavior, 14–15, 185–86; and civil liberaties, 165–66; and cognitive style, 170–76; dimensions of, 154–64; Foreign Service and military officers compared regarding, 166–68; and government involvement, 165–66; and political orientation, 112–13, 170–76; and religiosity, 170–76; and social origins, 170–71

Berelson, Bernard R., 39–40, 147
Birth, place of. See Geographical background
Birth, year of. See Age

Campbell, Angus, 115
Campboll, Donald T., 141–42
Cannon, Mark W., 167
Church attendance. See Religiosity
Civil liberties, 114–16; and foreign policy beliefs, 165–66; and government involvement, 165–66; and political orientation, 116
Cognitive style: dimensions of, 131–36; F[ascism]-Scale, 141, 143; and foreign policy beliefs, 170–76; Foreign Service and military officers compared regarding, 136–37; and political orientation, 139, 145–46; and religiosity, 139, 145–46; and social origins, 139, 143–46
Colleges attended: Foreign Service and military officers compared regarding, 72–73; representativeness regarding, 73–80
Conservative, and Republican (Rep-Con). See Political orientation
Converse, Philip E., 150, 153

D'Amato, Anthony A., 150
Defense, Department of, 4, 10; International Affairs Division of the Air

Defense (*continued*)
Force of, 26–27; International Policy Division of the Army of, 26–27; International Security Affairs (ISA) of, 26–28; Joint Staff of the Joint Chiefs of Staff of, 26–28; Operations 61 of the Navy of, 26–27; stereotype of officers of, 8–9. *See also* Foreign Policy; Military mind
Democrat, and liberal (DemLib). *See* Political orientation
Demographic characteristics. *See* Social origins
Dillehay, Ronald C., 131 n.4
DiRenzo, Gordon J., 144, 145
Dogmatism. *See* Cognitive style, dimensions of

Edinger, Lewis J., 3–4, 7–8, 184
Education, level of, 70–71. *See also* Colleges attended
Elder, Robert, 21 n, 23
Ernest, Raymond R., 141, 143

F[ascism]-Scale. *See* Cognitive style
Father's occupation: Foreign Service and military officers compared regarding, 65–66; representativeness regarding, 66–69
Foreign policy: and Defense Department, 5; and military functions, 3–4; and nonmilitary functions, 4; and State Department, 5. *See also* Beliefs, foreign policy
Foreign Service Officers (FSOs): as careerists, 17; representation of, in State Department, 18–19; sample and population of, defined, 21–23; sources of sample of, 25–26. *See also* Age; Beliefs, foreign policy; Cognitive style; Political orientation; Rank; Religiosity; Religious affiliation; Social origins; State, Department of
French, Elizabeth G., 141, 143
Fulbright, Senator J. W., 167

Geographical background: Foreign Service and military officers compared regarding, 42–44; representativeness regarding, 44–52. *See also* Hometown, size of
Government involvement, 114–16; and civil liberties, 165–66; and foreign policy beliefs, 165–66; and political orientation, 116

Hard-line, 11, 148–49, 151, 166, 174–75. *See also* Beliefs, foreign policy; Military mind
Harr, John E., 7, 17, 21 n, 22, 110–11
Haviland, H. Field, 27
Holsti, Ole R., 150–51
Hometown, size of: Foreign Service and military officers compared regarding, 52–53; representativeness regarding, 53–60
Horowitz, Irving Louis, 167
Huntington, Samuel P., 3–4 n, 27–28, 128–29, 166

Ideological identification. *See* Political orientation
Index of Dissimilarity (ID), 44–45
International Security Affairs (ISA), 26–28

Janowitz, Morris, 41–43, 53, 69–70, 95–96, 117–18, 124–25, 153–54
Joint Staff of the Joint Chiefs of Staff, 26–28

Kirscht, John P., 131 n.4

Lazarsfeld, Paul F., 39–40
Levine, Robert A., 151–54, 156, 159, 160
Levinson, Daniel J., 172–73
Liberal, and Democrat (DemLib). *See* Political orientation
Lipset, Seymour Martin, 114–15
Lovell, John, 95, 153–56, 159, 160, 177–78
Lutzker, Daniel R., 184–85
Lyons, Gene M., 138, 167

Matthews, Donald R., 14–15 n.11, 40
McCamy, James L., 20 n.3, 23 n

Index

McCormack, Thelma H., 141–42
McPhee, William N., 39–40
Military mind, 9, 128–31, 137–38, 147; and cognitive style, 136; and dogmatism and rigidity, 133. See also Hard-line; Beliefs, foreign policy
Military officers: sample and population of, defined, 26–29; sources of sample of, 29–30; stereotype of, 8–9. See also Age; Beliefs, foreign policy; Cognitive style; Defense Department; Military mind; Political orientation; Rank; Religiosity; Religious affiliation; Social origins
Millis, Walter, 9 n.7
Modelski, George, 5
Monsen, R. Joseph Jr., 167

Nationality: Foreign Service and military officers compared regarding, 62–63, representativeness regarding, 62–64
Navy, Operations 61 of, 26–27
Nonalignment, 11, 154–55; and anticommunism, and arms control and/or disarmament, 161–63; dimensions of, 160–61

Opinions. See Beliefs; Beliefs, foreign policy
Organizational characteristics, sources of, 35–39, 98–99, 126–27, 139–40, 176–82. See also Representativeness

Parents, nativity of, 61
Pearson, Drew, 43
Political party identification. See Political orientation

Political orientation: and civil liberties, 116; and cognitive style, 139, 145–46; dimensions of 112–13; and foreign policy beliefs, 170–76; Foreign Service and military officers compared regarding, 116–18; and government involvement, 116; and religiosity, 119, 126–27; representativeness regarding, 120–26; and social origins, 118–19
Postrecruitment. See Organizational characteristics, sources of; Representativeness
Prerecruitment. See Organizational characteristics, sources of; Representativeness

Rank, 31–32
Recruitment. See Organizational characteristics, sources of; Representativeness
Regional background. See Geographical background
Religiosity: and cognitive style, 139, 145–46; dimensions of, 100–102; and foreign policy beliefs, 170–76; Foreign Service and military officers compared regarding, 101–2, 106–9; and political orientation, 119, 126–27; representativeness regarding, 104–10; and social origins, 101–3; summary of findings regarding, 109–11
Religious affiliation: Foreign Service and military officers compared regarding, 88–90; representativeness regarding, 90–97
Religious self-description. See Religiosity
Representativeness, 12–13, 35, 98–99; and college attended, 73–80; and father's occupation, 66–69; and geographical background, 44–52; and legitimacy, 13; and level of education, 70–71; and nationality, 62–64; and parent's nativity, 61; and political orientation, 120–26; and religiosity, 104–10; and religious affiliation, 90–97; and size of hometown, 53–60; and social origins (summary of findings regarding), 82–87
Republican, and conservative (RepCon). See Political orientation
Rigidity. See Cognitive style
Robinson, James A., 5 n.2, 7, 184

Rokeach, Milton, 130 n, 131, 132, 134, 135, 143, 150, 172
Rosenberg, Milton J., 40, 173–74

Sapin, Burton M., 9–10 n.8, 128, 129, 137–38
Schoenberger, Robert A., 115 n.7
Searing, Donald D., 184
Simpson, Smith, 24–25
Smith, Earl E. T., 23–24
Smith, M. Brewster, 15
Snyder, Richard C., 5 n.2, 7, 9–10 n.8, 128, 129
Social origins: attributes of, 34–35; cognitive style, 139, 143–46; and foreign policy beliefs, 170–71; and political orientation, 118–19; and religiosity, 101–3; summary of findings regarding, 80–87. *See also* Colleges attended; Education, level of; Father's occupation; Geographical background; Hometown, size of; Nationality; Parents, nativity of
State, Department of, 4–5, 10; bureau and functional organization of, 18–21; country desk officers of, 23–25; stereotype of officers of, 8. *See also* Foreign policy
Steiner, Gary A., 147

U.S. Air Force Academy, 77. *See also* Colleges attended
U.S. Military Academy, 48, 77, 79–80. *See also* Colleges attended
U.S. Naval Academy, 77, 79–80. *See also* Colleges attended

West Point. *See* U.S. Military Academy
Wicker, Allan W., 185
Willick, Daniel H., 46 n.12, 73–74, 76
Wristonization, 17–18